PERCEPTIONS OF DEVELOPMENT

Perspectives on Development is organised by and
edited from the Centre for Developing Area Studies, McGill
University, Montreal, Canada. The primary focus of the series
is on economic, social and political development in third world
countries. The series includes works of a broad, comparative
and interpretive character as well as specific institutional and
empirical studies which stem from research activities of the
Centre. However, the series also includes other works judged by
the Editors to be valuable contributions to our understanding
of the development process.

Series Editors

R. Cranford Pratt, Professor of Political Science, University of Toronto,
Chairman
John A. Barnes, Professor of Sociology, University of Cambridge
Irving Brecher, Professor of Economics, McGill University
Peter C. W. Gutkind, Professor of Anthropology, McGill University
Ben Higgins, Professor of Economics, University of Montreal
Kari Levitt, Associate Professor of Economics, McGill University
Richard F. Salisbury, Professor of Anthropology, McGill University

PERCEPTIONS OF DEVELOPMENT

Edited by
SANDRA WALLMAN

CAMBRIDGE UNIVERSITY PRESS
CAMBRIDGE
LONDON · NEW YORK · MELBOURNE

Published by the Syndics of the Cambridge University Press
The Pitt Building, Trumpington Street, Cambridge CB2 1RP
Bentley House, 200 Euston Road, London NW1 2DB
32 East 57th Street, New York, NY 10022, USA
296 Beaconsfield Parade, Middle Park, Melbourne 3206, Australia

© Cambridge University Press 1977
Library of Congress Catalogue Card Number: 76-46863
First published 1977

Printed in Great Britain at the
University Press, Cambridge

ISBN 0 521 21498 X

Library of Congress Cataloging in Publication Data
Main entry under title:

Perceptions of development.

(Perspectives on development; 6)
Includes bibliographical references and index.
1. Economic development – Case studies. 2. Social
history – Case studies. I. Wallman, Sandra.
HD82.P443   301.24   76-46863
ISBN 0-521-21498-X

Contents

Contents

Preface

This volume is offered as an exploration, not an argument. It is an exploration of a theme which, although obvious, has been largely neglected. There were everywhere indications that the equation of *progress* with *material advance* was rooted in specific contexts of setting and situation and was not readily transposed into others. It was also evident that development issues had to be simplified to fit any one development model and that Occam's Razor most commonly excised the less quantifiable variables. Even explicitly 'social' analyses tended to be defensive about 'social' factors: they did, after all, interfere with the smooth progress of development. And if they did not lead to material advance, they could not be leading anywhere.

The impetus to this collection was a desire to see where else they might be leading; to consider the possibility that there was systematic evidence of progress towards – or the desire to progress towards – other goals. It is *not* intended as an anti-economic, back-to-the-spinning-wheel tract. It may be significant that I was less emphatic in this denial in the book's early stages than I am now. The cumulative evidence of the separate case studies makes it plain that the desire to enhance particular non-material qualities of life is not *instead of* material advance, it is *as well as*. The problems arise when the pursuit of one impedes or precludes pursuit of the other; 'successful development' occurs only in those (rare) instances in which the two are reconciled. While the cases included here are not success or failure stories as such, each illustrates some version of the paradox and of its more or less successful resolution. Our finding is that the measure of successful development varies within as well as between developing societies.

The theme for the volume was developed in graduate seminars in social anthropology in the Universities of Amsterdam (January through June 1974) and Toronto (1974–5). I want to acknowledge the critical stimulus of students in both places. I am indebted also to Professor Milton Santos for his encouragement of my then tentative notion that a collection of variations on the theme *Perceptions of Development* would make an interesting and useful volume; to Professors Y. S. Brenner and Ernest Gellner for their (separate) cautionary comments as the venture began; and to the Social Science Research Council (Research Unit on Ethnic Relations) for financial support in the preparation of the final draft.

Needless to say, the volume would not have been possible without the insights of the contributors, or without their tolerance of my use of their material. I can only hope that the whole does full justice to each of its parts.

London, *October* 1976   SANDRA WALLMAN

Contributors

Stanley Barrett Department of Anthropology,
University of Guelph, Ontario.

Jeremy Boissevain Antropologisch-Sociologisch Centrum,
University of Amsterdam.

Peter Harries-Jones Bethune College,
York University, Ontario.

Roger Krohn Department of Sociology,
McGill University, Montreal.

Michael Levin Department of Anthropology,
University of Toronto.

Marilyn Manzer Community Planning Division,
Nova Scotia Department of Municipal Affairs.

Ralph Matthews Department of Sociology and Anthropology,
McMaster University, Ontario.

G. E. Mortimore Department of Anthropology and Sociology,
University of British Coloumbia.

John Peterson Center for Community Health and Medical Care,
Harvard University.

Richard Salisbury Department of Anthropology,
McGill University, Montreal.

Sandra Wallman Research Unit on Ethnic Relations,
University of Bristol.

At each place was a safety razor, a washcloth, a package of razor blades, a chocolate bar, two cigars, a bar of soap, ten cigarettes, a book of matches, a pencil, and a candle. . . . So it goes.

Kurt Vonnegut Jnr
Slaughterhouse Five

La quantité des biens disponibles pour chacun ne mesure pas la qualité de l'existence.

Raymond Aron
Le développement social

The impact of the economic cycle on man can be positive, as when man is adequately fed and clad and sheltered; it can be negative as when the result is alienation from oneself and from others, a feeling of powerlessness. . .

Johan Galtung
The European Community

A firm refusal to identify *the* transition, big enough though it is, with the life story of the global totality, should free us from some of the excessive fears as well as from the metaphysical hopes. In fact we do not know much of the potentialities of industrial society, for freedom or for other values.

Ernest Gellner
Thought and Change

Introduction: Perceptions of development

The need to change the subject

Problems of non-development are as pressing as they ever were, and no less fashionable. It may be that writing about development has become for many of us a displacement activity, an alternative to dealing with the failure to solve 'real' problems and achieve 'real' goals. It has become necessary, in Dahrendorf's phrase, to change the subject: our justification for yet another volume on development is the ancillary need to address exactly those problems and goals – not as 'development experts' see them and perhaps must assume them to be, but as they are interpreted and dealt with by the non-expert in his various guises. We attempt in these cases to translate the *objects* of discussions about development into the perceiving *subjects* of its meaning and effect, and to analyse each perception in some relation to the social and/or economic context in which it occurs.

This last statement implies that we all know what 'development' is. In the economic literature, there is little ambiguity: 'development' is a perhaps inevitable but certainly unilineal movement towards a condition of maximum industrialisation, modern technology, high(-est?) GNP and high(-est?) material standards of living – the two last being popularly assumed to go together. Philosophically, however, we are on more hazardous ground: 'development' implies 'progress', which itself implies evolution towards some ultimate good – all of these notions being specific to particular times and places (Bury 1955; Gellner 1964; Redfield 1970; Sklair 1970; Wallman 1975, 1976). There is no reason why a condition of maximum industrialisation should be, or be assumed to be, the ideal moral condition; any relation between them is problematic (Firth 1964; Aron & Hoselitz 1965). Increasingly it is argued that industrialisation is not an economic *summum bonum* even for those who prosper (as Heilbronner 1974; Levi 1974; Schumacher 1973), and very obviously not for those who dont (Adelman & Morris 1970; Berger 1974; Critchfield 1974; Lewis, O. 1967).

But efforts to improve conditions in underdeveloped/developing countries continue to assess that improvement quantitatively – more is good; growth is progress – and to rate each area in terms of its shortfall from some implicit 'developed' goal – *we* set the objective which *they* have failed to reach. These notions persist in the plain face of two paradoxes:

(1) However successful a particular region's development effort, the economic gap between it and its industrialised, technological superiors

continually widens. 'Progress', far from being the explicit arrival point of the development process, tends to recede as one advances. Even the poor are beginning to realise that they cannot catch up with the rich. In many cases they are no longer trying.

(2) High GNP and/or rates of industrial growth are precisely *not* progress for the developed regions any longer – apparently bringing more ills than we yet know how to cure and certainly not 'satisfying' as such. It is as if quantities of things and qualities of life are not simply known (again?) to be distinct, but that they are even suspected of being mutually contradictory. Nor is this view peculiar to the very rich: there is evidence that even the poor may value the maintenance or increase of autonomy as much as they need more material goods.

Some of this evidence is brought together here: we are concerned to examine perceptions of development as they relate to concepts of boundary and autonomy. This should not be construed as a claim for the importance of 'perception' over 'reality' (see pp. 5, 11 below), but as an effort to isolate perceptions of development as a significant problem for analysis – however preliminary or imperfect. It is of little importance that such an enterprise be labelled and slotted into one or other philosophical camp, but it is essential that the values/aspirations/perceptions of people subject to the processes of economic development or non-development be taken seriously – however inconsistent they may appear to be, and however limited their power in the political-economic market place. We purport to be interested in the reception and effect of development planning, if only because failure costs money, and we should be attuned to all kinds of evidence for the potentialities of industrial/material advance whether good or ill.

It will be the purpose of this book neither to argue that things are getting better nor that they are getting worse. My own view is that the case is not proven either way. Our point is rather that we should not assume that we know, can predict or even agree on the criteria or the outcome of 'development' for a given people in a given context of time and place. We need instead to discover what that group, society or part-society wants and/or expects to gain from particular changes, and to recognise what it is likely to lose, or to perceive as loss, in the process. And we need to analyse conditions of non-development and/or the processes of economic and social change without inexplicit reference to the opposite ends of a simple and unilineal scale.

Because this has not yet, to our knowledge, been done systematically, the effort even to identify the difficulties inherent in doing it may pay useful dividends. Even if it does not, the cumulation of the papers presented here adds a dimension to the debate in which we all engage, with greater or less obsession, both as private and as professional people: given the options available to him, how best should man deploy his resources?

Each of these papers deals with a specific region, group or enclave of people, and with a particular development project or period. While all of the contributors are professional social scientists, they are not of one discipline nor of a single political or theoretical persuasion. The volume is therefore eclectic and multi-disciplinary. But each contributor has written his/her piece with the same perspective, and this focus, underlined in the writing and in the editorial links, provides the unity of the collection.

While no other framework was suggested to or imposed upon the separate authors, the recurrence of certain themes is striking. Three of these will be elaborated in the following paragraphs. Firstly, the logic of non-development may be distorted by normative reference to the opposite ends of a simple evolutionary scale: classifying societies as developed/underdeveloped or developed/developing (depending on the degree of optimism felt by the classifier) obscures a number of other-than-evolutionary issues. Secondly, any compendium of criteria of development must include the sense of autonomy/authenticity/integrity – some measure of social appropriateness – *as well as* the increment of material resources. And thirdly, the wavering or shifting of development priorities and objectives is neither erratic, nor is it the function of peculiar ambivalence or transition: inconsistency within a system is as normal and as essential as variation from one system to another.

Models, situations and perceptions

Good 'development' models – and not only those of the economists – tend to be evaluated in terms of 'tidiness' as much as of explanatory value: 'tidiness' is easier to assess. Since a real situation is never 'tidy' in this sense, any such model has necessarily abstracted from reality – according to certain (stated?) criteria and at some (chosen?) distance from or nearness to the data. For these reasons a 'proper' development model cannot deal with a number of crucial questions all at once. Who is measuring the development? Along what scale and according to which criteria? Is it synonymous with progress? with modernisation? with economic growth? with evolution? By what logic do changes in context, setting, situation alter its meaning – even for the same group or class? And (most galling of all) why does development not happen when it should?

The last question underlies many of the currently popular classes of development theory and the explanations of non-development that follow from them. It should work: why doesn't it?

A critical review of the literature is beyond our competence and purpose here, but the most influential of the various explanations of non-development are crudely summarised in the following sections. In the terms of this volume, each theory represents a particular perception of development, necessarily partial, necessarily governed not only by academic logic, but also by the historical and political context of which it constitutes a part. By suspending our own involvement and viewing them as all equally exotic (which is not the same as the moral trap sprung by the assumption that all social forms are equally good), we may see them on a par with the perceptions of development described and analysed in the papers following.

Scientific theory is not, of course, the same as 'folk' theory. But it is easy to misinterpret the differences. It is commonly assumed that scientific theory can be defined by its objectivity and logical consistency, and that precisely these elements are missing from the ordinary person's perception and explanation of events. On the contrary: '. . . the objectivity of scientific statements lies [only] in the fact that they can be intersubjectively tested' (Popper 1968: 44). And it is neither the logic nor the consistency of perception which makes it scientific: the logic of 'folk theory' however primitive, is usually impeccable. (See e.g. Ward 1965; Gellner 1973 and, classically, Evans-Pritchard 1937.) It is obedience to the methodological rules of the scientific game. Thus, particularly: 'He who decides one day that scientific statements do not call for any further test, and that they can be regarded as finally verified, retires from the game. . .' And: 'Once a hypothesis has been proposed and tested, and has proved its mettle, it may not be allowed to drop out without "good reason". A "good reason" may be, for instance: replacement of the hypothesis by another which is better testable; or the falsification of one of the consequences of the hypothesis' (Popper, *ibid.*: 53–4).

Theoretical perceptions of development therefore are – or should be – more systematically self-critical than their non-theoretical, non-scientific counterparts; and they are – or should be – persistent in the testing, reformulation and retesting of particular hypotheses. The difference between scientific and non-scientific is in the search for and the measure of 'a good reason' for changing tack in each case. A scientist is expected to specify and test the interrelations of a limited set of variables and to hold the rest equal or absent. The difference between theoreticians is in the problems they select, in the variables which they take to be significant – or most likely to be significant – to the problem in hand, and in the way in which these variables are controlled and combined in experiment. Their similarity is in the obligation – and the right – to order their priorities and to deal with one problem at a time. The essential difference between theoretical and 'folk' models is exactly here: theoretical models may not shift or are not required to shift their priorities and dimensions to fit the multiple constraints of ordinary life, as real people must.

These caveats apply equally to social science, but because the experimental limitation and control of variables is less feasible (not only for moral reasons), the issues are likely to be more plainly conceptual. Of the variables we know about, which do we take to be most relevant, significant, or likely-to-be significant to a particular set of social events? What criteria can we reasonably use to recognise the context in which those events occur? How are we even to delimit the situation which is to be analysed?

Gellner (1973) has underlined the difficulties inherent in circumscribing (or, as he argues it, refusing to circumscribe) the context in which a concept has particular meaning. The same difficulties pertain to any attempt to define situation: it is hard to know where to stop. Models for the analysis of situation are invariably built around notions of perception and/or structure, but few set out specific criteria of relevance or make explicit the logic of the boundary. For our present purpose the most useful exceptions are those of Goffman (1959 *et seq*; 1975) and Nadel (1957) – not least because each, while leaning toward one or other end of the perception/structure continuum, does so unambiguously. Jarvie's recent exploration of the notion itemises a thorough range of both perceptual and structural dimensions and stresses the effect that the various dimensions have on each other. He castigates both 'psychologistic' and 'holistic' approaches for ignoring these effects and so for denying the systematic importance of unintended consequences (Jarvie 1972: 3–36; see also Popper 1957 *passim*, and 1972: 78).

It is not a coincidence that scholars in economic anthropology are least prone to this fallacy. They are necessarily concerned with real phenomena, with the perception of those phenomena, and with the interaction between the two – all within the confines of a particular environment. Firth's successive statements on the tasks of the sub-discipline imply both a plea and a prescription for situational analysis and provide a logic by which the situation can be bounded (1939: 1–31, 352–65; 1951). His latest formulation is remarkably apt to the present problem: '. . . There is a structure at all levels – in the phenomena, as in the perceptions which order them and in the concepts which interpret their logical relationships; *and it is presumptuous to assign to one level more "reality" than to another.*' (Firth 1972: 38. Emphasis added).

I interpret this to mean that the phenomenon, the actor's perception of the phenomenon, and the observer's perception of the phenomenon are each integral parts of a situation, and that they act and react on each other in circular – perhaps spiral but not linear – sequence. If we want fully to understand non-development we must take all of these levels equally seriously – which demands that elements commonly neglected be brought into sharper focus. It is these other dimensions of development which are treated in the body of this volume. The theoretical perceptions are sketched as base line: in each there is evidence, if not open recognition, of the paradoxes inherent in 'progressive development'. But the need remains to distinguish the ways in which the paradoxes are perceived, experienced or resolved by particular groups in particular contexts of space and time; to deal with resources which are not economic in the narrowest sense; and to recognise alternative perceptions of betterment.

Theoretical perceptions of development

The bulk of these theories rest more or less explicitly on evolutionary assumptions; and they equate progressive development with material and/or technological advance. Non-development in this framework is explained by some impediment to the normal if not inevitable process of development. Since the evolutionary framework is so widely and variously used, the list of diagnosed impediments is very long. It ranges from inappropriate local institutions to the functioning of the international political-economic system – whether 'natural' or 'conspired'.

Other theories of development, and the explanations of non-development that follow from them, may be seen as spin-offs from or reactions to this evolutionary model. The explicitly anti-evolutionary approach which distinguishes between modernisation and development is important in allowing recognition of the unintended (and unexpected?) negative effects of 'material progress' on community, integrity, autonomy etc., and of the logic of more than one scale of advance; 'the limits to growth' debate in drawing attention to the inevitability of these limits, and to the danger as well as the immorality of the current zero-sum development game.

It is useful to group these theoretical perceptions in classes. The first is evolutionary, pro-development; the second is post-progress, anti-development; and the third and fourth are each equivocal in some way – one is anti-development for some, pro-development for others; the other anti-evolutionary and anti-modernisation, but strongly in favour of development. Each explanation of non-development entails a particular prescription *for* development, and each puts either a '*boo*' or a '*hurrah*' gloss on the concept (cf. Cranston 1954).

(i) The premise of the first and evolutionary class is that development normally follows a unilineal and progressive sequence. Any non-development is unnatural; each carries its own 'cure'. When non-development is explained by a lack of material resources in economically utilisable form, the treatments recommended are localised injections of material aid (as Rostow 1962), or buying power (Galbraith 1962) although the crass lack of money is seldom diagnosed (Valentine 1968). Suggestions as to where these extra material resources should come from tend to be vague – and nowhere more strikingly than in theories holding a shortage of people to account (as Wilkinson 1973).

Sometimes it is the absence of non-material prerequisites which is said to inhibit the progressive sequence. There may be a lack of organisational skills and attitudes (Brenner 1966; Tawney 1948) or of opportunity (Epstein 1962). Alternatively it has been argued that opportunities to 'develop' are there, but not grasped because of inappropriate traditions or institutions (Mair 1961; Spicer 1967), or because they are themselves inappropriate to – and so threaten – the traditional system (Bailey ed. 1973; Paul 1955). In the perception of the anthropologist, these traditions are *economically* sound where they form a rational and coherent system, even if *technologically* unsound to the extent that they are inappropriate to economic development (Firth 1939: 7; 1967 *passim*).

This logic entails the recognition of sub-systems or spheres – whether of exchange or of meaning – to which particular resources pertain, and between which they are not readily transposed, even when the material advantage of 'converting' them is recognised (Barth 1963, 1967; Leyton 1970; Wallman 1965). These notions are important (and are taken up again below) because they admit the plurality of perception and the possibility of levels or contexts of change. In this sense they are an advance on blanket notions of anti-change, anti-development societies or cultures (as Banfield 1958; Foster 1965), and necessarily more useful than narrowly functionalist models that were not designed to cope with change in the first place (Radcliffe-Brown 1952).

Either way, it is 'wrong' priorities which get in the way of economic development. Various 'cures' are proposed – improved communication (Bailey 1971; Goodenough 1963; Wallman 1965, 1968, 1969), new administrative structures (Batten 1968; du Sautoy 1958) and education (Spindler ed. 1963; Ogbu 1973) being the most common – although some argue that the excision of the very social scientists who make such proposals would be more effective (Deloria 1969; Frank 1971; Stavenhagen 1971).

The defining features of this class of theory are that development is progressive, that it is good (although sometimes painful!), and that it is normal if not inevitable. By these tokens successful cases do not require explanation (and will not be analysed), and the 'pathology' of non-development needs only to be diagnosed to be cured.

(ii) The second theoretical perception, in the terms we have designated, belongs clearly to a different era. The notion that there are limits to economic growth or to the *goodness* of growth (as in Mishan 1967) is introduced, and development, insofar as it remains inevitable and infinite, is bad. The most elaborate and extreme presentation of this view enters only technical-ecological factors into the analytic system (Meadows *et al.* 1972): given the finite nature of the planet, no more economic growth is possible to anybody without jeopardy to everybody; too much heat and population are generated, too many resources exhausted. Zero growth is the only hope and 'progressive evolution' must stop – each group or region fixed in the position it was when the ecological alarm sounded. It is evident that those who espouse this anti-growth, anti-development goal are likely to be urban and wealthy and technologically advanced. They are people with garbage to worry about, and their perception can be interpreted as elitist and self-protective. Certainly the model has no political dimension and neglects the possibility of redistribution as a cure both for over-growth and for non-development (Galtung 1973b; Chenery *et al.* 1974; Jahoda 1974), and of other inputs into the ecological or socio-ecological system (Cole *et al.* 1974; Mesarovic & Pestil; 1974). The clear inference of this model is that the world is developed enough, and that no further material growth, being the only salvation of mankind, is good – even if man must change his direction and/or himself to achieve it (Heilbronner 1974; and, more hopefully, Teilhard de Chardin 1955; Olson & Landsberg 1973).

No explanation of development/non-development is a pure statement about the way the world is; each is normative in some degree. But in the anti-growth/anti-development approach, the normative element is particularly explicit – probably because a vision of impending doom entails a sense of personal disaster which can only be alleviated by converting the haves and the have-nots to the same perception. Development theories have not previously carried this inference; what the poor did mattered little to the rich. Whatever the political implications of the change, it has affected the ground rules of applied academic discourse: development/non-development have become gut issues defended and opposed with none of the detachment once required of the genre.

(iii) The third and 'equivocal' class of explanation is contemporary with and shares the moral climate of the second. In this class, however, the effects of technical-ecological factors are minimised and emphasis put on political-economic relations. Inevitably the sense of involvement is partisan. According to the most influential of these theories, the international system itself can be held to account for non-development. The resources necessary to development are drawn off or kept away from the poor by the rich. The development of some entails the non-development of others. In some versions the process is automatic (as Myrdal 1968), or at least not directly intended (Amin 1973), in others it is conspired (as Frank 1969; see further Foster-Carter 1974). Either way the sobering notion that there are limits to economic development (as there are limits to ecological growth) is central, and even the most optimistic see the development process as a zero sum game in which an economic win for some constitutes a (relative?) economic loss for others. Where economic growth is based on external demand and external financing it 'always lags behind the current public expenditure that it made necessary' (Amin 1973: xii): where the rich get rich, the poor get poorer and (so?) more dependent on the rich.

The importance of this approach is in its shifting of emphasis from absolute to relative indices (and perceptions) of advance, and from differences in levels of development to the relations which cause and maintain them (De Kadt 1974: 4). But those that present development and non-development to be (only) the result of global structures of exploitation effectively take all decisions about the future out of the hands of those that they purport to champion: they invalidate the current efforts and perceptions of any but select academicians and supranational consortia.

Very likely this inference is not intended and follows from the politicisation of development issues. Because it is also a function of a macro-level of analysis, political and methodological issues are readily confused and academicians begin to dispute the *morality* of their separate perceptions. Thus: the (anti-development) *limits to growth* model and this (zero sum) *development of underdevelopment* model pertain to different political-economic camps, but both models represent development/non-development as globally determined conditions to be dealt with, if at all, by supranational effort, reform or revolution. By implication, analysis at the micro- and local level must be trifling unless it is deliberate 'mystification'. But if it is obvious that certain vital elements in the equation of poverty will only be altered by massive political-economic manipulations, it is also true that the smallest and poorest of local units has some amount of choice in and control over events occurring within its boundaries. To deny all significance to its perception and handling of the options facing it would be as patronising as it is impractical.

De Kadt's recent discussion of the causes and effects of neo-Marxist theories of development is concerned with different issues, but makes the same point: 'The exploited masses may be supressed by governments wholly dissociated from popular forces, but they are essential ingredients to the development process. Attempts at stage managing their demands from above are bound to fail: without the *active* participation of the majority, development is not possible...' And: 'mesmerised by the goal of economic growth, we have been left without the tools to measure the wider aspects of the development process...Perhaps "the system" can, indeed, only change through revolution on a world scale. But...meanwhile a lot of rather important problems need analysing...' (De Kadt 1974: 1–14).

A maverick addition to this 'equivocal' class of explanations (and the last of these sketchy examples) deals with smaller units and in greater detail, and is less categorical in its implications for 'cure'. Political and economic processes and structures parallel to those articulating the *development of underdevelopment* model are identified, but at a less than global level. The focus shifts to relations between the centre and narrowly defined local areas on the periphery – doubtless because the model was designed to explain economic disparities between specific regions of a single country (Schneider *et al.* 1972). The approach is anti-evolutionary insofar as a unilineal sequence of change is explicitly denied. All regions or part regions are not *either* traditional *or* modern *or* somehow transitional between the two, and a crucial distinction between scales of *development* and of *modernisation* is drawn. Elsewhere they are perceived as a single sequence (as above in this section and Dalton ed. 1971; Eisenstadt 1966; Lerner 1958; Wertheim 1973) in which negative effects are 'mis-developments' (Foster-Carter 1974) or unexpected hitches in a normally smooth process (Eisenstadt 1964); or they are perceived as analytically separate levels of a single sequence (Apter 1967).

In this two-sequence model the degree of freedom to choose between modernisation and development is not spelt out, but is apparently minimal. Their *either/or* entailment is predetermined and the form of change varies directly with pre-existing political-economic structures – particularly with those affecting local relations with the centre. Advances in modernisation and in development are, however, clearly distinguishable from one another. *Development* is seen as a consolidation of resources which will change existing forms of management and production toward greater independence of the outside. Development is, by this token, good. Modernisation by contrast is bad. *Modernisation* provides increased purchasing power and a higher standard of living, but at the expense of development. Indices of modernisation without development would include such things as welfare payments, tourism and remittances from migrants. These each allow more consumption and more short run goodies at home, but with all the profits and the long run developmental activity feeding back into a focal metropolitan centre away. Modernisation is not the *explanation* of non-development since each has distinct antecedent causes. But modernisation and development are inversely related to the extent that they are structurally incompatible and any advance in the first precludes advances in the second. This is an inference which those who want both – even if in different frames (Goffman 1975) – are unlikely to find appealing.

Perceptions and resources

With the exception of the *limits to growth* model which, bowdlerised a little, is concerned to stop development not to foster it, each of these theories or approaches 'blames' some thing or some one for non-development. To postulate a specific impediment in this way implies that development has specific cause(s) and objective(s) and that it follows an invariable sequence of events to a particular set of consequences. But in real life it is unlikely that a single factor will tell all, or that the same combinations of factors will pertain in every context. More important, there is variation possible in the selection of development goals; in the availability and recognition of alternatives to the development process; and in the actual consequences – intended and unintended – of similar development plans. Theoreticians – *qua* scientists or developers – may and/or should choose and concentrate on one priority at a time, and they may and/or should weed any factor extraneous to their particular model(s) out of account. But in real life people must manage a multitude of material and non-material resources which they value equally, whether singly or at the same time. They may perceive 'development' to be more of all these things and yet, and without contradiction, equate it with the alien package offered by theorists/planners/governments/outsiders. Our point is that the means and ends of development can only be prescribed *in theory*: both the *real* conditions of non-development and the *perception* of those real conditions will change with time, setting and situation (pp. 3–5 above).

It is important to appreciate the two levels together. The title of this volume expresses a reaction to the over-emphasis on material integers of development. Equally an over-emphasis on perception distorts the non-development issue. We have recognised in it two fallacies which we are determined to avoid. The first is a *simple life fallacy*. This appears in the tradition of the eighteenth-century Myth of the Noble Savage, but is updated by post-industrial malaise. The inherent fallacy is the assumption that a simple life *chosen* by someone exhausted by competitive consumption and by modern urban living is the same thing as a simple life without options. On the contrary: those who *cannot have* processed food, labour-saving technology, decent medical care and bright lights are likely to want them desperately – even if they also do not want to change the way they live. The second misconception can be described as a *fallacy of denied concreteness* along the lines that only perception is real and reality all in the mind. Such a view might be imputed to a discussion specific to the perceptions of development. But no amount of cultural relativism can deny the reality in scarcity, and we would have our case plain. We are not, in this volume, advocating 'the simple life', nor are we denying the iniquity and the inequity of poverty and backwardness. We are instead offering examples of the ways in which resources and the perception of resources form single and coherent systems in particular settings of time and place; and we are attempting to demonstrate that other developmental priorities may successfully compete with even the most vital need for material advance.

Autonomy and development

There is one set of priorities recognised in all cases described in this volume. The way in which it is ranked against or reconciled with the need or the desire for material advance is our pivotal point of variation on the development theme. Its parameters differ slightly from one case to another, but whether the priority is boundary; integrity; community; participation-in-planning; independence; social power; vitality or appropriateness – each of which is highly valued in at least one of these dozen examples – there is no doubt that we are dealing with generically similar things.

Galtung's (1973a: 33–46) 'mini-theory of power' allows these separate notions all to be seen as facets of *autonomy*. In effect he does so by postulating spheres of autonomy similar to the spheres of resources perceived by economic anthropologists (pp. 6–7 above). Briefly stated, his model distinguishes between *ideological, remunerative* and *punitive* power as threats to autonomy; and *self-respect, self-sufficiency* and *fearlessness* as the particular aspects of autonomy with which each is or might be counteracted. With *self-respect* it is no longer taken for granted that the ideas of others are superior to one's own; *self-sufficiency* follows from 'the ability to make do with one's own resources'; and *fearlessness* replaces anxiety about 'losing what one *has*, even losing what one *is*' (*ibid*: 35). Each of these stances alters the form and degree of dependence on those who have different or more-of-the-same resources, and progress towards any one of them will affect the choice and course of other kinds of development. There is therefore *some* relation between the development of autonomy and the development of material resources.

The co-variance of the priorities of autonomy and material advance is widely acknowledged, but there is no consensus on the way in which they vary. The recent plethora of development literature could in fact be classified according to the relationship seen, by each writer, between development and dependence (in the sense of autonomy lost or nullified). At one extreme is the view that development leads a country out of dependence; that this effect should be both the purpose and the function of development plans. The variation in choice of sector which should be given priority and developed first is itself germane to our theme (cf. Harries-Jones, Ch. 10 below). In this group we might include the more optimistic versions of the evolutionary approaches sketched above (pp. 6–8), but only by default: the explicit discussion of dependence in relation to development is relatively new (as De Kadt 1974: 2).

At the other extreme it is argued that economic development increases dependence, inexorably developing underdevelopment by increasing the gap between the rich and the poor and the dependence of the global/regional/ local poor on the rich who are one link ahead of them in a long chain of economic relations. Whether these links are perceived as fostering or in-hibiting development would seem to be an effect of the way one is facing in the dependency queue, but all versions of our last batch of explanatory approaches carry only the negative inference.

Using effectively the same evidence, some expect development to diminish autonomy, others say it does or will enhance it (compare e.g. Frank 1969; Lewis, W. A. 1966; Myrdal 1968). The reasons for such polarisation are also, in some part, the reasons for this volume. Firstly the relationship between the two processes is neither inevitable nor predictable: it can only be discerned by empirically-based analysis of the economic and political options and conditions pertaining to a particular case, and by taking an historical perspective appropriate to that case. Secondly and equally, the relationship depends on what development is perceived to be, by whom and in relation to what. Its meaning is largely assumed to be simply economic – despite the fact that even its economic value load alters drastically with setting: on the one hand 'development' is good for Zambia (Chapter 10); on the other, the 'developers' of downtown Montreal (Chapter 11) are, for some sectors of the population, the bogeymen of the decade.

Again: there is variation in the selection of goals, in the availability and recognition of alternatives to the economic development process, and in the actual consequences – intended and unintended – of similar development plans. And if both the real conditions of development/non-development and the perception of those real conditions can vary with contextual changes in a single setting, then 'development' may be a 'boo' notion and a 'hurrah' notion at once (cf. Cranston 1954 and p. 6 above).

These ambivalences appear 'in small' in our separate cases, and have convinced us that 'development' (for those who are subject of it rather than to it) comprises two distinct trends. It is a progression towards the (better?) meeting of basic needs, and it is a progression towards (greater?) autonomy and authenticity of self and/or nationhood. These are not necessarily comp-lementary processes. More often they are, on the contrary, no more than mutually corrective ideals: not the way development is, but the way it ought to be. Both ideals inhere in the various perceptions of development described in this volume. In some cases one is pursued and/or achieved to the complete exclusion of the other. Only a few achieve a combination satisfactory (to them) on both counts. Most commonly, both objectives are compromised and neither is achieved. From someone's point of view and in some respect, even 'successful' development is a double bind – such that: 'I got what I wanted, but it's not what I meant. . .'

Perceptions of loss and gain

The sense that 'I got what I wanted but it's not what I meant' is not the perception only of malcontents. The experience of loss along with gain is more universal than that. It is important to recognise that this is a practical, not a theoretical, view. *Theoretical* models of development deal with one side of the development coin at a time: it is at great thing, or it is a terrible thing; it is a great thing for some, but a terrible thing for others. But in *practical* terms most people sense that they stand to lose as well as to gain. This perception is occasionally conscious and articulate. More often it is expressed in ambivalence and inconsistency. It is worth teasing out a number of separate elements which are readily confused.

At one level, there is loss relative to aspiration. Once the notion of change as good, good as progress, progress as attainable has been admitted, new vistas of possibility open. The lack of some desired item may be endured, but it cannot be perceived as a loss unless and until the possibility of attaining it has been recognised. This form of loss may be suffered most acutely by people having an ideology of development without the means to develop, but insofar as the industrial machine needs us to need (as in Galbraith 1962), affluence is no cure. Certainly loss relative to aspiration is characteristic of an era geared to growth, consumption and 'progressive development'. Its intensity will vary only with the closeness of fit between aspirations (as perceptions) and available resources, and/or with the ability to refocus aspiration on to more attainable goals.

A second refraction of loss is relative to the gain of others. It may be endured without being perceived, or perceived by those who do not themselves endure it, but it is *politically* the most salient and the most hotly debated of development issues (as pp. 7–9 above). There is little doubt that development (as economic growth) benefits some more than it does others or that it has increased social and economic disparities within and between groups of people involved in or left out of the same process. These are effects which we have learnt to deplore if not (yet?) to prevent. But the fact that my own standard of living has risen 2% is a real gain; the fact that my boss enjoys a 20% improvement in the same period is 'only' a relative loss. Similarly a geometric growth of the centre does not always detract from the inching modernisation of conditions at the periphery. Conditions of brute ignorance or conspired privilege are not always sufficient explanation of the emphasis put on small real gains over large relative losses. It may equally reflect perceptions of advance and of appropriateness that have no necessary connection with economic development.

This brings us up against the third and most insoluble of the knots in the double bind: a gain in one means the loss of advance in other dimensions. To say that the choice of one option precludes the choice of another is not like saying that a house can only be entered through one door at a time. In the latter case there is only one house to enter; in the former, the 'houses' or objectives are likely to be many and contradictory. To assume only one objective is to confuse the logic of models with the logic of situations. Thus most of us want to live better *and* to live the way we have always done; to participate *and* to remain separate; to keep up with the Joneses *and* to distinguish ourselves from them; to give our children more options than we have had *and* to see them choose as we would have chosen. And most of us want to enjoy economic advance *and* to remain independent, authentic, appropriate to ourselves.

So at the most inclusive level, all change entails loss and all loss can be understood as a kind of grief (Marris 1974). In these terms, for example, it is probably inevitable that losses in other-than-material dimensions should be felt by any group enjoying better or worse material standards of life than they were brought up to expect – if only to the extent that the authentic way of doing things has been breached by change.

But the perceived effect of such change depends on the extent to which it can be incorporated into the identities (or meanings) of the past – i.e. on 'the balance between continuity, growth and loss' (*ibid*.: 20), and it is difficult to know what this balance will be before it happens. Marris distinguishes three kinds of change. The first offers no threat to continuity: the new is 'better but like' the old. The second entails growth (not, in this model, economic growth), but still maintains continuity since 'the familiar. . .is incorporated within a broader understanding or range of interests. . .[and does not] threaten the integrity of what has already been learned'. The third constitutes a 'crisis of discontinuity' and the 'discrediting of familiar assumptions' – a loss so fundamental that it must provoke either radical innovation or despair. It is important to recognise that economic development, modernisation and/or material advance could turn out to be any of these kinds of change. Our case studies might be classified accordingly, but we could not have predicted which would have resolved itself in which way, nor can we be entirely certain what the indices of entirely successful resolution should be.

Dimensions of non-development

In the framework of this volume the logic of development/non-development includes all the dimensions of perception and resource and of gain and loss which we have sketched here. Each paper is, however, distinct. The options available, and the ways in which choices are made and paradoxes resolved vary widely from one to another. The papers could therefore be grouped in a number of ways, each time to highlight a different theme. We have chosen to sub-divide them in terms of the perceived meaning(s) of 'development' and 'autonomy', and the way in which those meanings refract or react upon each other, and upon meanings proferred by or imposed from the outside. Other themes are signalled in the link paragraph preceding each essay.

In the first four papers the opposition between 'autonomy' and 'development' is quite clearly drawn. Those of Wallman and of Peterson imply a choice of 'autonomy' over 'development' – one in the proliferation of an elaborate series of conceptual and social boundaries against the outside, the other in the revival and maintenance of a nativistic Christian sect – although the title of the latter shows a proper scepticism of the reality of the options. The examples contributed by Barrett and Mortimore are more positive to the extent that 'autonomy' and 'development' are somehow reconciled. In each, economic development was directed and brought about by a leader astute or fortunate enough to prevent it distorting the meaning of the traditional system. The historical placing or sequence of events is especially important in these cases: the extraordinary progress of Barrett's people is over by the end of his paper, and Mortimore traces stages in the reconciliation of 'conservation' and 'development' goals.

All those in the second batch assess levels of 'autonomy' and 'development' relative to what they were or are in other times or places. In Levin's material the two are closely entailed and are associated with a particular leader. Whatever the reality of the past, the people perceive themselves to have lost on both counts since his death. Boissevain traces changes in the notion of 'progress' in one setting and relates them to 'development' measured against the perceived position of *others*, and to the loss of 'autonomy' felt when these relative positions change. Wallman deals similarly with different perceptions in a single setting, but this time the changes reflect a change of context or 'sphere'. The main paper offers a further example of 'development' measured against the position of *others* but in such a way that the enormity of the gap between *us* and *them* undermines the possibility of any autonomous effort to close it. There is nonetheless a perceived increase in autonomy: the companion piece discerns separate spheres of perception so that more than one measure of 'autonomy' and/or 'development' may be seen to operate at one time.

The last four papers take the notion of separate spheres or systems of perception further. Each deals with a particular project or series of plans which is perceived differently by different groups of people and/or at different points in time. In each case one perception 'triumphs' over another – whether by the exercise of power, by the resolution of paradox or by the compromise of opposite points of view. Each paper makes plain the bases of discrepancy or dispute. A common feature of all four is that the perceptions of the executive subjects and of the recipient objects of the project or plan differ crucially at some stage in the planning or implementation of development. In the contributions of Matthews, and of Manzer and Krohn, the differences remain (at the time of writing) unresolved; in those of

Harries-Jones and Salisbury we may discern the possibility of a happy ending.

Matthews' paper opposes the planners' view of relocation-as-development (where development is 'economic viability') to the people's view of relocation-as-underdevelopment (where development is 'social vitality'). Manzer and Krohn contrast the meanings of urban 'redevelopment' in the separate contexts of an official and an informal economic system – the crucial difference inhering in its perceived relation to 'autonomy' in the latter. Harries-Jones deals directly with the unintended consequences (on 'autonomy') of government plans for urban 'development', and with the conciliatory potential of participation-in-planning in such cases. The title of the last piece suggests the multiplicity of perceptions of a single project. Salisbury relates these to the interest groups concerned, to successive phases of the project, and to changes in the respective positions of the interest groups through time. The apparently successful resolution of the case came when the perceived threat to 'autonomy' gave way to the notion of 'development' as something in which *we* had participated as much as they. To the extent that this sense of participation integrates the notions of autonomy (as Galtung) and continuity (as Marris) with the economic advance that the projects are designed to achieve, it is a useful other-than-economic measure of successful development.

At this point we might do well to reprise the main themes. Firstly, the logic of non-development may be distorted or obscured by the assumption of a single and evolutionary scale of advance. Secondly, other-than-theoretical notions of development are likely to include criteria of 'autonomy' or appropriateness as well as the increment of material resources. And thirdly, the wavering or shifting of priorities is both normal and necessary to the development process. These themes are illustrated in the papers following.

1

*Each of this opening set of papers focuses on the 'autonomy'
of a particular group or enclave of people and illustrates a
different relation between 'autonomy' and 'development'. In
the first example, autonomy/non-development is sharply
contrasted with integration/development. A small community,
unlike its neighbours, appears to have opted for the first and
precluded the second. But since its members talk of wanting
both, the choice cannot be altogether conscious and deliberate.*

*To what extent do these western-Alpine Italians recognise
'development' to be hazardous to 'autonomy'? Are we
justified in assuming that non-development may be the
unintended effect of peculiarly resilient boundaries against the
outside?*

The shifting sense of 'us':
Boundaries against development in the
western Alps[1]

SANDRA WALLMAN

The River Varaita rises on the Italian side of the western Alps which form
the border between France and Italy. It has two sources which join at a fork
some few miles from the top of the valley. Above the confluence, the two
streams form two short valleys, separated from one another by a ridge of
mountains. Each side is known by the name of its settlement – Bellino Valley
and Chianale Valley – and each settlement is now a local government
municipality or *comune*. The two *comuni* are mutually accessible only via the
apex of the 'V' formed by their two valleys. At this point there is a third
comune, Casteldelfino, which is several hundred metres lower in altitude and
correspondingly further from France and deeper into Italy than either of its
upper neighbours. It is the site of a national hydro-electric plant, has a fair
variety of shops, a fulltime City Hall and a market once a week. All its
buildings are modern or modernised.

Given the dissimilarity of political and ecological setting, any difference
between this lower *comune* and the two above it is not unexpected. It is the
contrast between the two upper *comuni* that is striking and problematic. They
are comparable in every respect but degree of 'development'. The focus of
this enquiry is on the 'non-development' of Bellino. A brief description of
Chianale will underline the contrast.

Chianale is the more northerly of the two river sources. For some years
it has had the appearance of a modern alpine resort. The traditional dry-wall
stone houses are outnumbered by rectangular holiday villas and concrete-
block apartment buildings. There are several bars, restaurants and hotel
pensioni, some with modest neon name-signs, most with painted billboards
advertising the rustic and therefore recuperative properties of particular
alpine *liquori*. Commercially owned and operated ski lifts run up either side
of the valley for those who wish to enjoy the view from the tavern at the
top or the smooth ski runs to the bottom. There is a regular stream of
vehicular traffic, heavy with skiers in the winter and with trippers escaping
the humid lowland cities in the summer. A public parking lot concentrates
a large proportion of the visiting cars along the lakeside.

Superficially, Chianale is a bustling, populous village with all the evidences
of good but not luxurious touristic enterprise. Only in the context of this
discussion is it important that little of this enterprise or of the activity
associated with it pertains to or involves the original members of the old
comune. The great majority have dispersed to the lowlands. Since less than

half a dozen households persist in the old lifestyle, only a handful of residents are fulltime mountain-dwellers; three young children remain, and these must go to school in Casteldelfino. There is no resident priest – the incumbents of Bellino and Casteldelfino hear confessions and say mass in Chianale only in the tourist seasons.

Bellino, on the contrary, has lost so little of its traditional appearance that the provincial government has recently designated it a settlement of historical significance. Its over-wintering population had dropped by nearly half since the end of the second world war, but appears to have stabilised at about 450 people. This population is sufficient to maintain two two-room primary schools and a full-time priest. There is an accretion of people during the French and Italian summer vacation periods, but only a tiny minority of these are outsiders. The condition of many houses is original – the majority of winter residents still being dependent for warmth on the presence of cows in their basement stalls. Economic activity centres around these few cows, and the sale of calves is acknowledged to be the most important source of cash income. While there are certainly evidences of modernity and consumerism in Bellino, two characteristics distinguish it absolutely from Chianale – and, by extension, from generally expected trends. One is that it shows so few signs of socio-economic change or development; the other is that its boundary as a community is relatively intact.

The co-existence of these features suggests their co-relationship. But since the possibility of their co-relationship cannot be tested unless economic development and boundary maintenance can be dealt with in a single framework, they will be analysed here as parts of a single system of resources. This approach is readily justified: if the academic distinction between economic and non-economic resources relegates them to different levels of analysis, the people who are managing those resources must articulate them into a single system of options in which the cost of one alternative can be measured against the expense of another. By analysing the way in which Bellinesi perceive and manage their resources, it is possible to 'explain' the relative non-development of Bellino on the grounds that the preservation of boundary has equal priority with, or is given priority over material improvement; and to propose the more general hypothesis that autonomy and economic development are, or are seen to be, mutually preclusive. A tentative answer to the question of *why* Bellinesi should have accorded priority to boundary when so many comparable groups opt instead for development is suggested by the peculiar nature of that boundary. This is explored in the following sections.

Social-boundary systems

A social boundary is symbolic, although it may of course be symbolised by real things. Being symbolic, it is also situational, and responsive to changes in the relationship between the internal and the external systems – just as a balloon which bounds air, responds to changes in the relative pressure of air inside and outside itself. This elastic analogy (taken from Cohen 1969) allows the recognition that the size, quality and significance of a social boundary system will vary both with situation and through time. It does not, however, allow the possibility that items and influences may pass across a social boundary without jeopardy to it – for which theoretical purpose we may do better to visualise a tea-bag than a balloon.

Essentially we must be talking about a system of social relationships bounded on the basis of territoriality, or of ethnicity, or of economics or of symbolic identifications (Cohen 1969) such as value orientation and the like (Barth 1969). Changes in the criterion of inclusion within a particular system are quite normal; it may also be that the survival strength of a system varies with the ability to alter the form and content of its boundary appropriately.

If Bellino is examined as a social-boundary system, it is possible to account for shifts in its 'edge' by contextual changes in the criterion of inclusion (i.e. in the criterion of Bellinese-ness), and to explain the persistence of its boundary as a product of the management of those criteria as system-preserving resources. We are used to nesting models in which the bounds of political loyalty expand and contract with context (as, classically, Evans-Pritchard 1940), or the bounds of the economic system include ever-wider systems of relationships (as e.g. Malinowski 1922; Frank 1969). If we allow that resources of different kinds and degrees of measurability can be – or are – articulated in a single system, then we may allow that the boundary at one level is marked by criteria different from those marking the boundary at another level: 'nests' indeed there are, sometimes fitting inside one another as Nuer tribal segments are said to do (Evans-Pritchard 1940: 140–4), sometimes overlapping in whole or in part, but the criterion of inclusion, the test of membership in a 'nest', is not consistent throughout the system.

The notion of redundancy is suggestive. In the idiom of communication, so many criteria for inclusion within a system constitute as many 'messages'. If one message goes astray or is distorted, an alternative version has been or may be successfully transmitted and received; if one criterion of inclusion is inappropriate, one level of boundary threatened or breached, the system compensates on another level. The redundancy of boundary 'messages' in this case may be held to account for the curious durability of the system being bounded.

Hence Bellinesi use territoriality *and* ethnicity *and* economic and symbolic identifications as criteria of Bellinese-ness, varying them according to the logic of particular boundary situations, but consistently to the end of maintaining the boundary. I shall describe Bellino successively as a unit defined by territory; by language; by the form and usage of its family naming systems; by population; by economic organisation; and by aspects of life style. While these units are not co-extensive, I will argue that they constitute a single conceptual system for Bellinesi – which system involves sufficient redundancy to make it peculiarly resilient to pressures from outside and so peculiarly resistent to development.

1. Bellino as a geographic unit

The western Alps run north/south forming the border between France and Italy – between Provence and Piedmont. Three western alpine valleys on the Italian side are known as the Cuneo Valleys; the Vale Varaita is the northernmost of the three. It is about 50 km. long, and is enclosed at the top by the massive rocks of *Monviso* and *Pelvo d'Elva*. Along the valley there are thirteen municipal units (*comuni*) of which the total resident population in both 1961 and 1971 censes was stable at around 16,000 persons. The top of the valley is forked by two contributory sources whose topographic relationship is described in the introductory section.

Bellino is the more southerly of the two and the most remote point of year-round settlement in the *Vale Varaita*. The altitude of the highest hamlet is slightly under 1800 metres, of the lowest, about 1400 metres. At this altitude, a few hundred metres more or less make an appreciable difference in temperature, levels of mist and hours of sunlight, and the inhabitants recognise climatic differences between the upper and lower parishes. But the growing season overall varies only with the vagaries of a rain-shadow effect and is seldom more than two months long. Winters are extremely cold – occasional variations in degree serving only to alter the frequency of avalanche. The danger of avalanches has always been a primordial preoccupation in Bellino. The original pattern of settlement takes account of and so indicates their probable paths.

The *comune* comprises a cluster of nine small hamlets (*frazioni*) spread in a linear pattern along the main river. A narrow tarred highway, not infrequently blocked or broken by landslides in winter, now connects the hamlets to each other and to the lower valley. The road peters out not far above the uppermost hamlet. A trek over mountain footpaths in the same westerly direction would, within a few miles, bring one into France. This road was begun during the Second World War, presumably in a government effort to police Italy's border with France more effectively, but was finished only in 1948. Until that time Bellinesi could go east 'into Italy' down a track described as being wide enough for one mule. Some still remember treading awkwardly into the snow-prints of the person in front to avoid falling or missing the path altogether.

But while Bellino is less isolated than before, its topographic separateness is unaltered. As a territorial unit it is narrowly bounded to the north and south by the walls of the valley, to the west by the still higher mountains of the French border, and down the valley to the east by a bottleneck in the conformation of the mountains. From the perspective of Bellino itself, it is not the top of a continuous chute which runs down to the bottom of the valley.

It forms instead a boxed-in section whose edge marks a significant change in the form and use of the vernacular dialect.

2. Bellino as a language unit

Many alpine settlements along the French–Italian border were distinct political units as late as 1713, and there are still independence movements which testify to a continuing, if intellectualised, sense of separateness. More recently and more importantly, their position has entailed a switching back and forth between French and Italian 'nationality' as the border between France and Italy has been shifted in the resolution of wars, skirmishes or disputes. The latest change in the legal status of Bellino occurred in 1918, when it and two *comuni* below it were transferred from France into Italy.

The one real difference effected by this legal change is in the official language of school instruction: it was French, it is now Italian. Bellinesi above a certain age were schooled in French, those below that age in Italian. This switch is by no means unique to Bellino since it is entailed by the logic of national unification in Italy. What does appear to be unique, however, is the contemporary Bellinese pattern of language use.

Bellinesi all speak Italian, although often imperfectly, and some are semi-fluent in French. But these are second and secondary languages in every case. It is the vernacular Old French (*Provençal*) dialect which is used in all community contexts, and in all situations involving communication between Bellinesi of all ages. Such extensive use is now rare. European language scholars report that Provençal dialects are now spoken in Italy only by the very old and very young; that they are used by people who learned them as children, and by small children who spend their time with old people; that once they go to school they 'lose' the vernacular and communicate in Italian or one of its variants. In this respect Bellino is apparently unique.[2]

There is more evidence of the thorough compartmentalisation of language in the use of the provincial Italian dialect, *Piemontes'*. This is not only different from *Provinciale/Provençal*, it is also very different from Italian. While Bellinesi will speak Italian as well as they can when they must, they are explicitly reluctant to use *Piemontes'* in Bellino itself. It is as if they were anxious not to let it encroach into the territory of their vernacular dialect: being the geographically logical thing for them to speak, *Piemontes'* poses the greatest threat to the language boundary. The use of *Piemontes'* is accordingly restricted to commercial transactions with the lower valley. Where these are to do with the sale of cows or calves, the transactions take place in Bellino. The merchants who come to appraise and to buy are always from lowland Piedmont, and in this context Bellinesi will speak *Piemontes'*: they are on Bellino territory, but not in a Bellino context. Otherwise, and much more normally, *Piemontes'* is spoken in exchanges with non-Bellinesi on work sites lower down the valley or in Turin – never on home ground.

3. Bellino as a naming system

Within their vernacular dialect all Bellinesi have unofficial family names which they use wholly and only as terms of reference and address. Although these names are called in Italian *soprannome* and in French *soubriquet* – both terms normally being rendered in English as *nickname* – they are unlike nicknames in a number of crucial respects. They refer neither to personal attributes nor to past events and thus do not distinguish or censure individuals; they are inherited, usually from the father through an unspecified number of generations; and, being used in all community contexts and by everybody, they indicate no special occasion or intimacy (Wallman 1973: 129–30).

Just as the use and vitality of the vernacular dialect distinguishes Bellino from other Western Alpine communities, so this naming system is different, at least in its comprehensiveness, from vernacular naming patterns elsewhere in Europe. In other parts of Italy (and of France) *soprannomi* are not uncommon, but there are nowhere records of a contemporary community in which all families have *soprannomi* used so continuously and so systematically.

The relation of *soprannomi* to the official surnames (*nomi; noms de famille*) is crucial. The two systems are distinct both in form and in use. The official names number altogether twelve (eight being clearly predominant) and each over-arches some number of *soprannomi* which, in these terms, are sub-classes or sub-family names. The number of *soprannomi* is thus very much greater: seventy-eight are readily remembered, but only about fifty are still present; those no longer in use probably pertain to families who have left the area permanently.

While *soprannomi* are used in all community contexts, which is to say whenever the vernacular dialect is spoken, *nomi* are used by outsiders and/or in relations with the official world outside. Government censes, church records, birth, marriage and death certificates are always made out in the individual's official *nome*, and with no record of the *soprannome* appended. Similarly they are used in extra-Bellinese contexts outside Bellino in which Italian (or French) is spoken, and by stranger-outsiders on business in Bellino itself. In the latter case a handy confusion of the two systems may well confound the stranger's purpose altogether.

Etymologically, the *soprannomi* are largely Provençal, referring sometimes to an occupation, animal or place, often having no meaning at all. The *nomi* are unrelated in meaning and are etymologically (new) French. This distinguishes them also from their local Italian equivalents – as *Martin*, not *Martini; Richard*, not *Riccardi* etc. They are further distinct in form and by distribution from other French surnames in the lower valley and in adjacent valleys.

These distinctions are rooted in the history and relative isolation of Bellino, and it should not be inferred that they were or are deliberately

2

engendered for the purposes of boundary marking or maintenance. Nonetheless the two naming systems, each particular and peculiar to Bellino and distinct from the other, provide markers of contrast between inside and outside systems, inside and outside contexts, and so allow variations on the theme of 'us' and 'them'.

The significance of this boundary-marking function is underlined if we recognise that the *soprannomi* are not now 'necessary' in the way that they (probably) once were. While the origin of the *soprannomi* system is neither remembered nor recorded, its usage is clearly based in property relations. A person's *soprannome* is, and has apparently always been inherited from the father, as is his/her *nome*. But in the event of uxorilocal marriage residence the *soprannome* is taken from the mother. In such a case the child carries its father's *nome* and its mother's *soprannome* and the source of its residential property is plain. All contemporary families follow these patterns, even though the organisation of property has necessarily been altered and simplified by changes in the size and density of the population.

Speculation suggests another function, but one almost impossible to substantiate by contemporary forms: the *soprannomi* system may have served to reconcile Roman Catholic prohibitions against cousin marriage with the traditional endogamous preference of the Bellinesi. While the marriage of people with the same *nome* provokes no comment in Bellino and is statistically not uncommon, the union of two with the same *soprannome* is perceived quite differently. In effect the indigenous notion of kinship in particular relation to marriage distance is quite different from the official view. When local marital arrangements were made autonomously and without legal interference from outside, this local view would have increased the number of local marriage options, forbidding in-marriage *only* with partners of the same *soprannome*. But now that the Bellinesi are, in these matters, governed by outsiders, their perception of appropriate marriage classes may actually rule out options available to them as Catholics under Italian law: an Italian Catholic may obtain dispensation to marry *any* second or third cousin, whatever the congruence of surnames; a Bellinese Catholic would not apply for dispensation to marry a cousin of the same *soprannome*.

The contemporary expression of the *soprannome* system is not therefore explained by history: even a *satisfactory* explanation of origin (which I cannot offer) would insufficiently account for it. In the present context the comprehensiveness of the *soprannome* system must be related to the curious vitality of the vernacular dialect. In combination they symbolise the integrity and integrality of 'us' most crucially, and constitute the most explicit links between Bellino and dispersed Bellinesi.

4. Bellino as a population

According to the government census, the population of Bellino was, in 1951, 700 people and, in 1971, 450 people. But these figures do not represent the true extent of the community since the population boundary is systematically elastic. Bellinesi comprise three categories. There are, firstly, the all-year-round residents whose number is listed in government censes as *the* population. There are, secondly, the sporadic residents, the migrants to places of work in Turin, the uppers-and-downers who return home on weekends or on holidays, who may assist in and also expect to inherit a share in the paternal or parental property, and who usually talk of moving back home eventually. There are, thirdly, the summer residents. These are people of Bellino birth or parentage who have emigrated into France.

These two migrations apply to different periods. It used to be that all movement out was movement into France, frequently involving a permanent shift of main residence. But in the last couple of decades, temporary or target migrations to Turin and other parts of lowland Piedmont have become the pattern. The opening of the road must have contributed to the change: it is now easier to go down the road to the lowlands of Piedmont than it is to go over the Alps into France, but the effect of change in official language proficiency and the pull of industrial Turin must be more than negligible.

Because the French *émigrés* routinely return to spend the summer holiday in their ancestral home '*pour se reprendre*', the resident population is very much larger in the summer period than it is in the winter months. In 1973, in the largest of the nine hamlets, the population was three times as big in August as it was in May. All the people who were there were Bellinesi. They had *soprannomi*, used the dialect, called themselves and were called 'us'. Because the summer invasion is confined to people who can be categorised as Bellinesi, it does not present the threat to community that tourism is known to bring. The dialect, the naming system and real or putative kin ties are activated in such a way that the summer residents are perceived as full members of the community, and increased money and sociability can be enjoyed without hazard to the community boundary. These effects clearly underpin the economic and social survival of the *comune*.

5. Bellino as an economic system

The economic resources of Bellino are more extensive than the size or lifestyle of its resident population suggest. Bellinese own thousands of acres of land, but much of it is unused. This happens for a number of reasons.

Firstly their agricultural holdings are divided and subdivided by the rules of equivalent inheritance, so that many fields measure well under an acre, – some being no larger than a good-sized kitchen table. It is not possible to farm fields of this size 'rationally'.

Secondly, it is difficult to farm lands which are far from the valley floor.

The slope becomes back-breaking and the bringing down of the hay crop problematic. Land near the road which runs along the valley floor is therefore at a premium. Anyone leaving the area or cutting down work has no trouble renting out a low-lying, relatively level field. Land is rarely sold and rents are nominal. Bellinese-ness is prerequisite to land transaction and is itself enhanced by it: those resident away keep their stake in Bellino, those resident fulltime forge extra links with Bellinesi outside. Those who are committed to staying try to accumulate low-lying lands so that they may abandon their higher, steeper lands. The effect is that extensive acreage up the slopes and visible from the road is either uncultivated or uncut. As the population decreases it becomes easier for those who remain to farm because there is less competition for the more level lands: the ones who remain benefit – some quite explicitly – from the leaving of those who go.

Thirdly, the high pastures owned by the *comune*, said (by their elders) to be too remote for the peri-urban tastes of the younger cowherds, are in fact too vast for the present meagre holding of cattle.[3] While Bellino could rent its spare grassland to farmers from the lowlands each summer, it has steadfastly refused to repeal an ancient local law which prohibits the use of high pasture before the end of July each year; lowland husbandmen seek to escape the heat before the beginning of June. If this law made sense when the population was full and grass scarce, it does not make the same sense now; the grass remains ungrazed and unharvested. The neighbouring *comune*, by contrast, reaps enormous monetary advantage but retains no communal high pasture.

In economist's terms, there is a surplus of land in Bellino: there is land available which is neither used by its owners, exchanged for other goods, nor converted into money. This is not to say that the Bellinesi are not using it economically. They normally grow enough potatoes, barley and rye for their own needs, and they grow enough grass and reap enough hay to feed their small numbers of cattle. These are not a subsistence product: Bellinesi rarely eat bellinese beef and they regard themselves as living from the sale of calves. But they consistently maintain that they cannot increase their meagre holdings, that they have not the hay to feed more, that they cannot cut and carry more hay than they do.

On one level this is entirely true. The annual agricultural work must be carried out in a two-month growing period which, at that altitude, is all that nature allows. Much of the ground is frozen until the beginning of July; in July and August outside work is feasible (when it is not raining!),[4] but by September the mist rises so early in the day that it is perpetually chill and damp. Those who have not harvested by this time have little chance of doing so efficiently. The annual cycle therefore comprises two months of frenzied work to produce enough hay to feed a handful of cows throughout the eight months of winter during which nothing grows and the cows are confined to the basement stalls under each house.[5] Both the industrial Italian and the French summer holidays fall during this summer season, and the domestic labour force is at its optimum. But while the local definition of a well-off family as one with many hands to work in the summer and few mouths to feed in the winter fits these holiday schedules, few households achieve the ideal balance.

6. Bellino as a way of life

Hard as work is, the number of cows, the amount of hay, the acreage of cultivated land and the available work force fit each other perfectly well. If you were to ask a Bellinese why he did not keep more cows and so produce more calves and so make more money, he would say: 'I have not enough hay. I cannot keep more cows because I have not the hay to feed them.' If you were then to suggest that he might *buy* hay from the lowlanders who can reap two or three harvests of it instead of just one, he would say: 'I have no money.' And if you were then so bold as to ask why he did not rent or sell a house or some ground or something else that he did not use in order to buy the hay that would allow him to increase his production and lead a better life, he would be likely to avert his face and say simply: 'I cannot do that'; or 'We have never done that'; or perhaps 'That would be too much loss: those unused houses and abandoned fields are mine and they will belong to my children.'

Anthropologists at least are taught to expect responses like these, and a functionalist explanation of the management of economic resources in Bellino might well stop there. But since Bellinesi also talk of improving their lot and complain of the lack of modern comfort, even of the lack of progress and development, we must take their inconsistency seriously and go further (cf. Gellner 1973). Like most of us the Bellinesi want both things-as-they-might-be and things-as-they-have-always-been (as Marris 1974). They want an improved living standard, less work, certainly less back-breaking work, more comfort, less isolation. They want all the good things associated with cities and modernisation which they know of or have experienced at first or second hand. They also want to live and work as they have always done, in the way which defines them Bellinesi and distinguishes them from outsiders.

To be distinct is not always advantageous. The things which constitute Bellinese-ness and which identify a person as belonging to the mountains may constitute a liability outside the context of Bellino. In the city, mountain-dwellers have always been denigrated. They are mocked as *scarpe grosse*[6]; their accents are funny; they do not speak Italian as well as they should; they are perceived as lumpen, rural. Now that economic conditions are generally tighter, it is likely that they suffer the shortage of urban accommodation and the uncertainty of work more acutely than the city-bred (cf. Davis 1969).

While the young bloods of Bellino still migrate to work in Turin, few now expect it to be more than financially expedient, and that only in the short run. The bright lights of the city have not the appeal they once had: the city is not what it was and even the young are well-informed of its hazards. Members of the school-leaving class, asked to write short essays on what they would do or be as adults, pitched their extra-Bellino aspirations low – the boys at factory jobs, the girls at house-maiding – and they saw their out-migration as temporary: . . . One must go down and make a bit of cash, but no one would stay there. Not now. Not from here . . . The objective would seem to be to make enough money to live a little better, but without altering the way we live by doing so.

Conclusion

Despite a steady incursion of items and influences, the boundary persists. It is as if the management of social and economic resources were primarily directed to its maintenance, as if other priorities must be denied insofar as they constitute a threat to the sense of 'us'. The pressure to develop, coming as it does from the outside, must therefore be resisted. The resilience of boundary around Bellino accounts for the peculiar success of this resistance and the corresponding 'failure' of development.

Why the boundary should have this quality is more difficult to say. It may be that the Bellinese recognise that the optimum conditions of progress are unattainable and so choose to do something else – or do nothing (Wallman 1972). It may be that they have reached a compromise point: so far we have gained, any further we will lose. Life, certainly, is better than it was: the population is down and farming is easier; some things come back from the city; there is a road and access to the outside if one wants it; the children can read (and if they learn too much they will leave us!); there are television sets about, numerous tools and a bar or two . . . Bellino as a community had no contact with modernism and the outside until the road was finally finished in the late 1940s. It came upon the mainstream of development when it was already murky, and the backlash of progress, whether in Chianale or Turin, was plain to see. Maybe its resilience is the simple product of a set of social resources handily appropriate to boundary marking and maintenance.

Very likely all of these in systematic combination are necessary to the explanation of non-development in Bellino, and to an understanding of the peculiar tenacity of the community. Clearly the two things vary together. Hence the two naming systems and the vitality of the language; the relatively high proportion of year-round residents who have *not* left; the way in which summer visitors from France are reincorporated during their short visits, and are described and probably perceived as Bellinesi while they are away; the reluctance to convert remote lands and uninhabited houses into the cash that people claim to need; the stubborn refusal to repeal the ancient law that now prevents the *comune* making money out of its unused high pasture; the increasingly cautious view of urban wages and amenities. And hence the extraordinary contrast with Chianale.

Three general inferences may be drawn. The first relates to development: the process and therefore the concept involves the growth or diminution of autonomy as well as of material resources. The second relates to boundary: the sense of 'us' may be perceived and manipulated at various levels – the more levels, the more resilient to 'attack' from outside. The third relates to the explanation of non-development in cases of this kind: if a single scale of development and an uncontradictory set of priorities are assumed, non-development must be diagnosed as a hitch in the path of progress – a pathology if progress is good, a boon if it is bad. We tend *either* to enumerate what is to be gained by development *or* to moan nostalgically for what is to be lost. But development is not an either/or proposition, and the logic of non-development is both intricate and variable. In each case we must take account of available options and resources, but remind ourselves also that the way those options and resources are perceived will be crucial to the way they are managed.

2

'Autonomy' is not always inimical to 'development'. The remarkable autonomy of Olowo village was perceived in terms of non-worldly goods and benefits, but was expressed in fervent dedication to work and communal values. Over a very short period of time 'God's Kingdom on Stilts' became a model of rapid economic development. The people themselves claim that their religious beliefs produced their economic success. Hard work and economic progress were measures of faith and hence the means to salvation. The analogy with capitalism and the Protestant ethic is not, however, exact. During the period of its phenomenal material progress, Olowo's values were anti-individualistic, anti-entrepreneurial; and as communalism declined, Olowo's material and physical state deteriorated. It seems that cracks in the collective 'autonomy' undermined the process of individual as well as collective economic advance. Progress was past within one generation. But this intricate analysis of a brief success story illustrates the practical problems as well as the Utopian possibilities of 'development' and 'autonomy' unified.

Faith, work and autonomy:
The Holy Apostles and rapid economic development

STANLEY BARRETT

Olowo was founded in 1947 by Yoruba-speaking fishermen, and by 1969 had a population of over 1,200.[1] The village is located at the edge of the Atlantic Ocean in an area called Ilaje, which is part of the Western State of Nigeria. During the wet season most of Ilaje is covered with water. Houses are built upon stilts, there are no roads, and the main mode of transportation is canoe. Olowo is separated from the Yoruba mainland by about 50 miles of swamps and rivers, but in spite of its isolated location, harsh environment and brief existence, it has enjoyed unusual economic success. Shortly after the community was founded, a network of boardwalks on stilts was erected to connect every house. Bicycles, motorcycles, and even eventually a car for the *oba* (king)[2] were operated on them. This was a major innovation in Ilaje, for not only were there no bicycles in the other villages, but in order to move from one house to another it was necessary to enter a canoe.

As early as 1953 the community had purchased a generator for electricity; even in 1970 only two other Ilaje villages enjoyed this amenity. Within a few years several factories had been established, almost 20 large passenger boats that serviced the rivers and lagoons from Lagos to Cameroon had been built, as well as seven fully-mechanized ocean-going fishing trawlers – with almost no help from outsiders. As early as 1951, only four years after Olowo was established, it was described as Nigeria's most successful case of village-level development (Duckworth 1951). By 1957 it was said to have the highest standard of living of any village in the country (*Anon.* 1957).

One possible cause of Olowo's success was its religious beliefs. The village emerged from a protest movement against the killing of twins in Ilaje that began about 1942 and eventually produced almost 50 theocracies. Olowo people, who became known as the Holy Apostles, formerly were members of the Cherubim and Seraphim, which is a branch of the Aladura independent church movement that is widespread among the Yoruba (see Peel 1968). Olowo people themselves contend that their economic success was a result of their religious beliefs.

Another possible cause was the village's communal social organization. In 1948, one year after the village was founded, communalism was introduced. All personal possessions such as cash, jewellery, and watches became community property. Apparently even the extra clothing that wealthier members had brought with them was taken from them and distributed among those in need. From that point onwards no money was exchanged among members for goods or services. People worked in large gangs on projects selected by the village leaders, and all profits went to a central treasury. In turn, everyone was provided food, clothing, and housing. Food that could not be produced by the people such as yams, plantain and rice was bought in bulk by a trusted woman known as the community mother. Periodically clothing was distributed, and a small building called the Community Shop stocked minor items such as flashlight batteries and soap, which were provided without payment.

The communal system also affected the family. Not only did the wealthy have to relinquish their extra clothing, but men who had been accompanied by two or more wives were allowed to retain only one; the others were distributed among men who had no wife. This policy was necessary because apparently more men than women had joined the community. At two different periods marriage was banned entirely. Even when it existed, husband and wife did not live together, because the village was split into male and female sectors, separated by the central boardwalk. Although the rule was not enforced absolutely, children over five years old were not allowed to be raised by their own parents. Even before this age they spent most of the day in the kindergarten apart from their parents. The result of all these policies was to reduce the strength of the family and foster the communal system (Barrett 1974).

A third possible cause was Olowo's political organization. The village was not a democracy. A small group of men, led by the *oba*, constituted the elite and ruled with an iron hand. Religious and political authority were highly correlated, for those among the elite were the most powerful prophets in the village. The vast majority of members had no voice in their education, occupation, or choice of spouse. These decisions were made by the elite, who also directed economic activities, and took an active interest in social control. Laziness, disobedience and other forms of deviance were severely punished.

How to measure the influence of these factors on Olowo's economic success? Although Olowo emerged from a religious movement in Ilaje that produced numerous small theocracies, it was the only one to achieve unusual economic success. I undertook a comparative study with one of the other theocracies, which I call Talika, whose population in 1970 was about 900. Located about 12 miles along the Atlantic coast from Olowo, Talika had been founded by a prophet who had been a charter member of Olowo in 1947, but decided to leave in 1950. His decision was partly based upon his unhappiness with the communal system that had been adopted, and partly because he wanted to be the leader of Olowo; several members of Olowo followed this man to the new village.[3]

Olowo and Talika were similar in terms of religious and political organization. Both have their roots in Cherubim and Seraphim, and both emerged from the protest movement against the killing of twins. Members of the two villages claimed that their religious beliefs were identical, which I found to be essentially correct. Talika too was led by an *oba* and a handful of men who were the most powerful prophets. The outstanding difference between the villages was that Talika was organized in terms of private enterprise. People kept the profits from their work, and the extended family, which had not been suppressed, was the basic economic unit.

In this paper I shall focus upon the communal system. Because it was the basic difference between Olowo and Talika, it might appear to be the key factor in Olowo's success. My argument, however, is that while its contribution was important, it likely was no greater than religious beliefs and political organization. This has significant implications for the comparative method: while constants such as religion and political organization cannot by themselves explain why Olowo was successful and Talika was not, they cannot be eliminated, and indeed may be as important or more important than inconstants such as economic organization.

Finally, while communalism, religion, and political organization were the key sociological factors in Olowo's economic success, a number of other factors also were involved, the most important of which was the personality of the *oba*. He was a brilliant, innovative, awe-inspiring man, both loved and feared by his subjects; many of the innovations in Olowo, including the communal system, can be traced directly to him. In 1963 he died. The man who succeeded him was less capable, and the rapid expansion of the economy ceased. The second *oba* fell ill and in 1966 was replaced by a younger man who struggled to revitalize the economy, but never succeeded. This was due more to the fact that Olowo was a generation old than to the *oba*'s leadership qualities, for the force of the beliefs that had held the Apostles together had begun to diminish.

Physical structure of Olowo and Talika

The greater development and wealth of Olowo than of Talika is obvious from their physical difference. Although in 1969 their populations were similar, Olowo was much larger physically, with 566 as opposed to 196 buildings. The standard of construction in Olowo also was much higher. For example, the boardwalks in Olowo were wide and firm, and permitted the use of bicycles and motorcycles. Several were able to support the *oba*'s car. Talika also had boardwalks but these were precarious, consisting only of single planks or sticks strung together. In 1970 there were no cars, motorcycles or bicycles in the community, for it was impossible to use them.

In Olowo every house was constructed with a tin roof and a wood frame. In contrast approximately 85 of the 161 houses in Talika had thatch roofs, and the frames were made from the ribs of palm branches, which was the standard building material in the poorer villages throughout Ilaje. The same difference existed with respect to kitchens, which were small buildings used by the women to smoke fish and prepare meals. No woman in Olowo did this work in her house, for 214 kitchens existed for this purpose. In Talika

Table 1. *Physical structure of Olowo and Talika*

	Olowo	Talika
Dwellings	294	161
Kitchens	214	30
Other buildings	58	5
Total	566	196

the reverse was the case, for only 30 of the 121 dwellings in the female sector had separate kitchens. Finally, all the kitchens in Olowo had tin roofs, and were better constructed than the majority of houses in Talika.

Only five buildings existed in Talika other than houses or kitchens. These included a small building for their electric generator which was purchased in 1964, the church, a house nearby used by the prophets for healing, a shed, and a clay-oven bakery built in 1969. In contrast 58 other buildings existed in Olowo. Almost all of these were part of the industrial complex: factories, sheds, administration buildings. This variation in terms of buildings other than houses or kitchens in Olowo and Talika is an accurate index of their difference in industrial activity.

Occupations in Olowo and Talika

The main occupation in Ilaje in the past was fishing – both in the ocean and in the freshwater rivers and lagoons. Only men were allowed to fish in the sea, operating with nets from large canoes. Both men and women fished in the inland waters, which were highly regulated. For example, nets could not be used at the time of year when fish were carrying eggs. Inland fishing also was differentiated by sex: certain types of traps were used to catch 'women's fish' and could not be used by men. Fishing rights to specific sectors in the rivers and lagoons belonged to specific lineages. Some men also made a living from cutting timber and tapping palm wine, and women from making mats out of palm raffia.

When founded in 1947 Olowo too was dependent upon fishing. At first dug-out canoes were used, but in a short time enough funds were accumulated to allow the purchase of outboard motors and better fishing gear. Then in 1963 the village built the first of its seven fully-mechanized sea-going trawlers. In 1969 a large ice-making machine was imported in order that the trawlers could range further into the sea and remain out longer without fear of the catch spoiling. In 1969 fishing was still the main industry in Olowo, absorbing 37% and 56% of the men and women respectively (see Table 2).[4] Each trawler had two crews, but only when fishing was good did both of them work on a single day. About 40–50 men still fished in large canoes with motors. While their catch could not compare with that from the trawlers, it was similar to the catch obtained by other villages along the coast. There was a tendency for older and less educated men to work in the canoes. As in traditional Ilaje society, fishing in Olowo was differentiated according to sex: only the men went to sea, while the women dried and marketed the fish.

Table 2. *Occupations in Olowo*

	Male		Female		Total	
	N	%	N	%	N	%
Fishing	158	36.8	111	56.3	269	46.0
Passenger Boats	54	12.5	22	11.1	76	11.9
Carpentry and boatbuilding	55	12.8	—	—	55	6.6
Tailoring	17	3.9	11	5.5	28	4.7
Shoemaking	10	2.3	8	4.0	18	3.1
Sawmill	9	2.0	—	—	9	1.0
Bakery	5	1.0	2	1.0	7	1.0
Weaving	5	1.0	5	2.5	10	1.8
Soapmaking*	4	0.9	8	4.0	12	2.0
Laundry	1	0.2	8	4.0	9	2.0
Other†	88	20.5	18	9.1	106	15.0
Unknown‡	23	5.3	4	2.0	27	3.6
Total	429	99.2	197	99.5	636	98.7

* The soap factory actually has been abandoned, but in 1970 the myth persisted that the industry would be revived, and hence members insisted that those who had been formally assigned to this industry should be shown.

† Consists mainly of making mats out of palm raffia (women's work), jobs in the technical workshop, schools, and community hotel, and occupations involving only one or two people, such as the medical dispenser and postal agent.

‡ Consists of those who had several jobs, which made it hard to classify them.

Another major occupation was the passenger service on Olowo launches throughout the rivers. The first launch was completed in 1955 with the help of a man who had been hired from the mainland. After this the community constructed about 20 large launches on its own, which plied throughout the swamps to Lagos to the West, and prior to the civil war into Cameroon to the East.

In addition to the fishing and passenger industries, several factories gradually were established. The first to appear were the weaving, shoe, and tailoring industries. While at the beginning the equipment used was crude, by 1969 all had modern machinery. For example, the weaving department began with home-made handlooms, which were eventually replaced by 10 automatic looms. Raw cotton was made into cloth, dyed, and transferred to the tailors. The shoe factory was first located in a small house, with only manual equipment. In 1961 a new factory was built, and equipped with up-to-date machinery imported from abroad. The tailoring industry grew from a few manual sewing machines to 12 electric machines as well as numerous manual ones in 1969. In early 1960 a bakery was established. Unlike the older factories, it was equipped with modern machinery at the outset.

Early in my research some Olowo people told me that it was the policy of the village to circulate people among these various industries, so that they were proficient at many different tasks. A similar policy existed in the early American utopia of Oneida (Nordhoff 1971: 285). In an examination of 429 men and 197 women in Olowo, I found that 53% and 35% respectively had changed jobs at least once. These data, however, do not necessarily support the remarks of Olowo people. One reason is that the time-span is from 1947 to 1969, when the data were collected; it is reasonable to argue that a change of jobs during this period would be normal, rather than a result of a deliberate policy. A second reason was that I discovered that it was the elite, not the populace in general, who circulated among the various industries.

Table 3. *Occupations of Talika men*

	(N)	(%)
Fishing only	35	43.7
Trading only	4	5.0
Fishing and trading	22	26.7
Other	19	23.0
Unknown	1	1.0
Total	81	99.4

Table 4. *Occupations of Talika women*

	(N)	(%)
Making mats	18	47.3
Trading fish	6	15.7
Making mats and trading fish	6	15.7
Trading (not fish)	3	7.8
Other	5	13.0
Total	38	99.5

In Talika the main occupations were fishing and trading. Over 43% of the men were fishermen, which was slightly higher than the proportion of men in Olowo who did this work.[5] Talika people had no fishing trawlers, although some men had outboard motors. A number of Talika men also were traders, although 27% of them only traded part-time. In Olowo 50% of the women worked in some capacity connected with fishing, while in Talika only 15% did so full-time. The difference was the result of the much greater catch in Olowo, made possible by their seven fully-mechanized trawlers.

In Table 5 the occupations of the two villages are classified in terms of whether the work is done inside or outside the community, the latter requiring the person to live away from the community part or full-time on business not created by the community. Nobody in Olowo in 1970 – male or female – was employed in non-community business. This does not mean none worked away from Olowo. Such work, however, as on the launches, was always Olowo business, the profits of which went to the village treasury. Thus while outside, they were still inside in terms of membership and ideology.

Table 5. *Location of work of Talika and Olowo members*

| | Talika | | | | Olowo | | | |
| | Men | | Women | | Men | | Women | |
	N	%	N	%	N	%	N	%
Inside village	48	59	37	99	429	100	197	100
Outside village	9	12	—	—	—	—	—	—
In and out	23	28	—	—	—	—	—	—
Unknown	1	1	1	1	—	—	—	—
Total	81	100	38	100	429	100	197	100

In Talika all women also worked inside the community. As in the case of Olowo, some travelled to other villages to trade fish, but the enterprise originated in Talika, and these women had their homes in the village. The exception to this trend concerns the Talika men. About 40% worked outside the village full or part-time: 12% and 28% respectively. Of those who did so full-time 44% were traders. Of those who did so part-time 83% were traders. But when the number of those trading either full or part-time is expressed in terms of the total adult male population, the proportion is only 33%. The fact that 40% of Talika men worked outside the village at least part-time indicates the restricted opportunities of work in the village, and suggests that it was a less closed community than Olowo.

Income, investment, and consumption

Unfortunately I am not able to present precise economic data for Olowo, because this was a very sensitive topic. One reason concerned taxes. Because of Olowo's communal system, individual members had no money to pay taxes. The leaders of the village worked out an agreement with the Nigerian government to pay a lump sum annually based upon the number of adult members. The leaders were afraid that if the records on the economy became public knowledge the government might try to collect more taxes. Another reason peculiar to my period of fieldwork was that the third *oba* was sensitive to the criticisms of his subjects that his own reign was not as successful economically as the reign of the first *oba*. He was unwilling to make the records public, for they would confirm what his subjects intimated. My own attempts to obtain records of the first *oba*'s reign were unsuccessful, and even my most reliable informants failed to locate this information; indeed, some of them suspected that the third *oba* had destroyed all the economic records so that they could not be used against him.

It is quite clear, nevertheless, that only two of the several industries in Olowo were major sources of income: fishing and transportation. One of the best-educated young men in the village estimated that the annual income from these two industries was approximately ₦200,000–₦240,000 (in May 1974 one naira = $1.59 U.S.). Of the two, fishing was the greater source of income until the launches started to operate in the late 1950s, because transportation on the Nigerian mainland was not very efficient then, the passenger service was a lucrative source of income. After 1963 the fishing trawlers began to operate and this industry once more became probably the major source of income. An indirect clue to the income derived from these two industries in 1970 was suggested by the *oba*'s plans to build new roads, houses, and other buildings. He announced that the fishing industry would be required to contribute ₦800 per month for the construction of buildings, and the passenger industry ₦400 per month for the construction of roads, including cementing the existing ones. These figures did not likely represent the total monthly earnings of the two industries. For what it is worth, an article written on Olowo in 1957 (*Anon.*) suggested it had a capital value of ₦400,000. If this is correct, its value in 1970 was probably twice that amount.

The income derived from the other industries was small. The young man to whom I referred previously estimated that their total annual income was between ₦9,000 and ₦12,000. One reason for the low income was that outside markets were not established. This was true, for example, in the case of the weaving industry, although a few of its products were purchased by visitors to Olowo. The failure to establish outside markets may have been due to poor management. In 1970 the man who had managed the weaving industry was replaced. Before this was done it was rare to see more than two of the 10 automatic looms in operation. The new manager planned to increase production, establish links with agents on the mainland, and sell the product for a few pennies lower than his competitors.

For several years shoes were repaired in Olowo, but only about 1961, when the factory was expanded and the new machinery installed, were new shoes made in substantial numbers. The shoe factory then flourished for about five years. Its major product was the 'flip-flop' or rubber thong-sandal that is popular in Nigeria. Markets for thongs and sandals were established in Lagos, Ibadan, and as far away as the former Eastern Region. The boom fell sharply at the outbreak of the civil war, for the community no longer could obtain cheaply the raw material that was required. After the war ended in 1970, contacts were renewed. Former agents in the new East Central State placed large orders. More significantly, the shoe industry signed a contract with a wholesaler on the mainland, and began large-scale production again.

Some garments made by the tailors were occasionally bought by visitors, but this revenue was insignificant. An unsuccessful effort was made to sell bread to the neighbouring villagers, who said the bread was not good. Olowo people offered a different explanation: the outsiders could not afford to buy the bread. This reason may be closer to the truth, but the crucial factor probably was the hostility between Olowo and the surrounding villages.

It is clear, then, that there were only two major sources of income: the fishing industry and the passenger launches. Yet the other industries contributed by providing products for the village such as clothes, footwear, and bread that would have had to be purchased outside the community at a higher price. They also provided a variety of work for members, and created outlets for leadership aspirations, which may have reduced the temptation of the youth to run away.[6]

As in the case of income, I am unable to provide precise figures about investment patterns, but it appears that a very high percentage of the total income of the various industries was re-invested in the economy. This was made possible by the strict ascetic lifestyle led by the Apostles for the first several years. For example, the basic food eaten during the early years was cassava and fish. The latter were caught by Olowo people and were traded with outsiders for cassava. During this period Olowo people did not eat rice, beans, bread, or flesh other than fish. Clothing at the beginning was limited to simple working uniforms made out of khaki, and a suit of clothes to be worn when a person was not working. If a person had to travel outside the village, better clothing could be obtained from a central shop, but had to be returned after the trip.

Shoes were considered a luxury, and rarely worn, and there was a rule against having a wristwatch, socks, or cosmetics of any kind. Women were not allowed to plait their hair, nor to wear earrings or other jewellery. Nobody was allowed to smoke, but alcohol in moderation was consumed. Houses were well constructed, but the furnishings were simple: wooden chairs and benches without cushions, a table, and mats rather than mattresses on beds.

In addition to the austere lifestyle, the self-reliance of the Apostles contributed to the high percentage of the income that was re-invested in the economy. They caught their own fish, some of which they traded for cassava. They eventually made their own shoes and clothes. They cut the timber for their houses in the surrounding forest, and did their own carpentry work. As a result, the income from selling fish to outsiders and from the passenger service on launches was not seriously depleted by purchases of consumer goods.

Origin of communalism

Before suggesting the manner in which the communal system contributed to Olowo's economic success, I shall try to explain why it was adopted in

Olowo. To my knowledge, the only community in West Africa that was organized communally, had no private ownership, and did not use money among members was the Sect of the Second Adam in Ghana (Stoevesendt 1934). Although little data are available for this community, it apparently did not enjoy unusual economic success. The Sect of the Second Adam existed about 15 years before Olowo adopted communalism, but it is doubtful that anyone in Olowo knew of its existence.

Some collective economic behaviour existed throughout West Africa that might have acted as a model. Ames (1963), for example, describes the cooperative work groups among the Wolof of the Gambia and Senegal, and Goody (1958) documents a similar phenomenon in Ghana. In a comparison of Ghana and Uganda, Brokensha and Erasmus (1969) found that self-help work parties existed in pre-colonial times, and that these have been fused with present-day community development projects.

In Nigeria communal work projects and contribution clubs are prevalent among the Igbo. The Yoruba themselves are not devoid of collective economic activity: the *esusu* is a contribution club similar to that found among the Igbo, and among both ethnic groups cooperative farms have been established for several years. While these are not necessarily an expression of indigenous communal behaviour, they indicate that such models are not absent.

Schwab (1955: 357) has shown that within traditional Yoruba society itself the Yoruba lineage has semi-communal functions. Although lineage members did not normally work on a collective basis, they did help one another at certain stages in the farming cycle, and for large-scale projects such as the construction of a house. Moreover, the lineage was responsible for contributing goods and services during ceremonial occasions such as a marriage or a festival. Within Ilaje itself there was some communal activity. For example, villages cooperate with each other to clear the shallow rivers and canals that lead to larger waterways in the interior, and from there to the mainland. Each village is usually assigned a section of the river to dredge.

It is clear, then, that communalism is not alien to West Africa in general, to other parts of Nigeria, or even to Ilaje. The crucial factor, however, concerns the range of communal behaviour. The collective work gangs among the Wolof, the LoDagaba, the Igbo, and to a lesser extent among the Ilaje are hardly comparable to the Olowo case, for they amount to a small fraction of economic activities. In Ilaje, for example, one may contribute less than half a dozen days in a year to communal work. In contrast, almost all economic activity in Olowo consists of labour devoted to communal work projects or to the departments, with the profits being claimed by the treasury. Moreover, phenomena such as the contribution clubs and a few days of communal work do not modify the basic structure of the economy. People continue to be motivated by an economic system that gives priority to a self rather than a collective orientation. What this means, I suggest, is that the decision to establish communalism in Olowo cannot be explained in terms of pre-existing models.

Olowo people themselves stress that before the village was founded they had no idea they would adopt communalism. They say that this was done as a result of the first *oba*'s vision that they should copy the model of the early Christians. Until recently I have not been prepared to accept this explanation. One reason was that no other theocracy in Ilaje had adopted communalism, which suggested that the model of the early Christians was not crucial to the religious movement in general. Another reason was that the explanation was reduced to one individual: the first *oba*. I questioned the value of such an explanation, for it did not account for how *he* came upon the idea of communalism when nobody else did.

I am now inclined to accept the explanation of the Olowo people that the early Christians were their model, for some other communities such as the Hutterites appear to have acted upon the same stimulus. Even in their case, however, Bennett (1967: 38) has suggested that the Zadokite-Essenic communal sects rather than the Bible may have been their model. Moreover, in another utopia, the Zoarites of Ohio (Nordhoff, 1971), communalism apparently was adopted for explicit economic reasons, rather than for religious ideals. I also no longer see a problem in the fact that the innovation was the idea of one man. But this does invite a significant conclusion: the communal system – and hence, assuming that communalism was a necessary cause, the economic growth of Olowo as well – was basically fortuitous. Given the emergence of a village like Olowo in similar circumstances in Ilaje or elsewhere again, the probability of communalism being adopted is negligible, for it was a stab in the dark by a single individual. The fact that none of the other Ilaje theocracies adopted communalism supports this conclusion.

Contribution of communalism

A major contribution of the communal system in Olowo was to make labour and capital available to a central administrator who could direct them to specific economic ends. An enormous amount of work was accomplished within a few years of the founding of the village. The houses were built on stilts, an entire network of boardwalks linked every dwelling, and a canal seven miles long had been dug by 1949, which connected Olowo to the large rivers and lagoons in the interior. Without the supply of labour to the *oba* it is improbable that these feats could have been realized. The communal system also made the projects economically feasible, for the workers were supplied only with food and clothing. If it had been necessary to pay them a regular salary, this alone would probably have ruled out the projects. The profits derived from the labour of several hundred people in the fishing industry, who accepted only basic living necessities, were retained by the community treasury, rather than divided among the workers. As a result capital was soon available for investment in the economic infrastructure.

By making labour and capital available to the *oba*, the communal system allowed *early* innovations to be introduced. Funds were used to buy machinery necessary for improving the fishing industry and expanding the range of industry. For example, nets, boats and outboard motors were purchased, and in 1953 a generator for electricity was bought. This encouraged the mechanization of industries such as shoemaking and tailoring, and led to greater production. Because people still did not receive a wage for their work, the returns of the investments were quickly realized.

Organization and motivation of work

Any explanation of Olowo's economic success that failed to consider the efficient manner in which the activities of the people were organized and their willingness to work hard would be inadequate. Almost every hour that a person was awake was devoted to work that had been organized by the leaders. People toiled in large gangs at the beginning, but as the economy became more diversified and complex, work gradually was organized in three distinct patterns. The most important was departmental work. Every major industry such as fishing, weaving, and boatbuilding became a separate department. All adults of both sexes were assigned to a particular department, and even children of primary school age were included. After school was closed at 2 p.m. each child had to report to a specific department. While I am not certain, I think this usually was the department to which the child's guardian (i.e., landlord or landlady) had been assigned, rather than the child's mother or father. This permitted an early apprenticeship, and helped to socialize the children into collective working conditions.

A second pattern of work was carried out in large gangs. While this type was dominant when the village was first founded, its importance declined after the departmental structure emerged. However, communal labour continued to occur whenever a job existed that was too big for a particular department, or not the direct responsibility of a specific department. For example, people were often summoned to help the boatbuilders draw the fishing trawlers up on land for repairs, or to cut the long grass that quickly grew around the village. In 1970 communal labour occurred on an average of twice a week in the dry season.

A third pattern of work involved individual labour. For example, before the factories opened in the morning, and after they closed in the evening, people often waded into the sea with nets. The fish that they did not eat were sold in the village market to outsiders, or in nearby markets. Some members kept chickens and ducks, and attempted to grow oranges and bananas. This was the only type of work in Olowo that was not a collective enterprise addressed to a specific end chosen by the village leaders. The profits from all three types of work were claimed by the central treasury.

While in the conclusion I shall suggest that several factors including the political organization, the personality of the *oba*, and the religious base of authority contributed to Olowo's efficient organization, the communal system was extremely important in this regard. Communalism *per se* does not lead inevitably to good organization, but is a social type conducive to it. If private enterprise had prevailed in Olowo, it is unlikely that the outstanding projects such as the canal would have been completed. The obstacles to organizing hundreds of people, and to persuading them to cooperate, would have been insurmountable. Virtually every other village in Ilaje illustrates this argument.

Not only were Olowo people well organized, but they also worked exceptionally hard, as reflected in the following descriptions of a typical day of communal work, and a typical day of a particular member. My example of communal labour is a road-building project. In 1970 there was a plan to replace the boardwalks built upon stilts with cement roads. This was achieved by digging into the swampy ground and transferring the earth to the site of the new road, where it was pounded into a smooth surface. On the evening before this particular communal work was done, the town-crier circled the village and announced the project. At dawn of the next day approximately 600 men and women gathered at one edge of the village. From then until dusk they toiled with hardly a break, not even stopping completely to eat. Instead individuals would take a few minutes to drink water or eat the food provided by a group of women who had set up a makeshift kitchen next to the work site.

The work force was split into three gangs, each of which was given an equal portion to complete. In spite of the tremendous heat, the pace maintained was furious. The three gangs competed with each other to see who could finish first. On this particular occasion the leader of one gang periodically shouted encouragement. The result was astounding: a couple of hundred people who had been labouring without a break for hours would begin to run back and forth carrying huge loads of mud. By the time darkness fell a stretch of road about 150 yards long had materialized from the swamp. To put this in perspective, the nearest village to Olowo is not able to muster the will and cooperation in order to construct a narrow footpath from the main river to its primary school. In the wet season students and teachers must force their canoes as close to the school as possible, then trek through the mud the rest of the way.

My example of a particular member is one of the village's school teachers. At the time the data were collected, he usually rose at 4 a.m. and went to the technical school to teach four technicians who were preparing for examinations. At 5 he returned to his house and bathed. At 6 he attended a meeting in the palace, during which the day's activities were discussed. At 8 he began to teach in the secondary school continuing until it finished at 2 p.m. Then he returned to eat at his house, rested until 4 (unless there was communal work) and made his way once more to the technical department where he taught the same technicians until 6 p.m. From 6 until 9 he taught in the evening school. If he had a spare period he may have had time to eat. If not he would take his meal after 9, and try to get to bed by 10 or 11 p.m.

The young man was rewarded for his efforts. Not only was he invited regularly to the palace, but he also was selected among those to be sent to an institute for higher learning on the mainland. His case was rather extreme, for not all members worked with the same determination, yet the norm was not much lower. For example, the other teachers in the secondary school carried a full load in both day and evening sessions, took part in any communal work that occurred, and contributed what time remained to fishing or to some other economic activity.

The motivation of Olowo people was crucial to their success, but cannot be explained in terms of the communal system. This is why I do not argue that communalism was the key factor in Olowo's development. The only evidence I have that links communalism to the willingness of Olowo people to work so hard is very tenuous. Although there is doubt whether communalism was founded for religious reasons, it did take on a religious connotation after a few years. Some Olowo people even told me that it *was* their religion, and supported their argument by referring to the villages that surrounded them. In spite of the numerous religious organizations represented in them such as Anglican, Cherubim and Seraphim, and traditional Ilaje beliefs, Olowo people insisted the villages were without religion. This must be the case, they argued, for the outsiders were not organized along communal lines. The remarks of Olowo people can be interpreted to mean that the ideology of communalism occupied a central position in their village's value system, which meant that it became interrelated with other basic values such as economic progress.

Conclusion

Olowo's unusual economic success was partly a result of the communal system, which led to early innovation and to the efficient organization of village activities. However, communalism was not a sufficient cause of Olowo's development, for it does not explain the motivation of the Apostles. In concluding, I shall briefly consider other factors that contributed to development in Olowo, and then indicate the recent trends in the village that have brought it to the edge of dissolution.

Olowo people contend that their religious beliefs produced their economic success. Olowo was founded mainly for religious reasons, and the basic religious values were salvation and immortality. In 1947 Olowo people believed that their prophets had defeated death. This explains at least partly why they do not take their dead to the traditional burial ground in Ilaje, and do not have a burial ceremony or a marked burial ground. Indeed, burial is carried out under the cover of darkness, and a member's death is not a legitimate subject of conversation. The power of the prophets is reflected in their capacity to learn God's will through dreams and visions, to communicate with the holy spirit through *ede* or glossolalia (sometimes called 'angel language' in the village), and to cure sickness through prayer, or with water that had been blessed.

The basic religious values in Talika also were salvation and immortality, and they too did not have a burial ceremony or marked burial ground. Visions, *ede*, and spiritual healing also were characteristic of their beliefs. The main difference was that only in Olowo was it argued that hard work and economic progress was a measure of faith and hence a means to salvation.

This is a crucial difference between the two villages, but the explanation of it is much too complicated to be attempted in the remainder of this paper. All that I shall suggest is that for a number of interrelated reasons, the prospects of rapid economic development became realistic in Olowo. At that point most aspects of the social structure and the belief-system – including religion – became articulated with the goal of development. This is not to deny that development itself may have been conceived of as a means to achieve religious superiority over other Ilaje theocracies, and thus ultimately as a political phenomenon.

Economic development did not occur haphazardly in Olowo. Instead it was pursued with great deliberation and with single-minded dedication. The strong powers of the leaders were crucial in this regard, and I shall even suggest that the leaders intentionally defined development in religious terms in order to motivate the people. One implication is that while religious beliefs in Olowo may have enhanced development, their capacity to do so was no greater than the beliefs in Talika and other Ilaje theocracies. Another implication is that the Olowo case has little similarity to the Calvinist ethic, the relationship of which to rational economic behaviour supposedly was unintentional. For this reason it is not legitimate to evoke Weber's argument to explain the economic success of the Apostles.

The centralization of power and authority partly explains why the *oba* was able to introduce innovations such as communalism, and why his subjects were prepared to work so hard. Quite apart from the religious connotation of work, the leaders had the authority publicly to flog lazy people, and to refuse them food. Religion is important in this regard because it was a base for power and authority. Given the spiritual strength of the prophets, Olowo people were afraid to disobey them. Religion also contributed to social control in general; for example, the third *oba* once told me that the only reason he held church services was to make sure his subjects behaved well; by limiting disorder, religion indirectly contributed to the village's economic success.

While Olowo and Talika were similar in terms of political organization, there was a significant difference in the manner in which authority was exercised. Talika people were free to choose their job, education, and spouse. They also could leave the community at will, which was not allowed in Olowo. In other words the Talika *oba* had much less control over his subjects than his counterpart in Olowo. Whether this was due to personal capacity or interest is difficult to tell, but my judgment is that the more authoritarian nature of Olowo can be traced to the differences in the personalities of the two leaders. The effects of the Olowo *oba*'s personality can be seen on virtually every factor that contributed to Olowo's development. It was he who introduced and institutionalized the communal system. He also probably played the major role in defining development in religious terms, and hence tapping this source of motivation. Because of the fear which he inspired in his subjects, he was also instrumental in controlling deviance and persuading his subjects to accept an ascetic life style.

Two other important factors in Olowo's development were the village's technical workshop and the available economic resources. Founded in 1953 by the first *oba*, the workshop was soon equipped with modern machinery. Many Olowo people became expert electricians, welders, plumbers, etc., and were able to install the machinery in the factories, maintain the equipment in good running order, and even perform the sophisticated work involved in the construction of the large passenger launches and the fishing trawlers. Olowo was fortunate in that two potentially lucrative economic enterprises were available for exploitation: the passenger service on launches throughout the swamps and fishing in the ocean. However, Talika and the other villages in Ilaje also had access to these resources. The crucial problem again concerns motivation: why was it that only Olowo was unusually successful in taking advantage of these resources?

In recent years Olowo has been transformed. In 1968 private enterprise was introduced, and by 1972 hardly any communalism remained. At the same time the family became legitimate once more, and husband, wife and offspring began to co-reside. Since Olowo was founded there had always been power and status differentiation, but most people enjoyed the same material advantages. After private enterprise was introduced, the village began to be divided into rich and poor people, with the elite becoming the most wealthy by virtue of their control over resources in the village. By 1972 Olowo had begun to deteriorate physically; for example, the boardwalks were falling apart. By 1974 most of the industries had been abandoned, many members had left for the mainland, and this remarkable village was on the verge of disintegration.

3

Economic development increases the options and resources available to the 'developing' group and so opens the possibility of dispute over the way in which they are to be used. The people of 'Eagle Bay' have averted or resolved disintegrative conflicts by shifting their support between apparently incompatible objectives and principles, but always within a framework of consensus. A peculiar sequence of events – some intended, the others fortuitous – has allowed the groups' material advance without jeopardy to its sense of autonomy. Two points are nicely illustrated. One: it is normal for members of even the most unitary and cohesive group to have different perceptions and contradictory expectations of development, and for them to alter these perceptions and expectations with time and situation. Two: the dilemmas of advance are not always insoluble.

Sorting and cooling:
The politics of development on a
Canadian Indian reserve

G. E. MORTIMORE

Economic development plans for Canadian Indian reserves often fall far short of their goals. This may be because of inadequate resources, because of the people's resentment of the outside society and government, or because their experience of non-productive schemes which have been imposed from outside. Even when substantial resources are invested in programmes that appear to have the support of a large percentage of the population, the programmes often fail because of factional dispute and conflict of goals.

In contrast, some Indian groups achieve considerable success in reaching their own development goals. One of these is 'Eagle band' of Ojibwa Indians,[1] a highly acculturated group which holds a 40,000-acre reserve in north-central Canada. In the band's home village of Eagle Bay there is a clear consensus in favour of economic development, material comfort and life in a small community of mutually supportive persons in a place where there is access to fish and game. There are strong sentiments in favour of local control of resources and maintenance of Indian legal rights. The people of Eagle band have achieved and are continuing to achieve these goals.

Eagle band has a sizeable collective estate in cash, land and production equipment. It has a substantial capital fund remaining from the $1,100,000 which it received for the sale of the white-pine timber on the reserve in 1910, at a time when the band totalled 80 members. The band now has 232 members – 122 living on the reserve, 110 scattered to places as far apart as Sudbury, Toronto, Miami and Seattle. After a long period of isolation there was a stage during which band members were steadily leaving the reserve, resigning their Indian status and withdrawing their shares of the band fund. But Eagle band has now stopped the draining away of people, has lessened the outflow of capital money, and has linked itself to the outside world by telephone and hydro-electric power lines and an all-weather road. Since the building of the road, Eagle Bay people can comfortably drive to town and back within one day for shopping, medical service or entertainment, or to visit city friends and relatives. They are no longer called upon to opt *either* for life in a small community at the edge of the wilderness *or* for access to urban services: they can enjoy both. In a number of households, a substantial part of the meat consists of deer, moose and fish which is stored in deep-freeze units.

The band's collectively owned assets include a marina, tourist cabins, laundromat and handicraft shop, some remaining tracts of timber, many miles of waterfront in choice holiday country and several publicly owned vehicles, including a sewage pump-out truck and a road grader – both of which work for the band and are also available for commercial rental on contract. After some years in which outsider entrepreneurs drew the major benefit from industries which used reserve resources and labour, the band has launched into logging and tourism of its own. Many individual band members have private businesses in tourism, logging, construction and such varied enterprises as guiding, trapping, taxidermy, boat service, the operation of buses and trucks, and retail merchandising.

Band members are not individually wealthy; but with the aid of low-interest loans from band funds, and self-help and mutual help in construction, most band members resident at Eagle Bay have comfortable houses with modern plumbing. Most have motor vehicles and television; many have colour television. There is year-round work available for most heads of households at logging, guiding, construction and miscellaneous labour on development projects and winter works projects.

The tourist and logging industries have been developed with the aid of provincial and federal grants well in excess of $100,000 – but the sums conveyed to Eagle band in grants do not yet match the $170,000 which the band spent to build a road and hydro-electric line. These facilities made possible the expanded development of the surrounding non-Indian cottage and resort area.

Overview: social-ecological and political process

The relative success of development programmes at Eagle Bay can be explained in terms of two interlocking sets of social processes within an environmental framework. One set of processes involves the interchange of population between Eagle Bay and the surrounding society. Because these processes produce social consequences which are not intended by the makers of individual decisions, they may be called social-ecological processes.

The findings of the Eagle Bay study support the view of social behaviour as a compound of individual choices, a multitude of transactions, in which individuals make the best 'deal' they can perceive and can get in a process of bargaining both openly and tacitly with others – all within a particular social-ecological framework (Homans 1950, 1961, 1964b; Barth 1966; Inglis 1970: 195–264). Despite the fact that society is made up of individuals with widely different cognitive and emotional maps of the world, these individuals generate and make use of a number of more or less standard blueprints for behaviour in particular kinds of situation (Wallace 1970: 19–38; 109–20). We must notice both that there may be more than one set of blueprints governing behaviour, and that individual choices, actions, blueprints, do not necessarily have the results intended (Jarvie 1972: 1–33).

The processes of the second set are those by which group goals are pursued and decisions made regarding the framing of rules and the allocation of resources. This second set may be called political processes. These will be described as a network of reciprocal adjustments linking the leader and the led, and linking the village to its environment as the people collectively pursue common goals.

Both the processes by which structure and ideology are shaped and the processes by which decisions are made will be elaborated in this paper. However, the main emphasis here is on political and economic process. Specifically, the emphasis is on the politics of development.

Values and processes

It is central to the idea system at Eagle Bay that goals are valued above individual leaders. Members of Eagle band, while giving sometimes grudging credit to individual chiefs for leadership capacity and technical expertise, steadfastly argue that the band's economic achievements are the product of *collective* effort. This attitude has a long history. Letters from Hudson's Bay factors in the nineteenth century indicate that the Chief Eagle of the day, who was an independent trader in competition with the Hudson's Bay Company, regularly consulted his sons about important decisions. In modern times it is a firmly established tradition that important decisions are made at band meetings. Chiefs make it a practice to sound out band members' opinions privately before putting forward proposals. This reduces the likelihood of open and public conflict, which is regarded as undesirable.

Because goals are valued above individual leaders, and because there is a strong anti-conflict ethic, factions do not develop to the point where they are sufficiently strong and durable to be a decisive political force. Nascent factions that centre upon particular leaders are quite rapidly broken up because the people's attention is focussed upon goals and policies rather than personalities, and people tend to reject or accept a leader according to the degree to which his actions suit their goals. Nor do factions centred upon goals and principles last long. Serious divisions are pre-empted by the whole group shifting its focus to an alternative common goal.

Goals of the people of Eagle Bay may be divided into those which emphasise cohesiveness or 'togetherness', and those which emphasise states of being that the people wish to achieve in relation to their environment. 'Togetherness' goals are expressed both in what people say and in what they do. Residents of Eagle Bay are keenly interested in and concerned about one another. Gossip, anecdotes and jokes about individuals are the main material of social interaction. The people's concern for one another is manifested in times of crisis. When a man vanished on a trip by small boat across Lake Mallard in the spring, the entire male population of Eagle Bay ceased work and searched for his body until it was found. Families donated sums of up to $50 to pay for outboard-motor gas to finance the search.

Among people of Eagle Bay, life in a small community of mutually supportive persons is seen as desirable, and any decrease in the intensity of interdependence and 'togetherness' that might have been brought about by easier access to the world outside is explicitly deplored. The cohesiveness of Eagle Bay is partly a result of geographical isolation and the interdependence of its people. Because Eagle Bay is an isolated community of people sharing a common estate, its people tend to feel a sentiment of belonging together; because their relations are intense and multiplex, they have the capacity to reward and punish one another.[2] It is important therefore that they can dissipate tension by withdrawal and the avoidance of conflict-laden situations, and by frequent joking and kidding. The tendency is for troublemakers and victims of trouble and social stress to leave altogether, thereby eliminating a source of dissent or embarrassment. Those who leave are either pushed out by the pressures that are exerted against them or pulled out by the attractions of town life, or both.

Migration removes a variety of dissidents. First, it removes many of the chronically ill and disabled. Secondly, a big proportion of the persons who subscribe to an ethic of hard work leave. They tend to make long-range plans involving jobs, prosperity and a good education for their children, and to see reserve residents as lacking in ambition. Those who remain in or return to the community in fact comprise two very distinct categories which both subscribe to the idea of economic development as a source of benefit. These are the 'happy-go-luckies' who favour an intermittent or leisurely work pattern and expect economic prosperity to make life easier, and the 'serious moderns' who subscribe to principles of rational planning or efficiency, and see the reserve community and its resources as capable of being organized for the common good.

In this way, migration in and out of Eagle Bay sorts band members into an on-reserve bundle of people and an off-reserve bundle of people, each with its own particular patterns of belief and behaviour. Processes of migration have a sorting and cooling effect on the community, leaving the resident population internally homogenous.

The political-economic goals of Eagle Bay are the maintenance of a fairly high level of material comfort, but in the bush where there is access to fish and game; and in circumstances such that the people may exercise a high degree of local control over resources and political decisions. These goals are accomplished by a balance between conservation of resources and their conversion into consumer goods, and by a balance between acculturation and 'Indianness'. For the last 65 years the people of Eagle Bay have pursued economic development by the conversion of their lands' resources into consumer goods. For a longer time still, they have gradually moved their life style closer to that of the surrounding non-Indian population.

It is important that they have insisted on keeping control of both conversion processes in their own hands, and have maintained a steady pressure for the conservation of resources and of identity. This balance between conservation and conversion of economic resources has not been easily won. While no one seems seriously to have advocated the lease or sale of lands, the disposition of cash and timber resources has been a recurrent focus of political dispute.

Similarly the balance between acculturation and 'Indianness' has been marked by ambivalence and division. Acculturation seems originally to have been a political choice, an accommodation to the surrounding society. Eagle band might have chosen instead to remain culturally distinct (as did the Fox, see Joffe 1962), and might have mobilized political power in support of this position. But this would have been in opposition to the desires of the outside society. Indian agents' reports (in various Parliamentary papers, 1870–1910) show continuing sentiment for the continuing acculturation of Indians and express approval for Eagle bands' (and other bands') acceptance of non-Indian patterns – as, for example, in their acceptance of, and skill in, market trading – and disapproval of those that do not conform. Eagle band seems to have opted for some degree of acculturation as an intermediate goal, and with outside support and approval for this goal has been largely successful in achieving it. Nor can the sense of 'Indianness' be understood without reference to the 'outside'. Indians have suffered discrimination in respect of identity, language and culture, and physiognomy and have felt tension and uncertainty both manifested and resolved by joking about and avoidance of the issue (Radcliffe-Brown 1952: 90–116; Homans 1950: 263). But in areas where 'Indianness' returns clear benefits – as in the possession of the band's reserve land and the legal rights that go with Indian status – sentiments have been clear-cut and unequivocal. Now that Indian identity is beginning to pay dividends in social approval and even in cash (as from the sale of Indian handicrafts), Eagle band people are acknowledging Indian cultural identity with much less constraint and are seizing upon pan-Indian symbols like war bonnets to replace the lost Ojibwa patterns of the past.

In striking the balance between conservation and conversion the people of Eagle Bay explicitly recognize the need for leadership. They also recognize the need for technical expertise, even if it must be brought in from outside. While there is some contradiction between the need for leadership and expertise on the one hand, and the principles of equality and independence on the other, general goal consensus is maintained by collective values and by the sorting process of migration.

Despite general consensus however, specific conflicts develop over long-term versus short-term returns – investments for the future as opposed to profits now. These conflicts are embedded in a polarization of attitudes between an *efficiency* code and a *personal* code. The *efficiency* code consists in part of absolute principles, and in part of value preferences. These include: (i) Preference for band-membership loyalties above kinship loyalties. (ii) A view that non-Indians' obligations toward Indians are limited; rights must be defended and gains must be fought for. (iii) A concept of the leader and manager as a person who gathers consensus, but also has authority to give orders. And (iv), willingness to postpone gratification.

Individuals who tend to the *personal* code show on the contrary (i) Preference for kinship ideals as organizing principles: even brothers and sisters who espouse efficiency principles too strongly are counted out of the network of alliances. (ii) A view of non-Indians' obligations as unlimited. The debts of non-Indians to Indians are seen as an infinite, self-replenishing pool. (iii) An image of the leader as co-ordinator and gatherer of consensus, rather than as a person with a mandate to give orders. (iv) A strong inclination to avoid conflict. This is the prevailing anti-conflict ethic, but held with particular firmness. (v) Relative unwillingness to delay satisfactions; a preference for short-term solutions.

These notions are not held in pure form by anyone in Eagle Bay: persons tend toward one set of principles or the other, and a substantial number hover somewhere in the middle of the scale and move one way or the other according to circumstances. This makes a tidal movement between the two poles which combines with the responses and initiatives of leaders to provide the fine tuning of conflict-settlement and goal-seeking at Eagle Bay. The leaders make adjustments to compensate for changes in public support; they build programmes that integrate goals which had been in conflict at a specific or detailed level; they bring rewards and penalties to bear in support of their internal leadership positions and they use their skills to the group's advantage in bargaining with outside agencies.

Political processes

The unfolding of these processes in Eagle Bay must be traced in two stages: the *conservation* stage covered approximately the first 60 years of the band's existence after the Robinson Treaty of 1850 (Mortimore 1975). In this period the band made its living mainly by trade, and conserved its assets of timber, waterfront land and fish and game. The *developmental* stage has followed since about 1910. In this period, the band has been converting its assets into goods, jobs and cash.

For the latter period, the analysis of the interplay of goals and process is based on observation and accounts provided by living informants; for the former, on scanty historical records and the backward projection of contemporary processes.

The conservation phase (*c.* 1850–1910)[3]

The Chief Eagle of treaty time is believed to have attended a Catholic mission school where he learned to write an Algonkian language (similar to the one now known as Ojibwa) using French-style handwritten letters to represented the Algonkian sounds. He, the members of his extended family and some others, numbering 16 at treaty time, were involved in the fur trade as merchant entrepreneurs, while continuing to derive part of their living from subsistence hunting and horticulture. Their territories lay along an interface between an area of horticulture and an area of hunting and gathering. There was therefore a pre-contact trading tradition in which they had learned attitudes and skills appropriate to participation in the European fur-trade.

The history of Eagle band since the treaty consists of a series of adjustments, crises and readjustments in the pursuit of its major goals. The conservation period may be subdivided into four phases;

Phase 1.1: *The period of trade.* Eagle band maintained a canoe trading network spanning hundreds of miles from a base on the reserve of another Indian band. The government exerted pressure for the purchase of timber on the home reserve. Eagle band refused to sell (Mortimore 1975: 63–77) – although other bands, perhaps less prosperous than Eagle band, did sell. Nor did members of Eagle band send their children to school. The band refused to yield to forced conversion of resources, or to submit to group acculturation at the hands of outside agencies. The goals of independence, material comfort and life in the bush near hunting and fishing were comparatively well served in this phase.

Phase 1.2: *Crisis.* The advancing network of roads and railways made canoe trading obsolete. Material comfort was diminished. Independence and life in the bush were threatened.

Phase 1.3: *Readjustment.* In the closing years of the nineteenth century, the band moved to its own reserve on the Champlain River and lived by hunting, fishing, subsistence farming and wage-work in logging camps and in driving logs down the river. Some band members remained off the reserve and made a living by trade or wage-work in the growing towns. Some opted for a greater measure of comfort and lesser access to hunting and fishing. They stayed in town. Others had chosen a greater measure of access to hunting and fishing. Overall, independence, a measure of material comfort and life in the bush had been maintained.

Phase 1.4: *Crisis.* Population of the surrounding area increased. Prices of timber rose. Commercial and government pressure for the Eagle timber increased. The presence of holiday tourists, plus the return of absent band members, plus the knowledge of money available for the timber, created a sense of relative material deprivation. The goal of material comfort was perceptibly short of achievement. These pressures triggered the band's decision to sell its white-pine timber (leaving other species for future harvest). The timber sale in 1909–10 marked a watershed between conservation policies and development policies. The sale launched Eagle band into Stage 2.

The development phase (*c.* 1910–present)

Phase 2.1: *Readjustment.* When all returns were in, the band received $1,100,000 for the sale of its white-pine timber, and still had other timber in reserve. Unlike other bands under stress, Eagle band had sold none of its land. All members of the band were now receiving considerable sums of money each year in interest payments. The band retained a substantial capital fund, under federal trusteeship. People on the reserve built more comfortable houses, and acquired horses and other possessions. On the reserve, they could enjoy a good measure of comfort as well as ready access to hunting and fishing. If they wanted material comfort *and* access to urban services, they could move into town. The interest on their money gave them a financial cushion. Still greater material comfort could be enjoyed part of the time if people chose to move back and forth by seasons, as some did. The band was still refusing group acculturation in the form of schools, and the goals of independence, material comfort and bush life were all well served.

Phase 2.2: *Crisis*. A number of band members began to experience a shortfall in material comfort because they lacked 'white man's' education. Band members had been acculturating individually, at their own pace; it now became apparent that they could not enjoy life in the bush and at the same time acquire the skills they needed for bargaining for advantage over reserve resources and/or for getting jobs in town. There was pressure in favour of a school on the reserve.

Phase 2.3: *Readjustment*. A school was opened on the reserve in 1920. For several years it was a seasonal school, open in summer only. There was difficulty in getting teachers, but some progress had been made towards making good the shortfall in goals. People began moving in from scattered farmsites and hunting territories and concentrating at Eagle Bay so that their children could go to school. Because of better communication through a central point, it was easier for adults to get seasonal jobs. 'Togetherness' goals and processes began operating more intensively than in former times.

Phase 2.4: *Crisis*. A man-made environmental change – the building of a spillway for Mallard Lake waters after the Second World War – quickened the flow of water in the Upper Champlain River and delayed the formation of ice in winter. People had to take more roundabout and dangerous routes. A man was drowned. Another group narrowly escaped drowning. The consequences of isolation were more keenly felt. Because of diminished purchasing power in the inflationary period after the Second World War, the financial cushion of band interest payments was less useful in helping people to live comfortably in the city.

Up to this point, the accepted view had been that life in the bush on one hand, and a high degree of material comfort and access to city services on the other, were separate goals that belonged in separate geographical compartments, and could be tasted only in serial fashion, never both at the same time. Persons who rejected this view had tended to withdraw or muffle their opposition. Some left Eagle Bay permanently. Increasing numbers of them gave up their Indian status and withdrew their share of the band money. The outflow of people and money threatened an eventual end of the band fund. Pressure grew for a solution which would integrate the two sets of goals and make them simultaneously achievable.

Phase 2.5: *Readjustment*. An innovative chief who had earlier been rebuffed when he suggested building a road out, now got authority and a little money to build a horse trail connecting to the highway. It was built in the 1940s and provided a sketch or imperfect model of the possibility of goal-integration. This man was succeeded briefly by a conservative chief who in turn was voted out and succeeded by one Joe Eagle, elected by a large margin in 1953. Joe Eagle had once left the reserve because of his pro-development views and his own failure as a business entrepreneur. Now, under his leadership, the band built a road and a power line to the outside world. A number of people returned to live in Eagle Bay. Now band members went into the logging business for themselves and began to reap the large profits previously gained by outside entrepreneurs.

Phase 2.6: *Crisis*. The building of the road checked the outflow of band funds in one direction, but triggered a new outflow in another direction. About $170,000 in band money was spent on the road and hydro-power line, and the road made access by logging trucks easier. Together with the entry of band members as logging operators, this led to rapid and wasteful harvesting of much of the remaining Eagle-reserve timber.

Phase 2.7: *Readjustment and integration*. As a result of efficiency-code pressure for the restoration of wasted resources, Joe made two goal-integrative responses. He inaugurated a tree-planting programme which provided jobs and income for tree-planting labourers while it assured future timber supply; and he obtained provincial government grants to build a tourist industry on the reserve, thereby increasing band capital goods without further diminishing the band funds.

Phase 2.8: *Crisis*. When these grants were secured, Chief Joe tended to use them lavishly as a source of job income for band members, rather than sparingly in the interests of profit. His decisions here are clearly guided by 'personal' rather than 'efficiency' criteria. In building the band-owned marina, preparing the tourist cabins, and starting marina operations, he hired all available band members and their machines, apparently making no effort to keep labour costs down. There were suspicions that band funds as well as money from grants had been put into the marina which could neither be proved or disproved, because of loose record-keeping. A revolt was led by persons who cited efficiency criteria and backed by others bearing personal grudges. There was a stormy meeting at which Chief Joe's policies were fiercely criticized.

Phase 2.9: *Readjustment, integration and use of sanctions*. Joe attempted to deal with the criticisms by manipulating rewards and penalties within the Band, by securing an additional government grant, and by some largely unsuccessful attempts to introduce more efficient record-keeping and credit-control methods. He then died and was succeeded in 1971 by his nephew and adopted brother, Leslie – a successful small-scale private entrepreneur in logging and trapping who had served as Joe's 'Hatchet man', doing the unpleasant jobs which Joe preferred not to do. He had also acted as Joe's counterfoil by functioning as a critic from the efficiency viewpoint. Leslie now set out to make the reserve's business operations efficient. This involved pressing band members to pay debts, taking people to task for lax performance of duties, and sometimes issuing blunt orders and challenges.

Phase 2.10: *Crisis*. Leslie's behaviour angered a number of band members. There was a groundswell of resentment – a personal-code backlash.

Phase 2.11: *Readjustment*. Band members voted Leslie out of office. He was supplanted by Ronald Brunelle, husband of Betty Brunelle, the band administrator, whom Leslie had frequently rebuked for what he said was lax performance of her job. Ronald Brunelle was a personal-code adherent and strongly in favour of muffling conflict. From the start, his performance was criticized by Leslie. His reponse was to dodge confrontations, give no answers and suspend band meetings. Provincial government agencies created a band business corporation, separate from the band council, which was intended to co-ordinate interests and ensure continuity and more businesslike efficiency. But Ronald and his supporters gained control of the corporation and used it as an instrument for muffling conflict and suppressing criticism. Matters which would once have been discussed at band meetings were now declared to be the business of the directors of the corporation only, and so handled in corporation directors' meetings.

Phase 2.12: *Crisis*. Because of the lack of information about band business operations and the apparent inefficiency of band business management, band members became acutely discontented with Ronald.

Phase 2.13: *Readjustment*. At the end of Ronald's two-year term, band members rejected Ronald in the 1974 election and re-elected Leslie by a large majority. The efficiency code-to-personal-code-to-efficiency-code cycle had made one more tidal surge back to the efficiency pole. By this time, Leslie had learned more about leadership. He was less severe in his advocacy of efficiency principles, and tended to respond to personal-code opposition by modifying and softening his managerial approach. The likelihood is that he now will stay in office for a long time by the use of adjustive and integrative techniques and by the occasional careful use of sanctions.

Summary and conclusions

Metaphorically speaking, Eagle band and its reserve and the village of Eagle Bay have worked as a processing and sorting machine for human beings and inanimate resources. Because of circumstance and the application of political skills, both conversion processes have been controlled by the people of Eagle Bay.

The human raw material was a relatively unacculturated and ethnically distinct group of Ojibwa Indians. The output during the middle of the twentieth century has been highly acculturated Indian Canadians of the middle North, who have emerged in two different streams: the on-reserve stream with its division between personal-minded and efficiency-minded, and its apparent oscillation between the two poles to achieve better material conditions *and* to maintain independence; and the off-reserve stream of dissidents, troubled people, wage-workers and salaried employees, the elderly, disabled and ill. Despite acculturation, the people of Eagle Bay have a strong sense of group identity and an awareness of being Indian.

Eagle reserve is also a machine converting reserve resources of timber and waterfront location into money, jobs, consumer goods and capital goods in the logging and tourist industries.

There is only a cloudy line between social-ecological processes which are to a large extent involuntary and unplanned, and political processes which are to a large extent calculated and planned. Each kind of process contains some elements of its opposite. People leave Eagle Bay because they feel uncomfortable there, or because they see greater satisfactions outside. Decisions are individual. Yet the decisions are based on values, goals and preferences that are shared by others. The off-reserve setting favours the achievement of one particular set of goals; the on-reserve setting another. Individual decisions, viewed collectively, have social consequences which were not intended by any individual: individuals sort themselves into two population groups of different characteristics and the cohesiveness of Eagle Bay is strengthened.

The sorting-out process, by removing dissenters and concentrating certain kinds of people with certain kinds of ideas at Eagle Bay, has produced agreement about certain goals. Underlying the general agreement, however, there are conflicts about specific questions of development and the distribution of resources. Goal conflicts are solved by the integration of goals and by shifts in value positions between a particularistic and short-range pole and a universalistic and long-range pole. Leaders adapt to these pressures with varying degrees of skill, but political process consists of a double sequence of reciprocal adjustments linking the leaders and the led. The effect over time has been material advance with remarkably little loss of band autonomy.

4

Economic development as a variety of change creates a larger or different set of options or choices in a particular social setting for particular categories of people. In the case of 'Eagle Bay' Reserve (Ch. 3) difficulties of evaluation and decision-making were apparently overcome. But when the conflict and stress entailed by them become a dominant social theme, the society is faced with the dilemma quoted at the beginning of this paper.

The condition described is often referred to as cultural breakdown or cultural malaise. It can be expected to prevail until the society defines meaning and establishes value for the new alternatives, in a process analogous to that of mourning for the dead (p. 14 above). The success of the process is essential to the maintenance of the group's identity and its sense of 'social power'.

'Social power' is the result of members in the group being able to perceive common bonds and group unity, to act on common cultural rules for achieving common cultural goals, and to face its environment with a unified front. While 'social power' is therefore associated with political autonomy, political autonomy is not always available to or even desired by groups acting to develop social power. Such is the case with the members of the Hawaiian independent church of Ierusalema Pomaikai (Blessed Jerusalem). This group does not want, or is not able to seek political power, but has a sense of social power based in the supernatural. This form of 'autonomy' unites and supports individuals in the effort of dealing with the 'development' of their world.

If you can't join them – do something else: Hawaiian alternatives to progress[1]

JOHN PETERSON

> Human life is reduced to real suffering, to hell, only when two ages, two cultures and religions overlap. A man of the Classical Age who has to live in medieval times could suffocate miserably just as a savage does in the midst of our civilization. Now there are times when a whole generation is caught in this way between two ages, two modes of life, with the consequence that it loses all power to understand itself and has no standard, no security, no simple acquiescence.
>
> Hermann Hesse, *Steppenwolf*

The members of *Ierusalema Pomaikai* are very much a people caught between two ages, and their participation in their church is presented here as their attempt to deal with the ambiguity of their position. Hawaiians like many other ethnic groups in complex and colonial societies have become dependent on the economy of the wider society, but they have not become a totally integrated part of this society. This dependence on a non-traditional sector combined with the effort to preserve elements of traditional society has entailed some amount of accommodation so that new and old can exist side by side. Members of *Ierusalema Pomaikai* have sought this accommodation through their ideology. Thus participation in the church offers members help in adapting to the wider society and at the same time allows them to maintain social and cultural alternatives not available in the wider society.

The major objective of this paper is to examine this process of accommodation in members' participation in the church, and in their views of the economic development that has taken place in Hawaii over the last fifteen to twenty years. The process will be considered in the historical, social and cultural contexts in which it has taken place. The historical factors of greatest relevance here are the nature of contact between Hawaiians and non-Hawaiians over the years, and the recent advent of the jet plane and development of the tourist industry. Social factors include economic conditions, education and social structure, while cultural factors include church members' values and perceptions of the world in which they live. The final point to be considered in the paper is the way in which church members attempt to accomodate the old and new aspects of their world through their participation in *Ierusalema Pomaikai*.

A note on the terms 'Hawaiian' and 'Hawaiian Independent Church'

In a society like contemporary Hawaii, made up of many ethnic groups, the term Hawaiian may refer either to a resident of the state of Hawaii or to a member of the ethnic group that constituted the original Polynesian inhabitants of the islands. In this paper *Hawaiian* refers specifically to individuals who indicate Hawaiian ethnic affiliation. The emphasis, following Barth (1969), is on self-labelling, and thus Hawaiian ethnicity does not eliminate individuals who on grounds of biology or place of origin might be associated with another group. Rather, Hawaiian ethnicity indicates those individuals who behave or identify with social behavior that is generally defined as being Hawaiian. Thus within *Ierusalema Pomaikai* one could expect to find individuals who claim partial or total non-Hawaiian ancestry, but who are nonetheless Hawaiian.

The term independent church is used in accord with the definition given by Daneel (1971: 13). *Ierusalema Pomaikai* is an independent church because it is a religious organization that is not affiliated with any national or international religious denomination in its forms of ritual, belief, financing and organization. However, *Ierusalema Pomaikai* is one of a number of churches that combine to form a religion known as *Hoomana O Ke Akua Ola* (The Church of the Living God). This religion can trace its historical origins to the Congregational Church whose missionaries brought Christianity to the islands. Today other than in superficial resemblances such as use of a common hymn book, similar church architecture and organizational terminology, *Hoomana O Ke Akua Ola* and the Congregational Church (now known as the United Church of Christ) are completely independent of each other.

Hawaiian views of economic development and progress

Hawaiian views on economic development and progress during the twentieth century can be divided into two periods. The first period (1900 to 1959) is characterized by generally positive feelings but also feelings that change is inevitable. The second period (1959 to the present) is characterized by a growing realization of the negative consequences of rapid development.[2] In fact, these views largely parallel those of many people living in the United States; Hawaiian reaction to this reevaluation is an interesting variation on that of the rest of American society. In this section the views associated with these two periods and the causes for the change are considered.

As mentioned, Hawaiians are dependent on the economy of the wider society not only for jobs but also for many of the goods that they consume. Hawaiians, regardless of economic status, were able to take advantage of a large variety of consumer items as a result of nationwide economic innovation and expansion during the first period. The economic history of Hawaii is marked by a series of stages in each of which a dominant enterprise prevailed, starting with the supplying of whaling fleets, shifting to large-scale, single-crop agriculture and the servicing of military installations, and most recently to the extensive development of tourism. Hawaiians, like all people in the state, have been affected both positively and negatively by these enterprises. Through their involvement in the construction trades, Hawaiians have benefited most dramatically from the last two stages. The development of tourism, especially, has resulted in a general economic boom for the state, and opportunities for employment have increased an already high level of Hawaiian involvement in the general economy.

Because more jobs often resulted in the ability to purchase more consumer and luxury goods, Hawaiians generally looked favorably on this period of expansion. Their views were not totally uncritical of what was taking place but in this period any misgivings were generally expressed in terms of fatalism or overwhelmed acceptance of progress. 'We used to like to go to —, but there is a hotel there now. That's progress, and you can't stop progress.' Thus progress was considered inevitable, and even when the results were not totally agreeable, Hawaiians, like many others, did not feel that there was anything that they or anyone else could or should do about it. Progress was accepted with little anticipation of the effects or the long-range results. Additionally there seemed to be much more to gain than to lose at this time, and most individuals agreed with newspaper articles and other expressions of popular sentiment which stated that to impede tourism would be to kill the goose that laid the golden egg.

But rampant development in a group of islands cannot continue without treading on the toes of even the most forgiving people. The demands of the developing tourist industry were bound to come into conflict with Hawaiians in the course of competition for the same resources. Traditional Hawaiian culture and society, and only to a slightly lesser extent contemporary Hawaiian culture and society focus on the beaches and ocean surrounding the islands. Hawaiians look to these areas not only for recreation but also for subsistence. Many contemporary Hawaiians, following a traditional pattern, would like to live by the ocean at certain times of the year. This traditional pattern of behavior is reinforced by urban Hawaiians seeking to escape to the beach from their crowded and, in the summer, hot apartments. All of these activities have become increasingly difficult as the best beaches come under the control of hotels and resorts.

The rapid rise of tourism in Hawaii can be directly linked to the advent of the jet plane and the cheap air fares associated with it. A minister of one of the branch churches of *Hoomana O Ke Akua Ola* discussed this link in the following statement:

After 1959 when the jet plane arrived, it has been down-hill in Hawaii. Before the jet, life was simple. There were not so many people, people were happier and the government was simpler. If you wanted to get something done you just talked to to someone. Now the government is so complex that it is impossible to get anything done, and it is controlled by all of the outside people who have come here to build hotels. . .

There are several points of interest in this statement. Not only has the tourist population increased dramatically (*c.* 1,000,000 in 1969 to 2,500,000 in 1974), but the state population also has increased remarkably (21.7% between 1960 and 1970). This growth has resulted in raised land values and higher taxes to pay for expanded government services. To the Hawaiians who had already been alienated from their land, these increases meant diminished hope of ever regaining property in the islands.

The increased complexity of state and local governments also meant a significant loss of political power for the Hawaiians. While they rapidly lost control of the upper levels of government soon after European contact, Hawaiians until this point continued to participate in government through patronage and to influence the government in areas of immediate concern to them. Now even this limited degree of political power is diminishing. While at least two members of the church have held elective political office in the past (one on the state level and one on the county level) and many more claim to have personal acquaintance with various elected officials, the members who held elected office had done so twenty to forty years ago and political acquaintances were not often still active. Thus Hawaiians continue to drift to the periphery of society in the land that by tradition belonged to them.

The dramatic rise of tourism is associated with large scale real-estate development. This development was once seen as the harbinger of jobs and happiness, but is now evaluated more realistically by some. The following is the comment of a member of *Ierusalema Pomaikai*:

These people that want to build hotels on Molokai tell you that the hotels are going to provide many more jobs for the people, but when the hotels are built all the good jobs go to mainland *haoles* [outsiders, usually referring to individuals from the mainland United States]. Also they are going to build that hotel next to my place on the beach, and all those tourists are going to come over and look at my family and my house. I am going to have to move up to the mountains to get away from these people – but I would rather live by the ocean. . .

More and more people in Hawaii are realizing that jobs associated with tourism are made less than desirable by the irregular work schedules and shift in employment patterns they entail. Beach property values have gone up so rapidly that the few Hawaiians who still own property on the beach can no longer afford to pay the taxes. The many Hawaiians who have been renting beach property for a long time find that rents have increased beyond their means to pay, and that they have to move to less desirable areas without any compensation for what they have lost.

There are other issues in the clash between cultures that results from tourism in Hawaii. Contemporary Hawaiian life style on the beach rarely meets the expectations of tourists or the tourist industry. Outrigger canoes and Hula dancers are largely a part of the past preserved in plastic by the tourist industry. Hawaiians today are more likely to be working on a variety of cars parked in their yards and living in homes that outsiders feel 'degrade the surroundings'. High real-estate taxes thus serve to remove these 'unsightly' scenes from the beaches. Hawaiians are increasingly beginning to feel that they are losing privacy and freedom, and they are finding it necessary to act defensively. This goes against their much publicized tradition of warm and open hospitality usually referred to by both Hawaiians and by the tourist industry as the *Aloha* spirit.

When I first went to Molokai in 1969 the island was still removed from the extensive development that had taken place in the rest of the state. The people were open and friendly and lived up to the Hawaii Visitor Bureau's label for Molokai as the 'Friendly Island'. If I were walking along the road people would stop and give me a ride. On other occasions people were easy to meet, and, with only a few exceptions, willing to invite a stranger into their homes.[3] But by 1972 tourist development had started, and the island people were changing noticeably. Outsiders were now felt to be taking advantage of the local people, a feeling substantiated by many specific examples.[4]

The advantages taken by tourists were rarely willful or malicious, but more often the result of interaction between two groups of people with differing expectations. Tourists who had been told to expect the *aloha* spirit felt that they would meet an openly generous people. Hawaiians on the contrary were acting along lines of behavior suitable to a closed community in which a service rendered to an individual would be reciprocated in the future. This system of social exchange is converted to unwilling altruism by the tourist who steps into and out of the Hawaiian community without fulfilling expected obligations. Hawaiians on Molokai soon learned that contacts with people from outside their immediate community could not be conducted in the same manner as those within the community.

The residents of Molokai not only changed their views about tourists and tourism from direct experience, but also from seeing effects of the excessive development of the Waikiki district on Oahu and certain areas on the island of Maui. Here large numbers of hotels had turned the streets into hot, dirty, concrete canyons. People on Molokai did not want to see their island subjected to the same course of development. Problems of rampant development, culture clash and overcrowding result everywhere from increases in population and mobility and are not unique to Hawaii: people on Molokai knew only that they did not want to see their island subjected to this course of development.

Context of the views

The changes that have taken place in Molokai Hawaiians' evaluation of economic development in Hawaii have to this point been related to particular aspects of the tourist industry, but their views must be seen in a wider historical and social context.

Historically economic development was not particularly disruptive to the Hawaiian population of Molokai. The first twenty years of this century were marked by a series of unsuccessful attempts to exploit the limited resources of the island. Large-scale attempts at cattle ranching, sugar-cane cultivation and beekeeping failed in succession. However, early in the 1920s two events altered this unsuccessful economic course. The first of these was the passage of the Hawaiian Homestead Act (1920) which made land available on Molokai and other islands for people of Hawaiian ancestry. This land was intended to help Hawaiians establish themselves in family farming enterprises. While this objective may have been appropriate to social, economic and environmental conditions in parts of the mainland United States, it was of limited feasibility in the windswept environment of Molokai.

The second event which changed the course of economic history on Molokai also prevented the homesteading program from being a total disaster. This was the introduction of pineapple cultivation – pineapples being well suited to this dry land. Through planting agreements with two large corporation plantations, the Hawaiians were able to lease their land and thereby convert their agricultural plots from a resource of questionable monetary value to one which, at no effort to themselves, produced an income supplement. Pineapple plantations did not provide suitable employment for Hawaiians, however: they did not find the intensive hand labor and regular hours acceptable. This necessitated the importation of a labor force from Korea, China, Japan and most recently the Philippine Islands. Despite the presence of the plantations and the immigrant labor force, Hawaiians were not forced to accomodate the life they had been leading to these new elements. Changes could be avoided as long as the population of the island did not grow too large and as long as the major economic activity did not interfere with their usual routine of life. These conditions pertained until the recent influx of tourists.[5]

There are several social factors that play a part in the changed evaluation of economic development by Molokai Hawaiians. The first of these is their economic strategy. During the first period, up to 1959, Hawaiians had a limited involvement in the cash economy of Hawaii. For some the small income supplied by the pineapple planting agreements could be adequately supplemented by subsistence activities such as fishing and gathering the food resources that abound in various parts of the island. For others without homestead land, these subsistence activities were combined with work on the island cattle ranches, in state and local government jobs, and part-time as well as short-term jobs on other islands. As mentioned, Hawaiians shunned work on the plantations because of the regular demands it made on their time. When plantation work was sought, it was most often by women whose children were grown up or men seeking seasonal work. Indeed in all spheres employment patterns tend to reflect the Hawaiian involvement in subsistence activities. This economic strategy allowed great flexibility, the mobility to visit friends and relatives and to participate in various activities on other islands.

But the long-term consequences of this strategy may not have been so ideal. The lack of participation in the cash economy reinforced other trends pushing Hawaiians into a marginal position in modern Hawaii, and the lack of sufficient economic resources meant that Hawaiians were not able to protect themselves from rising property taxes. Hawaiians with land have found that to meet cash demands they must sell off these property holdings because they are unable to pay the taxes. Today, in spite of vastly increased participation in wage labor, the cost of living in Hawaii is so high and demands for cash so many that Hawaiians can hardly hope to regain their former holdings.

Church members have a particular interpretation of and reaction to their increasing participation in the general cash economy. The most significant symbol of their shift from a subsistence economy to a cash economy is the decrease in reliance on personal resources for the production of everyday necessities. A theme that appears frequently in sermons is the laziness of Hawaiians today who, for example, buy onions at the store rather than growing them themselves. Self-sufficiency is an ideal which Hawaiians can attain less frequently as larger numbers of them live in urban areas, but they continually look for reasons for their inability to achieve it.

Education is another factor that has led Hawaiians to revise their perception of economic development. While their change in attitude is in part due to a lack of participation in wider society, another part results, paradoxically, from greater participation in the educational process of the wider society. Among older church members formal education was limited to two or three years, the number of years of schooling tending to increase with the decreasing age of members. The older members when young apparently felt that attendance at school was not going to prepare them for what was important in their lives, but younger Hawaiians who see themselves as more dependent on wages are likely to stay in school longer. Compared to the general population church members still tend to have less schooling, but there is a noticeable trend towards increasing education. This seems to result in greater awareness of the effects of the development taking place in Hawaii. Since these effects are an important topic of conversation at the church, knowledge of them is spread among all church members.

In a complex society, differences in earnings and education determine social rank; the greater the deficiency in these two areas, the lower the social status. Hawaiians by these criteria are most often in lower social strata, sharing the social opportunities and orientations of other low-status groups in the United States. They have similar tastes in popular music and recreation, follow similar patterns of consumption, and have dietary habits similar in many ways to lower-class individuals on the United States mainland. Even Hawaiians whose income might allow their inclusion in a higher stratum engage in behavior similar to that of the less wealthy. They are defined more by their marginal involvement in the wider society than by such factors as education and income.

The basis for this marginal relationship can best be understood by considering contemporary Hawaiian culture, which for this purpose can be considered in two respects. The first includes those activities that are symbolic statements of cultural identity: the use of Hawaiian language, the consumption and enjoyment of food – especially traditional Hawaiian food, and claims to Hawaiian behavior and characteristics. A considerable proportion of church activities express these symbolic statements.

The second aspect of Hawaiian culture is the shared values which generate their behavior. Unlike other ethnic groups in the state, Hawaiians do not stress individual achievement but rather the individual's relationship with and contribution to the group. Cooperation is given greater value than competition, and individuals are socialized to subsume their activities within the activities of the group – be it an extended family, a church or other organization. Correlated with this lack of emphasis on individual achievement is the priority given to social relations above material wealth, and the emphasis on affiliation rather than achievement (Gallimore and Howard 1968; Peterson 1974).

The social values inevitably affect attitudes to economic development. They entail an economic strategy which is not compatible with an economy directed towards individual accumulation of material goods. Hawaiian use of money involves not its saving but its distribution among relatives and, in the case of church members, donations to the church. Since they do not accumulate money capital Hawaiians are unprepared for sudden demands for cash to pay taxes, car repairs, health care and the like, and this further weakens their ability to function in the wider society.

The relationship of Hawaiians to the wider society can thus be considered the result of incompatibility between demands for participation in the wider society and the cultural values of Hawaiian society. Contact between Hawaiians and outside cultures in the twentieth century could be characterized as a gradual encroachment of the new over the traditional, but not all Hawaiians have become fully acculturated nor are they orienting towards the new culture in the same way: many seem to be making a conscious choice not to become a part of *haole* society. Today members of *Ierusalema Pomaikai* continue to act out Hawaiian culture, despite the fact that increasing intrusion of *haole* society and culture is making this process of being Hawaiian more difficult.[6]

Within *Ierusalem Pomaikai* as a result, one finds individuals with their feet firmly planted in two different worlds. Through increased participation in wage labor and a dependency on the cash economy they are having to adopt strategies which will allow them to exist in the new world, but at the same time they seek to meet this world as Hawaiians. This necessitates the accommodation of the two worlds so that they can exist side by side. Members' participation in the church indicates two ways in which this accommodation takes place. First, members convert the monetary proceeds of their participation in the cash economy into means for obtaining the cultural ends of their

Hawaiian society. Second, the Hawaiian church provides an ideology which allows members to adapt to the wider society. It is significant that this Hawaiian ideology at once allows for adaptation and prevents assimilation.

Adaptation without assimilation

These attempts at adaptation without assimilation involve various activities in which members combine their efforts to meet and overcome the difficulties encountered in contact with *haole* society. But before discussing these activities, it is pertinent to ask why Hawaiian ethnicity should be maintained in a setting providing both a strong challenge to it and many alternative forms of social identity.

The nature and contemporary form of a group's identity are influenced by its previous form and by its contact with other groups. The fact that Hawaiian identity remains strong is therefore somewhat surprising. At the time of European contact, Hawaiian society was in a state of radical change: it had discarded its religion and was in the midst of political consolidation of the archipelago. This state of social disruption was compounded by a series of devastating epidemics that swept the islands in the early years after contact. Assaults on the cohesiveness of the Hawaiian people continued with the steady alienation of Hawaiians from their land, the weakening and ultimate dissolution of the Hawaiian monarchy, and finally the loss of political and economic power to new immigrant groups.

The effects of all of these events in Hawaiian society and culture were profound, but the Hawaiians did not disappear. Social identity is maintained as long as it serves the needs of individuals possessing the identity, and/or the needs of individuals from another group or groups. In this case, both internal and external functions are discernible.

Those functions external to the Hawaiian group are considered first. European exploration of the Pacific was started in the sixteenth century by the Spanish and Portuguese, but Hawaii was not 'discovered' until 1778 when Captain James Cook landed at Waimea on the island of Kauai. The Romantic Movement was heavily influential in European thought and exploration in the eighteenth and early nineteenth centuries. Thus when explorers and other travellers in the Pacific encountered the natives, the Europeans had a great respect for the islanders. This was especially true of their reaction to the various Polynesian groups with their elaborately developed political states.

This is not to say that European contact was entirely benevolent, but that Hawaiians were seen as worthy opponents. The imposition of European will on the Hawaiians was not justified by Hawaiian inferiority, but rather by European 'moral superiority'. This view laid the groundwork for a highly developed interest in Hawaiian society and its culture, beliefs, technology and arts, all of which were avidly documented and collected by explorers and (later) ethnologists. In turn these early collections of ethnographic information held the interest of an increasing number of people who today form the membership of *Hawaiian* clubs. While *Hawaiiana* has little to do with contemporary Hawaiian society, it is a very visible component of life in Hawaii today and forms the basis of admiration and respect for *ancient* Hawaiian people.

This admiration for Hawaiians and Hawaii had been increased in non-Hawaiians as a result of the development of the tourist industry. Not only are prospective tourists lured by attractive scenery and beautiful natives, but once in Hawaii, the tourist is constantly exposed to real and plastic artifacts of ancient Hawaii. Contemporary Hawaiians add to the tourist scene through their participation in hotel shows and other tourist-directed performances. A tourist's usually limited contact with things Hawaiian leaves him with an impression of the greatness of old Hawaii and the fun-loving good nature of modern Hawaiians.

Modern Hawaiians have to pay a price for the admiration of the *haole*. The emphasis on the past greatness of Hawaii and the grandeur of their culture only points to the fact that Hawaiians of today do not appear to measure up to their ancestry.[7] Perhaps this contrast between the power of ancient Hawaiians and the limited influence of Hawaiians in contemporary Hawaii reinforces the often played escape-role of the carefree, funloving person which is the modern interpretation of the romantic savage. This role has certain parallels in American Black behavior; however unlike Blacks, Hawaiians have not been removed from their homeland, and despite the possible negative consequences of the reminder of their past greatness, their past has been available to them as a source of pride and a focus of social identity.

Today some Hawaiians seek to establish their Hawaiian identity through the study and appreciation of their ancient culture; others are only incidentally Hawaiian, focusing their affiliation and social identity on aspects of their lives other than ethnicity. Church members have chosen neither this rear-view approach to life nor assimilation to the wider society, but are actively involved in being modern Hawaiians. This identity is not only supported by the external factors mentioned above, but also by a series of factors internal to the group.

For members of *Ierusalema Pomaikai* being Hawaiian and a church member are intimately associated, and both are of great importance in their daily lives. The life histories of church members give a clue to this importance. The membership of *Ierusalema Pomaikai* is made up predominantly of middle-aged (40 to 50 years of age) and older people, and virtually all of them spent a large portion of their childhood in the care of grandparents. As a result, many first learned to speak Hawaiian rather than English, which has been predominantly used in schools and most other public activities during this century. While simply speaking Hawaiian gave these individuals a strong attachment to Hawaiian ethnicity, language was not their only contact with traditional culture. Grandparents passed on to their grandchildren extensive amounts of information concerning Hawaiian remedies and healing rituals and lesser amounts of information about Hawaiian mythology, customs and technology. All of this information was introduced to church members early in life and has continued as a significant portion of their knowledge and understanding of the world.

Early exposure to this cultural knowledge does not however account for its persistence. While some cultural traits might be retained only for the sake of tradition, others persist because they are valuable in a particular environment. Hawaiian culture and ethnicity persist because they have value to Hawaiians; part of this value is found in the esteem in which their culture is held by non-Hawaiians.

The movement of Hawaiians between city and country further maintains the old culture. Traditional foods are an important criterion of Hawaiian ethnicity, and since most of these foods are gathered and prepared in the country an elaborate exchange system has developed between city and country which can be observed at the luggage pick-up counters of any of the airports in the state. Being in the country also offers the opportunity to engage in activities that are defined as being 'Hawaiian' such as hunting, fishing, going to the beach and, of course, visiting friends and relatives. Some of these are things that cannot be done in a city, yet they are activities that Hawaiians enjoy and consider an important part of being Hawaiian. More generally Hawaiians travel to rural areas for reasons which range from engaging in healing rituals to simply escaping the frustrations of urban life for a time. Some city-based Hawaiians even hope to return to the country permanently; over 75% of *Ierusalema Pomaikia* members have in fact done this.

These remarks about the countryside are not intended to de-emphasize the importance of the city or to give the impression that Hawaiians only live in the city because they must. Cities are exciting places to live, and they are places where good jobs can be found. At the same time the country is the place to do many of the things that Hawaiians like to do. Movement between city and country provides Hawaiians the opportunity to engage in activities that are important to being Hawaiian, something which is immensely enjoyable in itself.

But the question of ethnic continuity is not fully answered until its function for Hawaiians is more fully considered. Stated most simply, activities which define ethnicity are also adaptive to the need to live in two worlds. In the case of church members, the adaptation process can be seen in the interrelation of three factors: mobility, symbols of identity and economic dependency on the wider society. In the last portion of this paper the discussion of specific church activities indicates the way in which church members attempt to adapt to the wider society, and to accommodate the two worlds in which they live.

Ierusalema Pomaikai shows obvious signs of its historical connections with the Congregational mission-churches. But Hawaiians started forming their own churches 30 to 40 years after the missionaries arrived (in 1820), and

Ierusalema Pomaikai is a lineal descendent of these first independent churches. At times the combination of Hawaiian language and the sense of community that surrounds one at church services and other activities evokes the Hawaiian church of the nineteenth century. Beyond these first impressions however it is evident that *Ierusalema Pomaikai* is very much an organization of today, attempting to deal with contemporary problems of attracting and keeping members, unemployment, divorce, drugs and the place of the Hawaiian in the world today.

Some of these problems face all people in Hawaii and some are unique to Hawaiians, but the members deal with them all in a peculiarly Hawaiian manner. Church activities which deal with problems of particular significance to church members include the organization of state-wide meetings, money raising and mutual savings, counselling or healing, and the planning of and participation in general church activities. These will be discussed with reference to the general problem of accommodating the old and new worlds in which Hawaiians live.

Ethnographic accounts of Hawaiians after European contact indicated that they lived very mobile lives, moving within their home area in response to seasons and among the islands often according to whim. Such mobility continues today, but it is complicated by the present shortage of housing, and by monetary considerations such as cost of transportation and finding a job.

Members of *Ierusalema Pomaikai* attend several statewide meetings of the *Hoomana O Ke Akua Ola* religion each year. These meetings are held in Honolulu and on the outer islands and along with religious activities allow reunions of friends and relatives, the transaction of various types of business, and shopping – all of which seem to be given greater importance than the religious activities of the meetings. By attending these meetings, church members are able to maintain a network of individuals who can be called on for aid. Such aid is normally necessary when a member moves from one island to another, and can be in the form of temporary housing, help in finding permanent housing or a job, or help getting adjusted to the new community. In this way participation in the church enables church members to continue their traditional Hawaiian mobility while they contend with the problems of modern life.

A very large portion of church activities involve the raising of money to operate the church, and this money comes from individual contributions and group projects. The earlier reference to Hawaiian cultural values is relevent here: Hawaiians, like many other groups, place high value on group co-operation and low value on individual achievement. In keeping with these values, individual contributions are received with only limited recognition to the donor, while group projects, usually conducted by various clubs within the church, are enthusiastically supported and the group given prominent credit.

As in many churches, projects like church sales and church suppers provide money for building, maintaining buildings and support for church activities. In line with the Hawaiian predilection for mobility however the greatest proportion (about 75%) of the profits from these money making activities goes into plane fares for trips to church meetings on the other islands. Money raising activities are therefore also mutual savings activities which, since they often take the form of *luaus* (feasts or parties) which feature Hawaiian food and Hawaiian entertainment, also serve to reinforce Hawaiian ethnicity. At the same time, these mutual savings activities provide a culturally acceptable means of meeting the cost of transportation which members' usual economic strategies might preclude. The various types of healing rituals and problem solving activities of the church are a third means of accommodation of old and new worlds. These counselling activities include a formalized ritual called *hooponopono-kumuhana* through which members deal with problems ranging from ill-health to loss of a job. Problems of less severity are handled at testimony meetings and in casual meetings among friends.

Very often the problems of church members can be linked to their contact with the outside, non-Hawaiian society. These would include the effects of on-the-job accidents, and family problems that result from work scheduling or general frustration with life. But such problems are invariably translated into a Hawaiian idiom: an understanding of a problem in terms of Hawaiian spirits is sought, and a remedy prescribed which not only deals with these spirits but also with the cause of the problem in the wider society. In the counselling activities of the church, the accommodating process which combines ethnic symbols (Hawaiian spirits in this case) and problems which originate in wider society is most clearly observed: in counselling, as in other aspects of the church, a bridge is provided between the two worlds of Hawaiians.

Finally, the church provides a setting in which members can learn new social roles by planning and/or participating in church activities. Many individuals come to the church seeking help for a particular problem, and when the desired end is achieved they drift away. But those who stay to become active members pass through a sequence in which they start as observers of church activities, proceed to awkward participation, and finally become articulate and active participants. In the course of this progression members gain social skills valuable to participation in a group larger than that of their immediate family.

The development of new social roles as a result of participation in voluntary organization has been discussed by Little (1965) as being an important part of the acculturation process of rural Africans in cities. The skills of organizing meetings, speaking before large groups and planning long range activities all have potential value for Hawaiians. Certainly they could be brought to use in organizations other than the church, perhaps in the political arena. That this has not been the case thus far probably indicates that Hawaiians who are members of *Ierusalema Pomaikai* choose to emphasize the fact that they are Hawaiians, and see participation in other settings as a contradiction of this statement. In this sense the church seems to prevent assimilation and it may also prevent adaptation. However the changed attitudes noted earlier may provide members with the incentive to take action in the wider community in order to protect their interests. When they do this, because of their involvement in the church, this action will be in terms of their being Hawaiians.

Summary and conclusions

As a consequence of various historical, social and cultural factors, ethnic Hawaiians are at once part of and apart from the wider Hawaiian society. Hawaiians are dependent on the cash economy of the state, but culturally unable or unwilling to participate fully in the cash economy and the related society. The church members described here seek to accommodate the two worlds in which they live through activities in the church which both reaffirm their Hawaiian ethnicity and provide means for adapting to non-Hawaiian society. And in this process the church members have developed what was referred to at the beginning of the paper as social power.

The basis of this social power is in the cohesiveness of perceived common bonds and goals. From this cohesiveness or group integrity arise means for encountering the world: the group's evaluative standard is an important part of this integrity. That these standards can change in the course of forming group integrity has been illustrated here by the Hawaiians' changed views of economic development. Hawaiians changed these views as a result of increased awareness of their group integrity and from the realization that the course of these economic developments was in conflict with the goals and aims of their group.

Members of *Ierusalema Pomaikai* have developed their social power to the point of providing coherent knowledge and understanding of their world, but not to the point at which members exercise control over their future or can execute changes in their environment. Hawaiians' present interest in the future seems to be limited to protecting their life from further encroachment from the outside world.

Douglas Oliver has aptly stated that ' "progress" in Hawaii consists mainly in the substitution of one form of autocracy for another' (1961: 255). He uses autocracy in the usual sense of absolute power possessed first by the Hawaiian *ali'i* (chiefs) and later by the missionaries and their corporate descendents. But autocracy also means independent or self-derived power, and it is this second sense of the word that can be applied to the members of *Ierusalema Pomaikai*. The development of social power through their participation in the church is their alternative to the usual course of progress in Hawaii.

5

While the first four papers explored the interplay between 'development' and 'autonomy' within conceptually isolated units, the next batch deal with perceptions relative to other times, other places, other people. BaKosi provide an example of the way 'progress' looks from the distant periphery.

In the debates about development, underdevelopment and modernisation the unit of analysis is usually assumed to be a national society or national economy which, however small, is conterminous with the authority of a state. It is a mistake to take over these theories without recognizing chains of dependency within those states and without facing the question of whether the units we deal with, particularly as anthropologists, could ever be 'developed' or even 'modernised' (as pp. 5–10 above). What does it mean to say that a people, known to the colonial authorities as a tribe, favours development or is developed? 'Developed' in relation to what? In the perception of baKosi, 'progress' would be not more money, but a return to the 'autonomy' of the colonial past. While they recognise themselves to be materially better off than ever, the pinnacle of their 'development' is firmly associated with a long-dead leader. In this time their economic options expanded and/but their identity as a people was enhanced. Changes occurring since are construed by them in terms of 'autonomy' lost, not goods gained. For baKosi 'development' is loss and 'progress' is past. But this is not what is meant by the development of underdevelopment.

Progress in the past:
Dilemmas of wealth in baKosi

MICHAEL LEVIN

This paper considers the dilemmas and contradictions facing the members of baKosi society who have become relatively rich by growing cocoa and coffee. Unlike migrant entrepreneurs (Hill 1963) baKosi have become rich in their own lands by using traditional structures. But in doing so they have transformed these structures so that their success has created a new dilemma: how to maintain the solidarity of an increasingly stratified and occupationally mobile population? Aspects of baKosi society and history provide the context of this dilemma and constitute a rationale for present-day attitudes to change and to the future.

Traditional baKosi society can be reconstructed as a baseline from which to describe change. This reconstruction is a synthesis of several sources of information: informants' reports of how things were and how they have changed, and extensions of our knowledge of now-altered institutions by reference to societies similar to baKosi. It is not a description of baKosi at any one time but a synthesis whose heuristic purpose is to allow analysis of change and of perceptions of change. The term 'traditional' is used to denote forms of social organization that existed in the past and, if they continue to exist, are explained in terms of tradition: the reason given for doing things a particular way is that they have always been done that way.

If a list of 'changes' in baKosi were made up, it would include the usual hodge-podge of new things and lost things; trivial new consumer goods, new crops, diseases eradicated, better supplies of some essential goods, more freedom of movement, literacy, withered or suppressed institutions, ideas, attitudes and behaviour – some beyond understanding and others quite reasonable and very acceptable. Memory is one source of such a catalogue. The old ways and old times are often discussed and compared with the present until a picture or stereotype of an undifferentiated past is built up. This past is associated with admirable things but is not unambiguously evaluated: its loss, though regretted, is not uniformly mourned. 'The way things were' is undifferentiated in that the past is seen as a relatively static period, slow-moving, blending into one picture many things that occurred or existed at different times. For baKosi, the character of his past is in large part derived by contrast with the eighty years since Europeans first appeared. In one sense it is the time before things began to change; in another it is the time before change began to happen the way it does now. Either way, this view of the past provides an image against which to contrast new things, modern things.

Two major events mark baKosi history: the coming of Europeans in 1891, and the death of the Paramount Chief Ntoko Epie in 1932. The colonization by Europeans, first German, then British, ended baKosi independence and began the subordination of a people whose traditional social structure stressed autonomy at every level. The period of Ntoko's chieftaincy, 1916 to 1932, was one of gains in autonomy, a sense of growing solidarity and of increasing wealth.

The following focus on baKosi as a specific spatial and ethnic entity, as a bounded territory and population dramatizes what is most general and most significant about change in baKosi: the structural transformation of a relatively autonomous segmentary political system into a part of a national and world system. The two events described punctuate this process and are symbolically important in framing baKosi perceptions of time, change and tradition.

Traditional political autonomy

In the past baKosi were not isolated, but neither were they subservient or dependent. They fought wars, they captured slaves from, traded goods with and borrowed myths and institutions from their neighbours, but they remained distinct from them both politically and culturally. They were free, or more precisely, members of certain strata of baKosi society were free to enter into relations with others or to withdraw from them. The level of autonomy in most matters was the village group of lineages, and of political autonomy the clan.

Colonization and new tribal autonomy

This sense of independence continued into the colonial periods but was changed significantly. The initial contact with Europeans was in 1891 when German colonial agents first reached Nyasoso, their policy was explicitly directed against indigenous political institutions and their practice of forcefully recruiting labour left no doubt about where political power lay (Rudin 1938). British policy, especially in contrast to the German, had a different impact.

The British arrived in 1920. Their colonial style encouraged a self-conception of tribal[1] existence and autonomy, of free dealings between putative equals, two heads of peoples or nations. The major changes in inter-group relations in a colony[2] – the rights of free movement, working together in plantations and townships led to the development of an ethnic identity based on recognition of differences in language and culture, not principally on territoriality and political autonomy. Autonomy lost under the Germans was regained not at a lineage or village level but at a tribal and cultural level. The conception of autonomy was fostered not only by colonial policy external to baKosi society, but also by political and economic change within baKosi under the leadership of Ntoko. The policy of Indirect Rule and the evolving internal political structure generated by the Paramount Chief coincided and mutually fostered a sense of boundary – of a defined political unit.

Ntoko and political and economic change

As chief from 1916 to 1932 Ntoko created the basis for the economic transformation of baKosi and gained a unique symbolic place in baKosi perceptions of their history. Although the legitimacy of his claims to office was and continues to be disputed, his contributions to change are universally acknowledged in baKosi. BaKosi refer to him as Paramount Chief, although officially his title was District Head.

Ntoko was the younger brother of a German-appointed village chief whom he succeeded to office. In several deft moves about 1920 he claimed land which had been held in reserve for plantations. This land, regarded as part of the 'bush' hinterland of the baKosi villages, had been reserved by the German colonial rulers to be given to a railroad-plantation company in exchange for the building of a railway. The railway was finished, but only just before the First World War so that the company never received its payment. In 1920 Ntoko reclaimed this land under the British regime apparently without opposition, and proceeded to make the baKosi rich. By introducing cocoa as a cash crop and establishing farms on this reclaimed land, he and his elder brother became role models of economic innovators. As District Head, Ntoko was able to organize expansion into cocoa production and the settlement of the reclaimed land. This was done in the traditional manner: a newcomer was adopted or incorporated into a village by 'showing' him land. In exchange for being allowed to settle, the newcomer offered a small gift of money or European liquor. The gift was more important as a symbolic recognition of Ntoko's office and affirmation of his authority than it was of material value. The ritual recognition of his office and the act of allocating land created a pattern that continued to strengthen Ntoko's office and identify the economic expansion with his chieftancy. Once begun, however, the process of settlement and expansion of production had a political and economic dynamic of its own.

In the next decade this land – some of the most fertile in Cameroun – was converted from tropical rain forest to cocoa smallholdings. Previously part of the baKosi hinterland and some distance from the villages, this land was never bought but always allocated by the head of the community. This process is important for several reasons: politically it elevated the chief to a new and unique position in baKosi – a chief of all baKosi; economically, it clothed a radical transformation in traditional ritual; structurally, the separate changes in economic and political processes reinforced each other; and perceptually, an identity was established between growing political autonomy under Ntoko and economic expansion and growing wealth.

By 1930 a large area was established in cocoa and 'the farms' became the rainy season home for many baKosi. This established a semi-annual migration from the villages to the farms for the cocoa season. Penetration of cocoa into the village lands was prevented by the vulnerability of this crop to diseases made worse by high humidity of the village areas, and by its need for high average temperatures which were not maintained year-round at the altitude of most villages. An adaptation of the 'plantation model' of cash-crop production evolved in the development of the farms. The idea of employing labour in order to expand production was seized upon but the necessary forms of financing and credit which underlie plantation organization went unrecognized. Without sources of credit, wages could not be paid on a regular basis and other financial arrangements – leasing, pledging, share-cropping, tenancy – were used to employ labour and expand production and farm-owners' incomes.

In 1928 coffee, which can tolerate a wider temperature range, was introduced upland and spread as a cash crop throughout the villages in all parts of baKosi. The penetration of the cash-crop economy in these areas was slowed by adverse prices in the 1930s so that its full impact was not felt until later. The basis for the present-day economy of baKosi was, however, firmly laid. Its main elements were production by women of cocoyams in the farms and villages, and production by men of cocoa at the farms and of coffee in the villages.

This economic expansion has a singular place in the progress of the baKosi. It links modern agricultural production and traditional sovereignty. Ntoko is identified with the innovation of cash-crop production and is credited with bringing prosperity to baKosi. He had organized the building of roads, he had built a court-house and a two-storey stone personal house the equivalent of anything the Germans had built. The signs of his wealth still exist but the creation of the cocoa farms of Tombel plain is also regarded as his achievement.

In retrospect, this is an age of glory for baKosi. Economic expansion, strong political leadership and the assertion of traditional rights went together. In contrast to political life under the Germans, local and colonial politics were very active. The combination of these factors contributed to a sense of growing autonomy and collective identity. The growth of this autonomy and identity was brought to a halt by the arrest and suicide of Ntoko Epie (Vaux 1932; Ejedepang-Koge 1971; 121–5).[3] However much he had misused his own people in building up public works and his private property, and however dubious his traditional right to be or to create the office of Paramount Chief, the death of Ntoko is seen as an event which interrupted baKosi progress. This sense of growing autonomy was only partly an illusion. Although his power did not extend beyond baKosi nor was it sufficient to defy the British in the end, Ntoko did have power within baKosi and some power to limit direct British intervention in day-to-day affairs.

Many defeats are dated from his death. They add mundane elements, which in the historical retelling adhere to the specific and dramatic tragedy. In ending a period of dynamic economic expansion and political unity led and symbolized by him, the death of Ntoko Epie stressed the subservience of the baKosi to another power, another people. It marked an end to the period of rapid progress, and in retrospect is perceived as the cause of this change in fortune. The real and symbolic destruction of baKosi autonomy and of its evolving political system, colonial though it may have been, is seen as a turning point in baKosi progress. The downturn was not into poverty or chaos but to a lower level of expectations, a sense of less power to control the boundaries of baKosi as a community, society or polity. A reorganized local government system with local councils replaced the tribal head. The opportunity to identify a cultural tradition with political unity was now lost. The dependency that economic expansion had created was being felt in its negative aspects. As if also related to Ntoko's death, the loss of income and employment characteristic of the depression of the 1930s affected baKosi during this time. Cocoa prices had tumbled from 10.4 U.S. cents per pound in 1932 (Gill and Duffus 1968: 34) Employees had been let out from the plantations and employment opportunities declined (Ardener *et al.* 1960). The consequences of the continuing integration of rural areas into the colonial structure and of production for world markets were now becoming apparent.

Post-Ntoko baKosi

The notion of progress entailing both growing wealth and growing autonomy died with Ntoko. His death was neither the end of economic expansion nor of local political activity, but the consequences of modernization for baKosi, the growing dependency on production for sale, the growing powerlessness of baKosi in the colonial and later in the national structure were felt in a way they had not been before.

Political events since Ntoko's death are all of a piece: tension in political relations with the central authority, increasing penetration of national structures into rural social systems, competition in politics and for jobs, school positions, and public-work schemes. Reunification with the Republic of Cameroun (formerly East Cameroun) and national political independence affected local events very little, nor did the departure of colonial whites change the quality of rural life.

No single leader was permitted to emerge as the British administrators' ethnographic investigations had concluded that village councils were closer to the indigenous form of government (Arthur 1937; Vaux 1932). Even when Richard Mambo Ntoko, Ntoko Epie's son, was elected Paramount Chief and member of the Nigerian House of Chiefs, representation, not autonomy, was the issue. Today baKosi is seen as but one of many peoples in Cameroun, vulnerable economically to world commodity prices and politically dependent and subordinate to the government of the Republic.

The expansion of the cash crop economy into the villages has continued. Species of coffee especially adaptable to a wide range of temperatures have been introduced in higher altitude baKosi areas. By the late 1950s there was an established two-crop, market-oriented economy meshed with cocoyam production for domestic consumption. It involved a regular seasonal migration between the cocoa farms in the low-lying lands and the coffee in the upland villages. The seasonal migration was not new; the lack of convenient supplies of water on the farms had prevented year-round settlement.

The years of depression and the Second World War are unremarkable except as a contrast to the Ntoko years. No distinguishing events mark this period. Some returning wage workers established farms with funds saved during their employment, and although this was a prudent conversion of cash into capital, benefits were delayed until the post-war cocoa boom of 1947 to 1954 when cocoa prices increased ten times over wartime prices. They were relatively short-lived: by 1967 prices had dropped to almost half peak prices.

Perceptions of time, change and tradition

BaKosi history can be seen from one perspective as the interaction of tradition and change. The sources of change and the nature of the interaction define baKosi perceptions of time, change and tradition. Perceptions of time are discussed here as perceived periods of baKosi history. Change and tradition have been related differently in each one: change has been integrated with tradition; has been an attack on tradition; has sustained and disguised tradition; and has destroyed tradition.

Four major periods make up the history of baKosi in terms of present-day perceptions of the relationship of tradition and change: (i) the pre-European, (ii) European colonialism, (iii) Ntoko's chieftancy, and (iv) the post-Ntoko period. They are the times before and after the two major events in baKosi history: the coming of the Europeans and the death of Ntoko. As European rule and Ntoko's chieftaincy were concurrent, the 'historical' periods are chronologically concurrent, not consecutive. But the baKosi perceive them as distinct.

(i) The pre-European period is the source of tradition; it is the reference point on which discussions of baKosi tradition turn. The institutions and the rituals of baKosi were complete, the baKosi were autonomous and independent as a people prior to the coming of the Europeans. But, in retrospect they were poor in goods and knew very little of the possibilities of the world. This was not, however, a static period devoid of change. BaKosi legends of settlement tell of conflict and migration, of the desire for better lands and the creation of new villages. Wars were fought with neighbouring peoples – very likely, we can say now, to secure better access to trade with agents of the Europeans at the coast. Two major innovations originating outside baKosi were adopted during this period. One was the main secret society with police functions and rights of execution; the other was a new variety of cocoyam (*Xanthosoma*). The secret society was adopted through elaborate negotiations and cost a human sacrifice. The rules of its organization and operation were detailed, and access to them was heavily circumscribed. Membership in the secret society emphasized the inequalities ascribed by descent in the community. In contrast, the new variety of cocoyam was introduced by a slave, Nhasambe, and was adopted freely and widely for its ease of production, preparation and eating. Today it has replaced the older variety (*Colocasia*) as the staple food crop.

Two points are of interest. Firstly these changes were not considered disruptive of traditional structures. Change as such is not seen as incompatible with tradition, as bringing an end of tradition, nor as being anti-tradition. Secondly, innovative inputs were made both at the top and at the bottom of the status hierarchy, but in retrospect the innovations are appreciated independent of this status difference in their origins.

(ii) The coming of Europeans to baKosi is a major turning-point in their history. Change during this period is seen as dramatic and negative. Resistance to European rule was crushed and political autonomy was lost. Villages were reorganized from scattered compounds into two rows of houses along a central path. Village chiefs were appointed, and the people were forcibly recruited to bear loads, for local works and for the plantations. Certain institutions and rituals were banned. Peace between neighbouring peoples was enforced, but control over trade and the movement of strangers in one's territory was lost.

The positive changes seem to have been continuations of aspects of life that pre-dated the beginning of German colonial rule. Consumption goods became secure in supply and a wide variety of previously unknown items became available. The price of previously scarce goods such as salt and iron probably dropped significantly. Literacy and some trade skills are conceded to be uniquely European, but these could be learned and become skills independent of their teachers. These benefits, although recognized as associated with the European presence, are considered not directly dependent on colonial domination. BaKosi was seen as dominated by not integrated into a larger system, and peace and free trade as mixed blessings of the *pax imperium*.

(iii) The change from German to British colonial rule also marked the ascendancy of Ntoko as Paramount Chief. The contrast in styles of colonial rule and some of the consequences for baKosi are discussed above. Modernization of baKosi now begins to take effect and have an impact on the structures of baKosi. Although the integration of baKosi and the destruction of its separateness in an encapsulated state begins during this period, the process is overshadowed by the success of Ntoko who became the most important symbol of this period. At the time that modernization – i.e. increasing dependence on industrial centres as markets for cocoa and coffee and as sources of manufactured goods – is taking place, the political sense is of growing autonomy and a strengthening of tradition. In theory this synthesis of tradition and modernization would seem impossible, and in retrospect the identity of the two trends unmasked as a contradiction. Their unexpected unity is explained by two factors: by baKosi lack of knowledge of the world beyond Kosi physical and social boundaries, and by Ntoko's role as a political and cultural broker. The relative ignorance of most baKosi about the world outside heightened the sense of progress, the sense of autonomy reestablished, and the sense of relative power of baKosi under Ntoko vis-à-vis the British. Awareness of other peoples in Cameroun was slight and the feedback from those who had travelled outside was only beginning. Indeed, Ntoko's success depended on this sort of ignorance: more extensive knowledge would have encouraged neither Ntoko nor his followers. In his position as Paramount Chief Ntoko became a middleman between the British and his people, but he was also the middleman in introducing cash crop production to baKosi and adapting it to baKosi forms of land use and social organization. If the frustrated tone of reports of the A.D.O.s are any indication, Ntoko did stand up to the British. In this sense autonomy under him was not a complete illusion, but it is exaggerated in recollection. Today it is said he appointed village chiefs and tax collectors. Nonetheless, in bringing cocoa farming to baKosi there is no doubt that he modified the impact of innovation, making baKosi farmers comfortable with it, blending the commercial aspect with a traditional political form. This was of course, in his own political interest, but it did give baKosi work and cash incomes without their being required to work for Europeans or leave baKosi. The increasing dependency and the economic vulnerability implicit in the newly established relations were very likely not understood. The production side of the baKosi economy was growing much more rapidly than the demand for consumption goods. An innovation that gave freedom to spend was not suspect of costing independence. The push of modernization into baKosi was thus part of the centralizing of political organization under Ntoko and his traditionalizing of economic expansion.

(iv) After Ntoko, political organization was decentralized and economics was, in effect, separated from politics. The effects of colonial power were no longer filtered through the office of the Paramount Chief but felt directly through marketing cooperatives, village councils and a new District Court. The Depression and the Second World War were felt as the lull before the boom of the 1950s. But this lull served only to heighten the glowing impression of the Ntoko period, for in the fifties and sixties consumption caught up with income. Secondary-school fees, modern houses of cement and metal sheeting, an expanding range of consumer goods, rising bride-wealth payments – all these became new items of consumption for baKosi. Sharecroppers and tenants were replaced on cocoa farms by the owners themselves. In terms of actual work required, lost leisure and luxury expenditure, the baKosi cash crop farmer was worse off. With political independence, occupational mobility into civil service and teaching jobs became more rapid, but this, although lending prestige to the father of a successful child, put a great strain on his income during the schooling period.

Tradition is perceived less as a way of doing things than as a way of asserting ethnic identity within the Camerounian national heritage. The process of modernization which has made baKosi dependent on the larger system, and vulnerable to changes originating in it, is now apparent to them. Although there is ambivalence about the dependency created by cash crop production, and there is some desire for greater solidarity and autonomy of baKosi, the institutional and symbolic resources that might have provided some defense against incursions of the national and world systems no longer exist.

6

How does 'progress' look from the perspective of a small,
island state between Europe and Africa? How do the Maltese
interpret the economic differences between themselves and
other countries? What relation do they see between economic
growth and the quality of life? Despite Malta's small size and
relatively high degree of cultural homogeneity, there are in it
economic, political, generational and even regional cleavages
which make it difficult to speak of 'the Maltese view' on any
subject. In the reported statements of individual Maltese,
'progress' seems to signify movement towards that which is
lacking to each – whether a job, goods, or some quality of the
past. One task of government planning and rhetoric is the
equation of 'development' with a multitude of very separate
goals. The notion of a causeway (to link the less developed to
the advantages of the more developed) with a gate (to allow the
less developed to decide when to cut themselves off from the
disadvantages of the link when they choose) is suggestive of
the contradictions involved. National plans and the various
Maltese perceptions of 'development' and 'autonomy'
therefore alter with time and circumstance. They are shown
here to vary with changes happening within Malta, and in
relation to the perceived advances of those ahead and those
behind in the development queue.

A Causeway with a gate:
The progress of development
in Malta

JEREMY BOISSEVAIN

Malta comprises three islands, Malta, Gozo and Comino, covering a total area of 120 square miles. With a total population of just over 318,000 people and a population density of 2,600 persons per square mile, Malta is the smallest and most densely populated independent country in the world.

Malta's history has been greatly influenced by its small size and strategic location in the centre of the Mediterranean. For centuries it was run as an island fortress, first by the Knights of St John (1532–1798), then by France (1798–1800), and finally by Britain, to whom the French surrendered after rebellious Maltese had kept them penned inside the fortified capital, Valetta, for more than a year. The country received its independence from Britain in 1964.

If Malta's experience of self-rule was limited by the obvious difficulty of giving self-government to a fortress, it today provides what is probably the best example of parliamentary democracy in the Mediterranean basin. Politics in Malta are vigorous and cut deeply into all spheres of social activity. The intensity of social control and the ideological cleavage between the two major parties – the Nationalist Party and the Malta Labour Party – have worked against the formation of smaller parties. This has usually ensured stable majority government. Party politics in Malta have always reflected a strong class bias. During the recent past this was mixed in many fascinating combinations with nationalism and anti-colonialism.

The working-class-based Malta Labour Party replaced the Nationalist Party – traditionally the party of landowners, traders, civil servants and established professionals – after a hard-fought and very closely contested election in 1971. The Nationalist Party piloted the country through the difficult first years of independence. During most of its period in office (1962–71) it received considerable support from the Roman Catholic church in Malta which was and still is a powerful force among the overwhelmingly Catholic population. The church's impressive arsenal of moral, political and religious sanctions ensured Labour's electoral defeat in the early sixties. In 1969, however, the church and the Malta Labour Party overcame their differences and signed the equivalent of a peace treaty. This freed sufficient voters for the M.L.P. to gain a slender victory in 1971.

Malta's economy was for centuries based on the provision of goods and services to the military and naval garrisons of its rulers. In the early days of the Knights of St John the Maltese provided food and performed menial tasks, including physically defending the island against various aggressors. Increasing numbers of the professional classes were employed in the central administration. Under Britain, Maltese began to work in the garrison, the naval dockyard, and the civil service. The number of professionals and businessmen expanded as entrepôt commerce flourished following the opening of the Suez Canal.

The balance of power in the Mediterranean gradually passed from British hands. By the late 1950s this was reflected in the drastic decline of the defense establishment in Malta. Teams of advisors finally began to make serious attempts to find alternative economic possibilities. Foremost among these were plans to convert the giant, overstaffed, naval dockyard to a viable commercial enterprise. Attempts were also made to attract manufacturing industry. Britain had systematically kept such industry away to safeguard the monopoly of the dockyard and the military over local skilled labour. Steps were also taken in the early 1960s to encourage tourism.

In spite of these efforts, the economy was stagnant when Malta became independent in 1964. Discouraged by grim economic prospects and fearful of independence, more than 9,000 emigrated that year. (The annual average of the previous five years had been around 4,000.) But since independence Malta has proved to be remarkably robust. Not only has she become a diplomatic power to be reckoned with in Mediterranean affairs, she has also achieved a phenomenal economic growth. From 1965 to 1969 there was an economic boom, sparked off by the arrival of new industries and mass tourism. Since 1970 boom conditions have been replaced by a slower but still vigorous growth. A large number of foreign firms, attracted by various incentives, established themselves in Malta, increasing domestic exports between 1964 and 1974 eightfold, from just over £M4 million to nearly £M32 million per annum. (In 1975, at the time of writing, £M1 = £1.14 Sterling; £M1 = US $2.70.) During the same period annual imports grew much more slowly. They merely doubled, rising from £M34.6 million to £M67.2 million.

Because of measures taken by the newly independent government, Malta was able to capture an important portion of the wave of tourists which in the 1960s began cascading into the sunny Mediterranean from grey industrial centres in northern Europe. British currency restrictions for non-Sterling areas accelerated this influx: thousands of British discovered in Malta a Sterling island in the sun. Tourism grew from 23,000 arrivals in 1961 to 270,000 arrivals by 1974. The expansion of industry and tourism raised the Gross Domestic Product from £M47.4 million in 1964 to more than £M100 million by 1974. This increase was reflected in a considerable rise in the level of prosperity. Between 1964 and 1974 virtually every household bought a modern gas-cooker, a television set and a washing machine. During this period car ownership increased from 19,500 to over 45,000 – from one car for every eighteen persons to one for every seven.

But not all the benefits of economic prosperity were evenly distributed. Wage rates of white-collar workers and industrial labourers employed by government and established commercial and industrial enterprises lagged far behind those in tourism, building and manufacturing, and the disparity created considerable tension. Newly prosperous industrial managers, real-estate speculators and building contractors began to eclipse the traditional elite of professionals, higher civil servants and traders. The new textile and electronic industries tended to hire women, who were generally more likely than men to accept low wages and poor working conditions. This increased rates of male unemployment. Perhaps the most acutely felt development was the severe housing shortage created by the exploding demand for tourist accommodation. The shortage priced all but the wealthiest Maltese right out of the market, and in the process fed smouldering class-antagonism.

Malta has nonetheless become, both politically and economically, a viable and unexpectedly resilient nation. Even in a period of world-wide economic crisis, the rate of inflation and the cost of living have grown relatively slowly, and the rate of unemployment has risen no more rapidly than most.

Government and development

Some of the changes that have swept across Malta have been planned. There have been four development plans since it became evident in the late 1950s that Britain would evacuate Malta. These plans throw interesting light on the way the islands' elected rulers view development and so partly answer the questions posed at the beginning of this paper. Even a cursory comparison of the 1969–74 Nationalist development plan and the 1973–80 Labour development plan clearly demonstrates their different perspectives (see Appendix, p. 98). The most significant difference is in the ideological premises underlying the respective plans. As the extracts given show, the stated target of the last Nationalist plan was economic growth to achieve full employment and an increased standard of living on the assumption that as the economic pie grew, a better distribution of it would automatically follow.

In the Labour development plan the economic target was but one of several dimensions (Appendix, pp. 98–9). The interlinked objectives of the plan were to achieve (1) independence from power-bloc affiliations, (2) higher standards of living for all, and (3) specific improvements for socially disadvantaged categories. It was clearly recognized that a more equitable distribution of the fruits of progress entailed social reform. Moreover, the plan noted explicitly that economic growth was not an end in itself, '. . . since growth of GDP [Gross Domestic Product] is neither the appropriate aim nor an adequate measure of real development. It does not necessarily reflect changes in the quality of life, improvements in education, the diversity and satisfaction of work, increased social equality or greater national cohesion and independence' (p. 52).

Comparing the two plans, it is evident that development for the Nationalists meant economic growth. This was thought to be accompanied automatically by a rising standard of living for all. For the Labour Party development meant more than just economic growth. It also meant improvement in the quality of life, increased social equality, greater national independence – and so, social reform. It is worth noting, however, that the Nationalist plans were not debated in parliament and that vigorous Labour press did not criticize the Nationalist's narrower view of development as economic growth. From the limited debate in the press on the Nationalist Party plans of 1959, 1964 and 1969, it would appear that all those who publicly expressed their views, whether Nationalist or Labour, perceived development to be no more and no less than economic growth.

The significance of the broader concept of development set out in the Labour plan also escaped the attention of local press, radio and television commentators. With the possible exception of one editorial writer in the pro-Labour *L-Orizzont* (30 August 1973), all who commented in public and in parliament on the plan and its outline (published in August 1973) noted only its economic and political objectives. Even the Secretary General of the powerful and staunchly pro-Labour General Workers Union identified the 'principle target' of the plan as 'prosperity for all the people of Malta' (*L-Orizzont* 30 August 1973). The important social objectives of special aid to the disabled and aged, better housing and increased social equality were largely ignored.

Clearly, inspite of the way the drafters of the Labour plan viewed development, most of the opinion leaders who discussed it saw development only as economic growth.

Several Maltese advised me not to take the development plans as serious indicators of local attitudes to development. They argued that the plans had been drafted by foreign experts and only pushed forward by each sponsoring prime minister so did not reflect the views of a cross section of the population. But if a prime minister asks a conservative rather than a progressive economist to draft the national development plan, the choice reflects more than personal whim. The ideological premises underlying the plans are consistent with those of the parties sponsoring them and the views expressed are necessarily a compromise between the ideals and targets of the local and foreign experts, and those of the sponsoring politicians, whose own views generally closely resembled those of their constituents at the grass-roots level.

Grass-roots perceptions of development

When asked how they conceived of progress and development, people replied in many different ways. Some of their replies are noted below. While they are statements of acquaintances, and not the result of systematic survey, they may be said to indicate the views of many Maltese:

Progress is the incredible improvement in working conditions and social benefits achieved during the past half century [Pensioned skilled dockyard worker].

Progress is catching up with the rest of Europe in things like cars, social security, pensions, wages, etc. It is the fulfilment of a concept created by communication, the transmission of ideas; these concepts are transmitted and exploited by vested interests [Lecturer; the son of the dockyard worker above].

Development is whatever Mintoff [the Labour Prime Minister] wants. The Office of the Prime Minister decides everything [Professor].

Progress is being able to hold free discussions, being able to see films uncensored, being able to have free relations with girls [Lecturer].

Development is a better job and better pay [Unskilled dockyard worker].

Development is a job, good pay, a house and a better education for your children [Senior prelate].

I don't think the majority are mature enough to look at development as independence in the real sense of the word. . . On the whole the attitude is more about growth, it is more about employment. They are always thinking of it in employment terms. . . Their idea is more about real very near resources. They are thinking more individually than nationally. Or they think nationally as far as it affects them personally. . . We are really thinking in economic terms. We are interested in economic growth, for economic growth's sake and for what it means, more than for consumption as a mass. I think we are really interested in pounds, shillings and pence; in earning more to consume more [Economics student].

Progress is people realizing themselves, giving things to other people, to the poor, and helping various categories. All this has stopped under Mintoff [Wealthy landlord. He noted specifically that progress was *not* catching up with the rest of Europe: 'In the north they have made a mess of things.']

By and large progress and development to the average Maltese means *more*; more security, economic growth, and employment; more pay, houses and cars; and more and better education for their children. This is fully consistent with the definition of development formulated by the national planners, with which they have been indoctrinated during the past fifteen years. It is also consistent with their own experience, especially during the past ten years, with the economic boom, its decline and aftermath and with the growing scale of social changes of which they are slowly becoming aware. In relative terms most working Maltese have gone from what they consider relative poverty to relative prosperity in the course of a generation.

But if most people see progress in terms of material welfare, some, and especially the older ones who have worked with their hands, see it as emancipation. They compare their present comfort – now that they are pensioned, insured against illness and cushioned against unforeseen crises by savings in the bank – to the incredible poverty which they recall surrounded the old age of their own parents and grandparents. They also see great progress in the way in which their own and their children's dependency on the professional classes has been reduced by better education, welfare measures and greater general prosperity. They say there has been great progress, for the gap between rich and poor has closed somewhat. For them progress is more than money: it is a greater sense of freedom, a sense of autonomy and dignity.

Economic growth and the quality of life

For most Maltese the recent economic growth has brought with it relative prosperity – a better life in material terms. Only intellectuals are actually heard talking about 'the quality of life'. As a young university lecturer noted, 'Though "the quality of life" seems on everyone's lips in the north of Europe, you hardly ever hear of it in Malta.'

But if only a few use the term, many are aware of the environmental pollution that has come with economic growth. They complain in conversation and in 'Letters to the Editor' about the rising level of filth deposited on Malta's shores. Those who live or swim near sewer outlets are conscious that more houses, more hotels, more tourists mean more toilets, more sewage, more pollution. All Maltese are aware of the congestion and noise of a threefold increase in the number of automobiles in the last ten years. But most Maltese, like people everywhere, seem quite prepared to put up with the negative effects of their newly acquired gadgets. Hence the limited success to date of two pressure groups *Din L'Art Helwa* (This Beautiful Land) and the Malta Human Environment Council which is concerned to alert public and government opinion to the connection between economic growth and environmental, social and cultural pollution.

Only some old men openly regretted 'progress', and tried to explain that the simpler, slower, rhythm of life forty years ago was more congenial. While admitting the benefits that political and economic developments have brought, they lamented the passing of a life-style. It does not surprise them to hear that in the north of Europe people are moving from the frantic tempo of congested cities to try to obtain something of the way of life which they once knew. But in Malta their children and grandchildren cannot understand this. For most of this generation progress still means more growth, more things.

The inhabitants of Gozo, Malta's isolated rural neighbour, are probably more conscious than most Maltese of the relation between the quality of life and economic progress. They have thought about it, for they have been asked several times for their opinion on the desirability of a causeway linking them to Malta. They have still, perhaps, their destiny in their own hands. Gradual but increasingly rapid developments have eroded Gozitan customs and life-style in ways that no one foresaw. Yet Gozitans are ambivalent about the causeway. Though it was a political issue before the 1971 elections, and the government was placed under severe pressure to achieve it, Gozitans today are more reflective and less certain about it. Every Gozitan is fully aware of what it would mean to be linked directly to Malta. It would mean access to the job market in more industrialized Malta. It would also mean that industries could be more easily established in Gozo. This would mean that perhaps fewer Gozitans would have to emigrate. Finally, with a causeway, Gozitans would be able to share the cultural activities of Malta, and would be able to transport the seriously ill quickly to the central hospital in

Malta. On the other hand, Gozitans also see that the causeway would open their picturesque, quiet and immaculate island to the hordes of Maltese picnickers who have so polluted their own countryside. On Malta there is now hardly a rural lane, a quiet field or rocky promontory that does not have deposits of plastic jetsam, rusting tins, bags of household rubbish, bottles, bloated mattresses, bursting pillows, and over-stuffed armchairs. Though most prominent Gozitans publicly proclaim they would like the causeway, many in private express grave doubts. They do not want to sacrifice their tranquillity and the rustic beauty of their countryside to waves of refuse-dispensing Maltese. A hotel receptionist summarized their dilemma neatly when she said, 'It would be nice to have a causeway in bad weather and during weekdays if we could close it during weekends and holidays.'

Development gap

Most Maltese and Gozitans perceive themselves to be less well off than north Europeans, about whom they have learned a great deal from television in the last few years. They have also considered themselves to be far better off than people in most countries in Africa and Asia. They have learned about these not only through television, but also from active missionary fund-raisers. Just as Malta is located geographically between Europe and North Africa, Maltese see themselves at the comfortable middle of the development continuum. Although they define progress as the state of north Europe, few believe that Malta will ever catch up completely. Nor have they worried much about doing so. It is a secure feeling to be able to look down upon people. Many Maltese look down upon the Gozitans. They regard Gozitans as quaint, sly, backward hayseeds. Most can cite examples of some crude everyday expressions Gozitans use, and of the extreme suspicion with which they treat the inquiring Maltese. Many townsmen in Malta also look down upon those who live in villages, regarding them as less civilized than they. But all, at least in the past, have been able to look down upon North Africans and those in the mission zones as truly backward.

Some friends, economics students, commenting on the development gap between Malta and other countries, summed up the situation as follows: 'We are happy to have Britain for an example', the first said. 'We have this sort of...Well it's not quite an inferiority complex. It is more like a daughter, you know, who has got respect for her mother. She does not want to be richer. We are quite happy to have England better than us. Because it is sort of a natural thing, a natural state of affairs. It is as if Northern Europe were our mother. But we are better off than the missionary folk. We always think of Africans as barefooted and hungry.'

The second added: 'We start worrying only when we see countries like Libya getting ahead of us. Then we really start worrying. In the past we have always said that we were worse off then anyone else. But we were always ahead of the Arabs. In fact, we have used the Arabs as a scapegoat. We have always turned our wrath on the Arabs.'

'We've always learned that they're all filthy, you know', the first interrupted. 'They're really dirty.'

'Then we start thinking', the second student continued. 'Christ! You know it really looks like we're falling behind. They start coming here with their fancy cars and spending money. When they come here we start hearing more about them. When they actually buy or put out more literature or contribute to the mass media, then we start becoming aware that they are one up on us. And that they are not really so illiterate as we thought they were.'

Most Maltese and Gozitans thus have not thought of themselves as particularly underdeveloped. The Nationalist Party, in fact, has occasionally critized the Labour government for playing the role of underdeveloped nation and begging aid from wealthier nations. While much of this critique is political rhetoric, it also reflects the differing views on development and the identity of the country referred to above. A frenetic effort lies behind much of the Labour government's success in amassing grants, development loans, used military equipment, books, saplings for reforestation, technical advice and so on from a variety of places including Nato countries, Libya and the People's Republic of China. This effort is a resource that many Nationalist leaders failed to muster while in government. Nonetheless, the belief that Labour prime minister Dom Mintoff is lowering the prestige of the country by defining it as underdeveloped and asking for aid strikes a sympathetic chord with some Maltese, especially those who are better off.

It is to be expected that perceptions of progress, development and underdevelopment will shift from class to class. The well-to-do, who are largely strongly anti-Labour, may not see much difference in lifestyle between their Malta and northern Europe. Trips abroad demonstrate to many professionals that they live more sumptuously than many foreign colleagues. (Or at least they did so before the Labour government started collecting income tax more systematically: between 1971 and 1974 the annual revenue from income tax rose from £M4.5 million to £M11 million.) Why should Malta then proclaim its underdevelopment and beg for aid?, they argue. The lifestyle of wealthy foreign residents in Malta and of the growing hordes of middle- and working-class tourists from northern Europe emphasise the relative poverty of the poorer Maltese who cannot afford to travel abroad in the same style. Aid from wealthy European countries who have in the past used Malta harshly for strategic purposes is a right, they argue, and it will help to narrow the development gap. These different perceptions of foreign aid are quite logically related to the class composition of each political party.

The Labour government's broader development perspective and its greater emphasis on foreign aid may also reflect a growing uneasiness about multiplying signs of rapid development in Libya. Increasing employment opportunities in Libya for Maltese; expanding cultural and diplomatic activities; and the growing numbers of highly visible, free-spending Libyans who come to Malta in search of alcoholic and sexual adventures denied them at home are indicators that Libya is rapidly catching up on Malta. These changes affect the way Maltese view their position relative to others. To stay in the middle of the development continuum, they must move ahead. This calls for a broader emphasis on development.

Conclusion

It is very difficult to generalize about the concepts of development and progress in Malta. There is no single perception. Most people think of development and progress in terms of their own personal concerns. The working-class Maltese, who has probably suffered unemployment and has close relatives who have been forced to emigrate, thinks of development as security, as a good job with good pay. Somebody from the established professional classes has a different view, for he faces different problems. The same is true for intellectual and non-intellectual, young and old, Gozitan and Maltese. Perceptions vary not simply with the eye of the beholder, but with social and economic position.

It would also seem that perceptions can be imposed. The differing concepts of development of the Nationalist Party and the Labour Party are cases in point. Their development plans reflect dominant opinions within the parties. Thus when a party controls the government, the particular view of development that it holds becomes national policy. It is promulgated and people have little choice but to accept it. In time it may become their own perception of development. Thus notions of development, of pollution, of the quality of life can be formulated by an influential minority and then spread through mass media, political indoctrination and government policy over a much wider body of people.

There is no doubt that Maltese perceptions of progress and development have changed and are changing. The different points of view of the Nationalist and the Labour parties have already been referred to. There has been a logical succession of development concepts. The view of development purely as economic growth is slowly being replaced by a broader concept that includes political and social goals. This sequence is not random, nor does it result from the periodic changes of political party in power. The succession of one party by another is itself based on developments taking place in society. In Malta the insecurity and lack of development of a new nation have been replaced by self-confidence and relative prosperity. It is not surprising that with these changes, perceptions of progress and development have also changed. Many of the urgent, short-run goals have been reached. Having obtained basic necessities, people are now shifting their vision to a wider framework. With this shift the concepts of development and progress are also being redefined.

Perceptions of development and progress are related not only to differing social position and political affiliation. They also reflect the level of economic, political and social development of one country relative to others. The Maltese experience seems to suggest that once a certain level of material prosperity has been achieved relative to other countries, development and progress can no longer be expressed by national leaders purely in terms of economic growth. Sufficient time must elapse for people to see that even though they may be better off than before, the stronger continue to take the biggest pieces of the growing economic pie. Once they perceive that they remain deprived relative to some, their notion of progress changes. Towards the end of the boom in Malta it was becoming evident that economic development was by-passing many – in particular the socially handicapped, the many salary earners and the growing number of engaged couples unable to marry because property speculation had priced housing out of their reach. By the time the boom ended many had begun to realize that resources were limited, that progress was more than just economic growth, and that basic structural changes were required if they were to achieve a slice of the pie.

Thus the wider concepts of development and progress held by the Labour leaders, by growing numbers of Maltese and, especially by Gozitans, reflect both the boom and its abrupt end. These broadening concepts also indicate growing uneasiness with the way North Africa, long the epitome of under-development, is catching up.

Appendix: excerpts from two Maltese development plans

The 1969–1974 Development Plan[2] (Nationalist)

Aims of the plan

'The Third Plan will pursue the same broad objectives of strategy that have motivated the previous two plans. It will be aiming to achieve a high level of employment, through a further conversion of the Maltese economy, by 1974, and it will be endeavouring to do this by creating new activities relevant to Malta's overriding objective of long term viability' (p. 3).

'The immediate task of the present Plan is to achieve a rate of economic growth high enough (a) to provide jobs for virtually all who seek them; (b) to build up those areas of activity within the economy which can be effectively developed and which contribute to the achievement of Malta's planning objectives; (c) to raise standards of living in line with increasing productivity of labour' (p. 55).

The human dimension

'In a development plan the human factor must be taken into account. The increase in economic opportunity and the resultant increase in real incomes should lead to a better distribution of resources and rising living standards' (p. 60).

The 1973–1980 Development Plan[3] (Labour)

Aims of the plan

'*Political objectives*: The Labour Government is determined that Malta should find her identity and place in the community of nations. Malta will do this by discarding the centuries-old role of a fortress in the interest of a long succession of imperialist powers, by disengaging from power-bloc affiliations and dedicating herself to economic and social progress through peaceful collaboration with all...

'*Economic objectives*: One of the primary objectives of the Plan is to increase Malta's productive activities to an extent which would make it possible for Malta to dispense after 1979 with the economic returns accruing from defence arrangements negotiated with foreign powers...

'The economic purpose of the Plan is to secure the country's self-reliance and self-determination through diversified relationships with other countries, far and near, so that no single country's decision or economic trouble could seriously affect Malta's welfare.

'*Social objectives*: The Plan contemplates a steady improvement in the living standards of the people within the limits of available resources. Society is a single whole, and all parts are closely related to others. The division into political, economic and social objectives is ultimately arbitrary. There is an organic unity in all the objectives of the Plan. The Plan expressly recognizes that the ultimate objective of development must be to bring about a sustained improvement in the well-being of all, and especially those who, through illness or other misfortune, cannot without help from the State secure a fair share of the fruits of economic progress. If undue privilege and social injustice persist, development will only accentuate inequalities and social unrest will eventually jeopardize all economic gains' (pp. 49–50).

The Human dimension

'Stress has been laid on the economic objectives of the Plan, the policies by which it will be stimulated and guided, and the vision which inspires the whole Plan. This is a Malta standing on her own feet, sustained by the ingenuity and resourcefulness of her own peoples and containing within herself the economic power and sinews to maintain self-reliant growth. Economic growth in the abstract is not however the end of a rational economic policy: it is its result. If the economic and social objectives of the Plan are achieved, growth of national income will be registered. The target growth rate is the resultant of the specific human improvements that the Plan aims to achieve...

'The test of success of the Plan is not the attainment of some particular growth rate but whether the basic-felt needs of the mass of people, and especially the poorest and least fortunate, have been met' (pp. 61–3).

7

The small British dependency of Basutoland became the sovereign state of Lesotho in 1966. Like the Maltese, the Basuto perceive their 'development' relative to the development of others. But in their case, only one 'other' is significant and it is so far ahead in the development queue that the Basuto set little store by their chances of catching up. Poverty pushes them to migrate and migration exaggerates and confirms the country's economic backwardness. The perception and the reality of non-development act and react on each other in a closed and vicious circle of non-development that even massive injections of money would be unlikely to break. In the perception of the Mosuto villager, 'progress' is industrial South Africa: there is none in Lesotho because there is no wage work and they see no way of bringing it home. Like the baKosi, the Basuto place 'autonomy' in the past. The need to migrate to work for industrial wages has sapped it since.

The bind of migration: Conditions of non-development in Lesotho[1]

SANDRA WALLMAN

The argument offered in this paper emerges as one aspect of material collected in Lesotho where I was concerned with problems of rural development – or, more correctly, of non-development. The extraordinarily high rate of failure of development projects in the country was and is, striking. Before independence it was normal for colonial government schemes to fail; since independence it remains largely true that somewhere between planning and execution every project undertaken has broken down. I shall try to show here that some substantial part of the failure can be attributed to a combination of social and economic factors which constrain the individual Mosuto in such a way that he will make no effort to improve conditions in his home village and so none towards the country's economic advance. Nor, by extension, will he co-operate with any 'improving' agency planning and/or implementing change for him. While this particular syndrome pertains, it would appear that significant economic progress cannot occur – whatever the level of development aid or investment.

The component factors in the non-development syndrome are not consistent in kind, nor are they conceptualised at the same level, and I am quite conscious of their imperfect synthesis here. Nevertheless, an analysis of Lesotho's (economic) reaction to the presence of South Africa enters a caveat to the theory of 'aspiration effect' (Firth and Yamey 1963), extends the concept of 'frustration gap' (McLoughlin 1970), and adds a dimension to the cognitive map of 'migrant ideology' (Philpott 1968). More important, it may increase our understanding of economic problems in Lesotho and in regions sharing certain characteristics with Lesotho. The dangers of eclecticism are therefore compensated by the possibility of practical advantage.

The necessary characteristics of this non-development syndrome are three:
(i) a poor, entirely rural domestic economy;
(ii) a geographic position next to or near to a thriving industrial complex;
(iii) an established pattern of temporary migration to the city.
Lesotho, as exemplar, may be briefly described.

Lesotho

Lesotho is a stark, mountainous country entirely enclosed by the Republic of South Africa. Its total area is less than 12,000 square miles. A maximum of 1,500 of these are suitable to cultivation: nearly two-thirds of the land area is made up of rugged foothills and mountains, which are ideal for the raising of sheep and mohair goats but are generally inaccessible to the plough. Seventy per cent of the people live in the lowland third of the country.

The present population of Lesotho numbers about 800,000, of which it is estimated that 45 per cent of men and a steadily increasing number of women are absent at any one time. The migration of Basuto to work in South Africa is therefore a fundamental factor in the life of the country. The closing of the border on the South African side (as of 1 July 1963) has affected this population movement to the extent that migration can no longer be a matter of unregulated individual choice, but the dependence of Basuto on wage-paying jobs in South Africa is no less desperate. Indeed, Lesotho might be described as a dormitory suburb of peasants who regularly commute to work across the border for several months at a time. They do not regard Lesotho as a place of 'work' (i.e. of money-making) any more than the big city suburbanite would think of setting up shop in his own front garden. It is significant, of course, that Basuto are commuting across an international boundary, and that the laws of the receiving country preclude extended visiting and prohibit immigration. Whatever the level of frustration at home, the outlet of permanent migration is virtually closed to even the most enterprising of them.[2]

The national economy presents, on the whole, a dreary picture (Pim 1935; Morse et al. 1960; Elkan 1963; Halpern 1965). Lesotho has no immediately marketable resource other than unskilled labour. It has virtually no indigenous industry or entrepreneurship. Its traditions of land use are technically inefficient and are vitiated by population pressure and soil erosion. The high rate of out-migration entails a shortage of manpower in some areas so that the country is effectively both over-populated and under-peopled. Further, the fact of being land-locked by the Republic of South Africa restricts any possibility of independent economic action.[3]

But existing analyses of the national economy do not fully account for the persistent failure of rural development projects in Lesotho. An appreciation of its refraction upon the individual is lacking. It is the purpose of this paper to demonstrate that the economic facts of village life are perpetuated by their effect on individual villagers.

The closed circle

Provided that no single cause–effect sequence is imputed, this non-development syndrome may usefully be visualised as a closed circle. This is shown in the figure at the top of p. 104.

The various factors can then be grouped, sometimes arbitrarily, under the headings Poverty, Migration, Ideology.

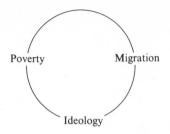

A. Poverty

By poverty is meant lack of any necessary economic resource – non-material as well as material. *Time*, for example, is an essential non-material resource often left out of account in economic analysis.[4]

Simple observation of ordinary village life shows that the mere business of survival at subsistence level so fully occupies the day that improvement or innovation may be ruled out for lack of time alone. The most prosaic and fundamental tasks are the most time-consuming; producing and preparing food, finding and preparing fuel, fetching water. . . Because there is no accessible mill, a woman may spend half the day grinding sufficient maize for the household's evening meal; with no piped water each bucket used may mean half an hour's walk to a spring and another half an hour's walk back. Multiply this time-expenditure by the number of buckets necessary to the most frugal of families and a sizeable chunk of someone's man-day is spent. Numerous other tasks can and should be computed in the same way – if only to correct the impression that the poor sit about a good deal, apparently having nothing to do.

The most glaring and obvious material shortage is of arable *land*. Every Mosuto householder has a traditional right to three fields on which to grow a subsistence crop, but not everyone has the full complement and something like 10 per cent have no lands at all. The amount of land available is further reduced by the fact that, of the fields claimed by individual villagers in a particular season, one-quarter of the total had not been planted. Various reasons were given for non-use, but the majority cited lack of a plough or the strength to pull it, and lack of seed or the money to buy it (Table 1).

Lack of draught power and/or of manpower (an overall shortage of physical *strength*) is then another important element of village poverty. In lowland Lesotho there is a critical climatic period of between 40 to 60 days for ploughing and planting since a late-started crop runs the risk of being caught by frost before it has matured. But the operation depends traditionally on able-bodied men who are largely absent, and on oxen whose condition at this season is so poor that even several span cannot turn drought-hardened lands. Ploughing must begin as soon as the first rains fall, and there is no grass to build up the strength of the cattle until several weeks after the rains have fallen. Many villagers therefore plough and plant too inefficiently or too late for a good harvest, and some simply give up hope of working their lands at all.

A poor harvest, of course, entails other shortages. Most dramatically, it means a shortage of staple *food* for that year; more insidiously, the shortage is perpetuated by the fact that there is no *seed* to plant the following year either. On this basis it is at least logically impossible to recover from one hitch in the subsistence cycle. Production never catches up. And sub-subsistence production in a region which normally grows no other food generates an inescapable need for *money*.

Table 1. *Lands*

Total number of fields claimed: 221	Number 'enforced fallow': 54
Dispersion by households:	
No. of fields No. of households	Reasons given for non-use:
0 13	22 'no seed'
1 16	12 'too hard'
2 36	9 'no plough'
3 41	11 'hoping to plant wheat later'
4 3	
Average per household: 2.03 fields	Percentage unused 1962/3:
	25% of total

Employment for cash wages in the village is chronically scarce. One person has a regular job at the trading store three miles away, another is paid a monthly wage to work in the village café-store. (The proprietor also runs a bus service but drives his own vehicle.)[5] One small group of men get casual employment sheep-shearing at the trading store twice a year (Wallman 1969: 50). They are highly skilled; the same ones get taken on every season for about a fortnight. They are paid at the rate of two cents (one-fifth of a shilling) per sheep shorn and, working at incredible speed, can make up to seven shillings a day. Everyone else can expect occasional per-diem cash employment 'at the Chief's place' (*Moreneng*), always at the daily-paid rate of two shillings. This work is most likely to be offered at the height of the hoeing season when everyone is, or should be, fully occupied in his own lands. It is none the less popular because two shillings gained is not measured against a day lost: time itself is not valued in cash and is not marketable.

These are the only village-based jobs involving a cash wage. Outside the village, opportunities for earning in Lesotho are virtually non-existent. Given the effective absence of a private sector in the country's economy, the Mosuto peasant automatically looks to South Africa for cash employment.

B. Migration

(i) *Effect on local organization.* Whatever the attractions of 'the place of the whites' (*Makhooeng*: usually visualized as Johannesburg), and however strong the pull of the industrial bright lights, the brute truth is that village poverty pushes the peasant over the border and is the immediate cause of his migration.[6] But while his absence from the village allows an injection of cash which may bring his family over the subsistence line,[7] it directly adds to the shortage of strength which is an element of the poverty that makes migration necessary. Further, it upsets the demographic balance of the village (Table 2) and entails the disruption of traditional organization in many other spheres (Table 3. See further Wallman 1975).

Table 2. *Population*

Total number of villagers: 552					
Male		Female			
Age in years	No.	Age in years	No.	Total number of absentees: 75	
Under 17	127	Under 17	139	Male	
17 to 49	104	17 to 49	118	Unmarried men (non-adult)	20
50 and over	31	50 and over	33	Married men (adult)	40
Total	262	Total	290	Female	
				All married, adult status	15

Patterns of communication at the Chief's court and at village meetings alter to the extent that villagers are ill-informed of communal matters and the Chief's authority is diminished (cf. Ashton 1952: 88; Wallman 1968). Family authority, customarily vested in the oldest male, must devolve on someone else or crumble in his absence, and there are numerous examples of non-viable families whose permanent disruption may be attributed to the repeated temporary absence of a crucial member. The frequent instability of marriage may be both cause and effect of the fact that the traditional procedures of bridewealth are rarely observed (Wallman 1969: 44).

It is, of course, true that many successful compromises may be/have been made. On the economic side, for example, one may occasionally see a woman herding cattle when tribal tradition strictly forbids (functional?) females any contact with kine (Schapera & Goodwin 1937: 138, 149–50; Ashton 1952: 141–2), and there is no doubt that non-kin co-operate in productive tasks when they find it necessary and possible (cf. Southall, 1961: 62–6). Contrary to some expert expectations, however (Gonzalez 1961: 1273), I see little evidence of specific and consistent institutions created to cope with the exigencies of absent members: in Lesotho, most of these adaptive arrangements appear to be made on an *ad hoc* and temporary basis.

(ii) *Effect on consumer preferences*. Extensive individual migration affects village organisation in the ways described above, but also affects the individual which, by cultural accumulation, impinges on rural life in another way. Exposure to the industrial complex of Johannesburg and 'the Reef' (Witwatersrand); the bright, bustling bureaucratised city; the plethora of manufactured consumer goods and diversions; the variety of processed food; even the clockwork organisation of the gold or diamond mine which is central to his urban experience – repeated exposure to these things gives the migrant the tastes and preferences of a full-time urbanite.

Table 3. *Households*

Total number of households: 109*			Heads of households		
Size:	Average	4.9 persons	Male:	present, not earning	43
	Smallest	1		present, earning	2
	Largest	17		absent, earning	34
	Mode	4		sub-total	79
			Female:	widowed	22
				divorced/deserted	5
				sub-total	27

* Note that only 106 household heads were reported – 3 being said to 'borrow' the heads of others.

All but the poorest households manage to indulge these to some extent. It is significant in this context that while any standard 'urban' item can be bought at the local trading store, villagers constantly complain of inadequate quality or range. By contrast, things bought in the cities of South Africa have, whatever their quality, a certain cachet. It is not unusual for even large pieces of furniture to be carted hundreds of miles home by train, bus and pony from some mining town in the Republic when the equivalent is available locally.

Anything or anyone conforming to urban South African standards is described as '*semate*' (corruption of 'smart'). A considerable part of the most meagre household budget is spent on this value (Wallman 1969: 61–72).

The attraction, however, is not only of prestige, nor are all *semate* things necessarily frivolous. Urban South African food is, for instance, *semate* because city fare is more satisfying in terms of variety and nourishment than the indigenous village diet could ever be. Of the tinned and processed foods bought, nearly all will contain the animal protein or sugar which malnourished villagers crave as fundamentally as they do prestige. In the lean summer season (December–March) most families must buy food or they will starve, just as in the fat winter season (June–September) they must buy blankets or freeze. The buying of urban manufactured items is often essential to survival, but the brands and styles bought will reflect the *semate* ideal.

C. Ideology

If, in the occasional outfit or household item this ideal is attained, the village world and, by extension, the country as a whole never make it. On the contrary, the situation generates tensions which are manifested in apathy, hypochondria, and the fear and/or fact of violence.

On the verbal level, a stranger to the Sesotho language and to Basuto village life is struck by the number of times certain words recur in the course of conversation. He gets an aural impression that villagers spend their days visiting, feeling ill, resting or looking for work (*ke chaketse; kea kula; ke phomotse; ke batla/kopa mosebetsi*). Observation shows these to be the preoccupations of people who in fact spend a great part of the day on the more prosaic business of survival, but the ideological content (and probable changes in it) are readily inferred.

Visiting has always been an important social activity for rural Basuto and has been extensively described in its 'traditional' form (Ashton 1952: 90; Lestrade 1937: 119–30). These descriptions imply that visiting is positive, purposive activity. Indeed, the linguistic concept of visiting (*ho chakela*) combines the notion of walking about (*ho chaka*) with the idea of purpose and forethought (applicative suffix – *ela*). In the present context, however, it is often quite aimless; a woman may buy a return bus ticket to Mafeteng for four shillings, spend only an impulsive two shillings when she gets there and speak of the busride itself as the visit; a man may walk some miles to visit a village-in-general only to wander about in it when he gets there – 'in case something is happening'. The element of planning emphasised by Ashton (1952: 90) is commonly absent.

There is no set time for visiting. Some days, notably Sunday, are entirely devoted to it and any ceremonial or enforced holiday will probably follow the same pattern; no one time of day is preferred as long as essential chores are not too seriously impeded, but villagers are reluctant to walk about after dark unless there is a bright moon. They say it is dangerous, that there are cliffs and rocks to fall over, dogs and city toughs (*tsotsis*) to attack wayfarers, and unnamed spirits of the dead to do unnamed things. They will begin to go home when light fades, whether at dusk or when clouds come up: time is gauged according to light (Wallman 1965).

Not all their fears are groundless; injuries from falling and assault form the bulk of cases in the out-patients' department of Maseru Hospital, and the possibility of medicine murder (Jones 1951), though seldom mentioned, cannot be ruled out. Some people claim to remember a time when Basuto did move about freely after dark, but nocturnal social life must always have been inhibited by the treacherous walking surfaces and night frosts.

The etiquette of hospitality has more certainly altered. Traditionally friends and strangers alike were received openly and generously, and any visitor would be given something to eat and drink and a place to spend the night if he wished it. Nowadays not even the verbal pretence of such hospitality is kept up; villagers will stress instead their own poverty and the perfidy of strangers. There is always a current cautionary tale to tell of some local person robbed or damaged by a stranger passing through. Even those who understand and sympathise with the plight of men back from 'the place of the whites' (*Makhooeng*) without work or the money to buy food and blankets, and perhaps with no land to plough, have themselves too narrow a margin of survival to risk much on casual acquaintance. The questions that have always opened a conversation between people on any way – 'Where do you come from? Where are you going? What is your business there?' – are no longer just the small change of social intercourse and idle curiosity, but are as often undisguised evidence of acute suspicion.

Litigation reflects the same ambiguities. Most of the cases brought before the local Chief's court during (e.g.) March 1963 concerned trespass. In one typical instance, a woman stoically sold two oxen to pay a fine of £18 imposed (at the rate of £2 per head) after her nine animals had escaped from their kraal one night and grazed a neighbour's lands. She continues to insist that some 'enemy' must have deliberately let them out. Since this is a popular modern alternative to sorcery, she is generally thought to be right. None the less, the responsibility for the damage is hers alone, she must pay for the advantages of owning stock. Although the traditional code of behaviour between friends is observed as far as possible, no one expects loans or donations in times of monetary crisis (cf. Bailey 1957).

Women may visit each other 'only to gossip' (*Ho seba feela*); for men the supply of beer is crucial. The heavy inebriation that comes with drinking *joala* can be found somewhere in the village at any time. When beer is plentiful, not a few villagers – women as well as men – exist in a perpetual drunken lethargy. *Joala* itself is quite nourishing (the really dissolute apparently live for years on nothing else) but spiked with 'white' spirits or with more dubious mixtures invented in the *shebeens* of Johannesburg becomes impure and even lethal. Perhaps fortunately, few villagers outside the narrow circle of the Chieftainship can afford these addenda and drink only substantial amounts of *joala*.

Lesotho is singularly free from endemic diseases. Despite intestinal and lung infections – the latter engendered in South Africa – the Basuto are considered extraordinarily tough.[8] None the less, the tone of village life is apathetic. While it is true that the diet is unbalanced and *joala* drunk to excess, the lethargy and physical malaise characteristic of villagers cannot be ascribed only to malnutrition (as did Munoz 1960) and alcohol; it includes a strong element of hypochondria. Small illnesses and aches and pains are endlessly discussed and analysed, cash is squandered on an enormous range of patent medicines and paid to herbalists, 'witch' doctors and 'white' – i.e. white-skinned or white-trained doctors. All three categories are called *lingaka*. No special popularity attaches to any one group. Many people consult all three, making their decision according to the complaint to be diagnosed and the intricacies of availability and price: e.g. 'white' doctors' charges are standard and often cheaper, but 'sesotho' doctors customarily divide their fee into two parts and only demand the second if and when a cure is effected. Villagers may spend any unscheduled time doing the rounds of all accessible doctors to find a cure for some largely imaginary complaint. A charlatan with a hypodermic syringe of distilled water is as likely to bring relief as is a bottle of medicine from the Government Hospital.

Consonant with a morbid interest in sickness, the verb 'to be ill' (*ho kula*) is widely and imprecisely defined. It is used to describe manifest physical disorders and any degree of mental breakdown, including the 'good' psychological trauma that partially qualifies a person to be a 'witch' doctor. It may also refer to the vague depression that allows one to sit and do nothing – sometimes drinking and talking a little, often staring mindlessly at the horizon. In this context, only its psychosomatic aspect distinguishes it from *ho phomola* – to rest, to stay still.

The meaning of *ho phomola* is less diffuse and more objective. It can imply only that for some reason outside oneself one is not working; the weather is bad; the harvest is in; it is Sunday. But it is most commonly used to denote that one has no paid employment, exactly as members of the theatrical profession in England talk of 'resting' between contracts. In Lesotho the line between being on holiday and being unemployed is as narrow. The lack of paid work and the nagging need for it (*ho batla/kopa mosebetsi*) are the most fundamental preoccupations of lowland villagers and absorb the time and energy of many:

The ruling here is not like other countries; here there are no jobs. Here, to buy a blanket only, I must go to Johannesburg. And when there is hail or the fields are spoiled there is famine. Only to eat we must take work with the Boers.

This desperate economic dependence has obvious political overtones which have been sharpened by the closing of the border (July 1963):

We used to go to the Whites whenever we needed anything because it was easy to find work. Now they are chasing us away. I have been here, stuck, for six years without work. Now they have closed the gate and we must have another Pass to go in. They say we must go to our own country. But there are no jobs in this country; I see no work between here and the grave.

Conclusion

The peculiarly wide gap between what is known to be possible (in the city) and what actually is (at home) is crucial to the economic pessimism which dominates the rural Mosuto's world view. Migration to the thriving industrial complex shows him that the poverty of his village is relative as well as absolute, and relative to something as rich as industrial South Africa, what chance can there be of alleviating that poverty? The gap between 'home' and 'away' is so vast that any effort to bridge it is seen to be fruitless. On the other hand, the involvement between 'home' and 'away' is so complete that the possibility of small improvements which are necessarily far below 'away' standards provides no incentive to development effort: the contrast is considered unalterable.

Rural life in Lesotho is therefore a particularly unhappy compromise. The villager's aspirations are continually stirred by industrial enterprise over the border, but his opportunities are strictly limited to an unsuccessful subsistence economy at home. Every migration creates greater consumer wants and diminishes the chances of satisfying them at home – both because lands are 'neglected' and because the idea of Lesotho being self-sufficient becomes increasingly preposterous.

Hence the retreat into lethargy, the drunken brawls that follow a party, the endless litigation and the accusations of treachery and sorcery characteristic of everyday life.

Hence also the lack of fit with the 'aspiration effect' model. Firth and Yamey (1963: 382) postulate that contact with people and products of wealthier societies will either encourage consumption at the expense of saving and capital accumulation[9] or will stimulate new enterprise and effort. In Lesotho, neither alternative obtains. In the first case, the rate of consumption is geared to subsistence and is anyway very low. It cannot therefore be at the expense of any very significant saving; the capital accumulation possible in the meagre context of Lesotho's present economy would not of itself be sufficient to real economic growth. In the second case, the stimulus of South Africa's wealth tends to draw enterprise away from Lesotho so actually inhibiting its progress.[10] While the border was open, 'aspiration effect' was detrimental to the country's economic development to the extent that the more enterprising Basuto preferred to live in South Africa. Now that the border is closed and virtually all migrants are obliged to return home after each labour contract, the more enterprising are readily identifiable as the most frustrated.

McLoughlin (1970) suggests that a 'frustration gap' of this kind will spur the individual to even greater economic effort but adds that if the gap becomes 'too large for enough people, frustration, political unrest and other social problems will of course arise' (McLoughlin 1970: 30). The pessimistic rider becomes appropriate to the Basuto case if we add the necessary ideological dimension: viz., the extent to which a too large gap affects the migrant's view of his own home.

Philpott (1968) defines the migrant ideology as 'the cognitive model which the migrant holds as to the nature and goals of his migration' (Philpott 1968: 474). Where the analysis is concerned, as his was, with the effect of migration on the sending community, recognition of the home-denigrating facet of ideology which I have described here would seem essential.[11]

In sum, non-development in Lesotho is a function of a complex of poverty, migration and ideology, and can only be successfully treated if attention is paid to the whole syndrome. It is easy to prescribe negatively: economic development will not be assured by an injection of cash to cure the poverty, nor by a tourniquet to stem the flow of migrants, nor by an amphetamine to lift the pessimism, nor by any one specialist effort alone. More positively – and therefore more diffidently – I would venture that the present emphasis on agricultural development for Lesotho will continue to be nugatory in so far as it exacerbates the unfavourable contrast with urban South Africa. It is even possible that development funds spent on the subsidy of a sizeable industrial complex in Lesotho would allow the villager to think of his home as a place of money-making, of progress, and so would encourage him to improve his rural lot.

The facts of rural life are both cause and effect of non-development and will not be altered until the closed circle of their interaction is broken. Without a break, even the most expert development planning will continue to fail for want of local support.

8

According to Galtung's formula, development comprises two distinct trends: it is a progression towards the (better) meeting of basic needs, and it is a progression towards the achievement of (greater?) autonomy, authenticity of self and/or nationhood (p. 11 above and Galtung 1973a).

In these terms, a narrowly economic definition of development may distort the realities of backwardness – even where social/psychological variables are admitted. My own piece on 'Conditions of non-development in Lesotho' (first published in 1972 and reprinted above) apparently does so: a number of Basuto, while tolerant of the analysis, have contested the pessimistic inference. I have since attempted to deal with this discrepancy by taking the Basuto sense of advance as seriously as I there took measurable improvements in GNP and/or in material standards of life. The following note recasts the case of Lesotho in terms of advance or sense of advance in autonomy. No disclaimer of the previous analysis is intended: the present piece constitutes only a coda. It is another perception of the same set of conditions.

A different progress:
The modernisation of dependence
in Lesotho[1]

SANDRA WALLMAN

Just as the notion of 'non-development' is used (as Ch. 7) in relation to *economic advance* or the lack of it, so the word 'dependence' refers most narrowly to *political status*. On this basis the British dependency of Basutoland became the independent state of Lesotho in 1966. But neither (non)-development nor (in)dependence is necessarily confined to a single sphere. The manner and extent to which any territory is made, or is perceived to be made independent by Independence varies widely from one sphere to another.

While Lesotho has seen changes in manifestations of dependence since 1966 and some small economic progress may have been made, Lesotho is, in very significant ways, no more independent than it was in the colonial past. But since its present forms of dependence are more modern, more 'developed' than pre-Independence forms – reducing the difference between Lesotho and other small territories in Africa or in Europe – they may themselves be regarded as indices of development.

Spheres of dependence

Lesotho achieved *de jure* political autonomy in October 1966, after 130-odd years of somewhat ambiguous tutelage to Britain. This change of political status has affected Lesotho's external relations in important ways, but cannot be said to have made the country economically independent or to have lessened its vulnerability to the friendly and/or unfriendly pressures of South Africa.

This paper will separate the various aspects of Lesotho's dependence on Britain and on South Africa and examine recent events in the light of an expanded concept of 'development'.

It is useful to define three spheres of dependence – the political, the economic, and the ideological, and to consider them in turn. It should be emphasised that the spheres are only analytically distinct, and that the empirical data are bowdlerised by brevity.

(a) Political dependence

The Basuto nation was founded by Moshoeshoe I in the first half of the nineteenth century. According to history (Hailey 1953, Sanders 1975,

Thompson 1975), Moshesh brought together remnants of various Bantu tribes escaping the ravages of the Zulu wars. His powers of leadership were matched only by his talent for diplomacy: he virtually 'achieved' the protection of Queen Victoria as a means of avoiding defeat at the hands of the Boers. But the negotiations were complex, and the dependent status of Lesotho always ambiguous. Two points may serve to summarise this ambiguity.

Firstly, the Basuto were the last of the Bantu tribes to go under and have always taken a justifiable if sometimes exaggerated pride in that fact. They had been 'allies' of Britain against the Boers and saw 'protection' as an arrangement between equals, not as colonial subjugation of any kind. The result was a pre-Independence political system in which the formula for indirect rule was inapplicable, and in which a single locus of responsibility for government could not be identified (Wallman 1969: Ch. 2).

Secondly, Britain never wanted the territory. It was – and is – expensive and difficult to administer, yielding few economic or strategic returns. Only when her hand was forced did Britain take it over, but on a *pro tem* basis, just to keep peace until disputes with the Boers and later the Union/Republic of South Africa were settled. For this reason Lesotho missed out on the usual perks of dependent status: Britain never accepted responsibility for its future, even in the short-term. It is pertinent that the majority of Basuto seem to have been unaware or not cognizant of Britain's lack of commitment to their cause (ibid.: 32–8).

Lesotho's present relations with South Africa can also be rooted in its history. The Basuto were from the beginning a thorn in the flesh of the Boers. The pioneers of both nations competed for the same resources long before *apartheid* was invented and the Basuto have always had good reason to be jealous of their land and their nationhood. No non-Mosuto has ever owned land in their country. In terms of contemporary economic development, the fact that the Basuto are reluctant to grant leasehold to a foreigner is said to be a significant single impediment to foreign investment.

Important aspects of Lesotho's recent history are a function of her being caught in political crossfire between South Africa and Britain. Although always politically independent of South Africa, Lesotho's diplomatic relations with that country had (until 1966) to be mediated by a British High Commissioner. When South Africa left the Commonwealth in 1961 the then High Commissioner became also Britain's Ambassador to the Republic. The ambiguity of Lesotho's dependent political status *vis-à-vis* Britain, extended at that time to its political status *vis-à-vis* South Africa. It may well have affected events since 1966, as, for example, in relations between political factions in Lesotho, and in their various dealings with South Africa.

(b) Economic dependence

This influence apart, Lesotho's dependence upon South Africa is most cogent in the economic sphere. The dimensions of her economy are sketched in the previous piece (pp. 101–12). It is significant that its most fundamental limitations are natural – the constraints of topography and climate – but the most galling are those effected by juxtaposition to South Africa.

Thus: soil erosion is Lesotho's most serious and urgent *technical* problem. Natural factors combine with traditional farming practices and with an increasing pressure of population on the land to erode the soil at a rate which suggests there may be none left for the next generation. Despite the obvious fact that this ecological niche is quite unsuited to agriculture (see De Kiewiet 1941: 258; Wilson 1971), Basuto confine their productive effort at home to subsistence farming. Maize is the staple food and the main crop, grown by every family who have any possibility of scratching any field. But with rising population on the one hand and with arable areas dying of exhaustion and misuse on the other, there are simply not enough fields to go around. And, in Lesotho, to be without fields is not only to lack the rights of citizenship, it is to go seriously hungry.

The 'push' to South Africa's mines, factories and farms is not therefore the product of a relatively luxury need to pay taxes and buy blankets and cash goods. In many cases even the family's staple food ration must be bought for cash. With few local sources of cash wages, migration to work in South Africa is essential to the survival of the country. The absence of a large proportion of the able-bodied entails a shortage of labour essential to the agricultural cycle and in its turn exacerbates the shortage of food.

These economic conditions are intrinsic to Lesotho and have no necessary reference to the presence of South Africa as such – except insofar as it gives Basuto an option as a source of cash. Others are extrinsic – at least to the extent that they are direct products of the juxtaposition and relative wealth of South Africa. The matter of communications is striking in this respect. The only railway in Lesotho is a short length of South African Railway line running into the capital. There is a system of roads in the lowlands – the main road running north–south, and a 'Mountain Road' which runs east–west into the foothills but stops well short of traversing the country. Private motor-traffic can and does use the lowland roads, but drivers who are allowed to enter the Republic can also use the generally much better South African highways. These run most conveniently round the border and have been, on some stretches and in some periods the only roads between adjoining districts in Lesotho: the driver goes out of Lesotho into the Republic, drives along a South African highway parallel to the border and turns back into Lesotho at the required point.

Air transport too is entwined with South Africa. A commercial airline based in Maseru runs schedule and charter small plane services to and from the mountains of Lesotho and nearby airports in South Africa. The impossibility of these small planes linking Lesotho with the outside world without the use of South African airports – and so the implicit approval of that country – has been painfully underlined in the experience of political refugees who may flee South Africa only to be incarcerated by the borders of Lesotho (Halpern

1965). Telecommunications are similarly restricted. And while Lesotho profits monetarily from the Customs Union with Botswana, Swaziland and South Africa (see Turner 1971), its strictures are made inescapable by the fact that Lesotho is entirely surrounded by South Africa. Even so, the very existence of a Customs' Union is taken by some to be evidence of the *inter*dependence and, by implication, the equal bargaining power of the four states.

It would be wrong to imply that no positive economic changes have occurred since Independence. The launching of the Ox-Bow Hydro-Electric Scheme and the fostering of tourism are important cases in point. In bald economic terms, however, both these enterprises depend for their success on the patronage of South Africa and South Africans. It is in terms of decisions made and negotiated that these economic changes constitute real advance.

(c) Ideological dependence

The Basuto sense of national pride and integrity should not be underestimated. Nor does it preclude ideologies and constraints of dependence in other spheres. It is to be expected that the *perception* of the conditions of political and economic dependence described will alter in context and through time, and that they will not necessarily vary with the facts of dependence. In one sphere we may take pride in autonomy, in another, and perhaps simultaneously, we have no control over our lives. The inconsistencies are important, and we do the Basuto no honour by pasting over them (see Gellner 1973).

The habit of second-class citizenship as an effect of dependent status is well documented (as Mason 1959, Fanon 1967) – even where dependence has been confined to a single power or a single area of activity. Having been doubly dependent, on Britain and on South Africa, Lesotho's recent history has been characterised by a pessimism concerning the possibility of successful Basuto initiative. A case in point would be the reluctance of villagers to follow the lead of a Mosuto innovator: whites have always been the source of modernity and progress. They also hold the key to it. *They* are responsible: it is not soil erosion which makes us poor, but South Africa which could make us rich. And since the (perceived) cause of the problem is out of our jurisdiction, it will not be amenable to our efforts at solution. Related to this is the conviction that Lesotho is neither a place of 'work' (i.e. of money-making), nor a centre of 'progress' (i.e. of industry) – although it is arguable that this non-development syndrome is more clearly a product of Lesotho's being so much less industrialised than South Africa than it is a direct effect of dependence (pp. 104–7).

Either way, an ideology of dependence is a significant inhibition to development, and is not readily altered by a simple change in political status. But it is in direct dealings with South Africa – the context in which the close fit between economic and political dependence has shown most vividly in the past – that an effective difference can be seen. The fact that the Basuto government is recently said to be taking a harder line towards South Africa on a number of issues certainly reflects some change in ideology, but it does not necessarily indicate any lessening of economic dependence. Nor does it bear any necessary relation to development.

Development?

The last statement implies that we know what 'development' is. The problems raised by this assurance are discussed in the Introduction (pp. 1–16). Our perspective must be wider. In this case it is relevant to ask whether decreasing dependence is a necessary condition of 'development'.

The constraints of Lesotho's geographic position and natural resources make it extremely unlikely that she could ever be economically independent of South Africa. It is pertinent to the Basuto, however, that the pattern of her dependency has altered since Independence. Under the tutelage of Britain she could not negotiate economic agreements with countries other than Britain without the mediation of Britain. Nor could she bargain with South Africa on her own account, and, in the pre-Independence period particularly, Britain's own economic relations with South Africa seriously constrained Britain's mediating role.

Now Lesotho negotiates her own economic aid and can exploit her position as 'an island in the middle of the South African sea' in whatever ways the Basuto leadership sees fit. This political change has some implications in the sphere of economic dependence, but is most clearly crucial to Lesotho's measure of her own position – to her sense of advance. The pattern of Lesotho's dependence is now so much more like that of small territories in – say – Europe (as Galtung 1973a) that progress may be said to have occurred.

The assumption that increasing economic independence is the only measure of development is our assumption. It may not be theirs.

9

In the previous cases, perceptions of development have been those of particular groups of people in specific contexts of place and time – the first batch of examples looking inward, the second looking backward or outward to other times, places or people. In the four that follow, the focus shifts to particular projects or plans. Each of the groups involved in any of them may perceive it differently, and their various perceptions may change with time and circumstance. Certainly the ' autonomy' of the various protagonists will be differently affected by any 'development'. Fundamental to all four is the contrast between the perspective of the planners and of the people who are subject (and essential) to their plans.

The first of this group presents the problem as an opposition between 'economic viability' and 'social vitality' as goals of 'development'. In the context of a plan to move people from 'backward' rural areas into urban 'growth centres', the planners concerned themselves almost exclusively with the economic indices that they were able to measure, the people (not quite so exclusively) with the social fabric of their lives. In the terms of this volume, the planners' pursuit of development as economic advance came into conflict with the peoples' perception of development as the enhancement of their 'autonomy'. The conflict was painful and costly for both parties. More important, the author argues that it could have been avoided.

'I'd sooner be here than anywhere': Economic viability vs social vitality in Newfoundland[1]

RALPH MATTHEWS

This essay focuses on an economically backward region of an industrialized country. It examines some of the implications of planned economic and social change in rural Newfoundland, one of the least industrialized areas of Canada.

My interest in the development of Newfoundland began in 1966 when I was involved in a sociological assessment of a program of community relocation then being organized under the sponsorship of the provincial Government of Newfoundland and the federal Government of Canada (Iverson and Matthews, 1968; 1970; 1973; Matthews 1970; 1975a). The program was an attempt to lure the people of small fishing villages into larger 'growth' centres. Throughout its operation both governments claimed never to pressure any community into moving. They argued that many rural Newfoundland communities were no longer 'viable' places in which to live, and were glad that many rural Newfoundlanders took up their offer of assistance in moving from them.

But one feature of that program was a regulation that no assistance would be granted until at least eighty per cent of the households in any community signed a legal commitment to move. Though many rural Newfoundlanders did move, my research revealed that resettlement often occurred as a result of fear and intimidation within the community and was hastened by rumours of future government neglect if they did not move.

Throughout that early study of resettlement there was a striking contrast between the description of rural life proferred by various governmental officials, and that of the rural people themselves. The planners tended to distinguish between viable and non-viable ways of life by the criteria of economic self-sufficiency. From their comments there could be little doubt that rural Newfoundland did not pass the test of viability. Most of them could see no alternative to moving the people where they 'could become part of the manpower stream of Canada'. On the other hand, the people who did move generally spoke with feeling and affection for their former way of life. Most readily admitted that the traditional economic basis of their communities had declined, and they had moved because they could see 'no future for the children'. But many indicated that they would have chosen to remain had that option been available. They liked many aspects of their previous life but they moved 'because everyone else was moving'.

This difference in outlook between 'the planners' and 'the planned' led me to undertake a second study of rural Newfoundland communities during 1970 and 1971 (Matthews 1975b). The time my focus was on communities which had *not* chosen to resettle and which had even refused encouragement to do so. The people of these communities refused to accept that their way of life was non-viable, and had expressed the view that they were 'there to stay'. The discussion contained in the following pages is based on this more recent study.

While some rural Newfoundland communities are no longer self-supporting and require subsidy far in excess of the income they generate, it seems improper to judge a way of life in terms of a cost-benefit tabulation. Such an analysis makes sense when applied to a business corporation whose inputs and outputs can be balanced, but a large portion of the 'product' of a rural community is actually consumed by the community and will not appear as income generated. More important, the assessment of a community in terms of economic viability overlooks the social and cultural character of the community which may be both vital and viable.

This is not to say that we should reject economic development. Certainly the inhabitants of the communities I studied have no wish to do so. Like most rural Newfoundlanders they realize that it is impossible for them to survive in their home communities by living in the past. Indeed, they are no longer willing to sustain the inconvenience and hardship that would be involved in doing so. Rather they are attempting to meet development on their own terms, in a way that will not totally undermine their present way of life nor force them to abandon it entirely. They want a style of development related to their own goals and values. Perhaps their outlook can best be understood by saying that they are inclined to focus on *what is happening besides development in most development programs.* They see what is to be lost through development, in addition to what is to be gained.

This paper is an examination of the criteria by which we judge the viability and vitality of rural life; of the strategies which are being employed in developing rural regions; and of the values which underlie these strategies.

It is my belief that most regional development policy for eastern Canada is primarily based on criteria of *economic viability* which ignore the *social vitality* of the communities themselves.

Economic and social considerations in regional planning

Regional planning will be based on economic considerations because regional disparity is thought of in economic terms, and economic disparity is obvious: when the majority of people in a region have insufficient goods and are without jobs, the region in which they live is economically disadvantaged. It is much more difficult to determine whether a region is socially disadvantaged. Even if people lack schools, hospitals and other modes in infrastructural amenities, it may be that these needs are met by the traditional culture.

Even the selection of criteria to determine social or cultural poverty is problematic.

Moreover, a strong case can be made for the primacy of economic considerations in regional development. The first concern must be the satisfaction of physical needs. Only when people have satisfied their basic needs for food, clothing and shelter can they begin to think in terms of human excellence. I am therefore not arguing that we should neglect economic concerns or that economic disparity should not be a central consideration in any strategy of regional planning. My concern is that most regional economic planners focus so fully on economic considerations that they neglect to consider the social structure, culture, and values of the people they are planning *for*.

Economic planners may hasten to point out that most good works on regional planning devote considerable space to the 'social factors' in development. Indeed they do. But such social factors are usually considered as obstacles to be overcome or altered if the economic policies are to be successful. One of the clearest expressions of this viewpoint is to be found in the opening address of the president of the Development Centre of the Organization for Economic Co-operation and Development (OECD) at its annual conference in 1966. Speaking on the relationship between economics and the other social sciences, he says,

the economic sciences study rather the 'necessary' – that is to say what should theoretically allow the fastest development, and *the social and human sciences study the 'possible', that is to say the social and psychological resistance which may manifest itself, and thus make it possible to discover ways and means of overcoming it* (emphasis mine) (OECD 1967: 12).

This approach is only slightly more frequent than the tendency to begin with a broad statement concerning the inseparability of economic and social development, and then to neglect social considerations throughout the remainder of the work.

Not all regional planners take this tack. Myrdal has long complained that 'economic theory has disregarded these so-called non-economic factors and kept them outside the analysis', and has advocated combined socio-economic approaches to regional development (1957: 30). Most recently a leading Canadian regional economist has rallied to the cry.

The main point is that in economic analysis, and particularly in regional analysis, explanations are offered in economic terms when in fact many of the elements are non-economic, cultural, social, political and psychological (Firestone 1974: 213).

He argues strenuously for a consideration of 'social indicators' of all kinds in regional development.

In its widest sense, regional social disparity is concerned with how people as individuals and as a community feel about their way of life. And this relates to differences in aspirations, wants, attitudes, satisfactions, motivation, behaviour, cultural traits, and involvement in community affairs . . . In effect, regional social disparity relates not only to social circumstances which may differ from region to region *but also how people feel about these differences* (emphasis mine) (*Ibid.*: 213).

Like Firestone, I am concerned that all aspects of social life be considered in regional planning. I am particularly opposed to thinking of the social, cultural and psychological factors as obstacles to be overcome. I am aware that those who argue for a consideration of social factors in the formulation of social-planning programs are often accused of being biased, or of deliberately manipulating the evidence for their own benefit. Thus it has been said that the sociologists and anthropologists who have written about resettlement in Newfoundland have been 'driven to rationalize arguments that will seek to conserve or restore the rural environment to which they have formed an emotional and intellectual attachment' (Copes 1972: 147). I have attempted to answer this criticism elsewhere (Matthews 1975a). The point to be made here is that indifference to the plight of those disadvantaged by social planning programs is not a value-free stand, but itself institutes a particularly precise perception of development. Our industrial culture has come to accept economic-growth objectives as the only rational ones. When sociologists and anthropologists oppose economists in debate over regional development policy, they seem to be arguing in terms of 'irrational' social factors in the face of 'rational' economic considerations. If sociologists who stress social considerations are accused of being 'pie-in-the-sky' dreamers and are chastised for proposing solutions which are 'not realistic' because economically costly, the charge cannot be countered. The only way to offset these criticisms is to emphasize that all planning rests on values and to attempt to provide perspectives on the economic objectives of regional planning which do not entirely neglect social considerations.

Canadian directions in regional development

In comparison with most countries, Canada has a long history of regional development programs. The earliest dates from the 1930s when the Government of Canada passed the Prairie Farm Rehabilitation Act.

This was an attempt to revitalize western Canadian farmland after several years of crop failure brought on by drought (Buckley and Tihanyi 1967: 11). It was undoubtedly also an attempt to overcome some of the rural hardship and out-migration caused by the world depression of the 1930s. Over a decade later a similar program for eastern Canada was established under the Maritime Marshland Rehabilitation Act. Both programs focussed on land use and were concerned to rehabilitate existing farm land and to open up new land for agricultural use. But if neither program was directly concerned with social development, both had important social repercussions. At a time when small prairie farms were being phased out by mechanization, programs such as these enabled small farm operators to remain in business and to withstand the pressure to sell out and move to the cities. From an economic viewpoint they served simply to keep alive economically non-viable farm units.

The next major effort at regional development in Canada shows the same confusion between economic and social goals. The Agricultural Rehabilitation and Development Act (ARDA) was passed by the Government of Canada in 1961. While far more ambitious than its predecessors, ARDA in its early stages continued the directions begun by the previous programs. It focussed on 'land-use' projects designed to 'salvage lands abandoned as agriculture retreated from marginal areas' (*Ibid.*: 18). Most of these were small-scale projects: little sense of comprehensive planning is evident in the list of ARDA-financed developments in the mid-1960s when a co-ordinated farm-consolidation and rehabilitation program was worked out for rural Ontario (*Ibid.*: 21). This was followed in 1966 by the launching of comprehensive development programs in several areas of the country (*Ibid.*: 22). These were made possible by the Fund for Rural Economic Development (FRED) Act which provided $300 million (Canadian) in federal funds for a comprehensive attack on regional disparity (Poetschke 1971: 272), on the grounds that nothing had yet been done to help backward areas reach the 'take off' for self-sustaining growth (Rostow 1956, 1964). Hence the FRED financed programs were designed to shift away from agriculture, 'land acquisition, drainage, and land development. . .into the broader field of industrial structure' (Brewis 1969: 128). For the first time attention 'shifted decisively in the direction of education, training, and the provision of employment in non-primary occupations' (*Ibid.*). Moreover, the FRED programs were conceptualized in terms of total and integrated social and economic planning. They were seen as long-range planning strategies between Ottawa and each of the provinces. No programs would be formulated until a research phase had 'isolated the main problems and potentials of [an] area'. This was to be followed by a program-development phase in which strategies of development would be worked out between the two levels of government. Only then would the implementation phase be entered (Poetschke 1971: 273).

The new approach to regional development received massive support from a study of programs published by the Economic Council of Canada in 1967 (Buckley & Tihanyi 1967). It was highly critical of the land development strategy of ARDA and its predecessors.

The farm assistance policies advanced by ARDA are remarkable for their tendency to evade the question of what might constitute an effective solution for marginal farm units. . .ARDA farm programmes are judged unlikely to have had any appreciable impact on the problem of low-income farming. (*Ibid.*: 16–17).

This report provides two alternatives for promoting per capita *economic* growth in any area. The first was assistance with 'development projects', while the second, described first as 'labour force adjustment' and later simply as 'adjustment', covered measures designed to encourage the movement of population out of areas of under-development (*Ibid.*: 17). The authors of the report spoke strongly in favour of this latter alternative.

In the long run, departures from the area of origin will tend to improve the local balance between labour and physical capital (including natural resources) in favour of the latter, making possible the attainment of higher productivity for the remaining labour force.

Under the conditions prevailing in most parts of Canada, it is likely that a low-income rural area must rely heavily on downward adjustments in the size of its labour supply before significant increases in local productivity can be hoped for (*Ibid.*: 17).

Indeed, it would appear that the authors of this study regard 'adjustment' as the goal, and seem to contrast this with 'development' projects which are largely the result of local pressure and may compromise *economic* principles.

ARDA cannot remain immune from the pressures to provide 'development' of a locally tangibile nature even if programme planners themselves realize the strong need for 'adjustment'. This pressure can easily lead to situations in which economic principles are compromised and projects are accepted for ARDA financing even when they are economically unsatisfactory (*Ibid.*: 19).

The value orientation of this study is clear. The goal is an increase in *per capita* economic growth, a goal which can only be achieved when large numbers of people are removed from rural areas. In the authors' perception, the solution to low farm incomes is farm consolidation with surplus farm labour channelled into urban industrial occupations. If they are concerned about the social consequences of these policies, their concern is tempered by their belief that economic gains will compensate for social loss. Indeed, their greatest worry is that local resistance to the proposed 'adjustments' will 'compromise' their economic principles. They judge that one of the greatest accomplishments of the ARDA programs has been to wear down this resistance and 'soften' the opposition to programs of out-migration.

It is a major accomplishment of the programme that it also helped to soften public attitudes toward genuine adjustments in the rural economy (*Ibid.*: 19).

Their work directly fits the description of development planning which considers social factors only when they hinder economic goals.

The framework used in this study seems to have been uppermost in the minds of the developers of the FRED programs. Thus the 'research phase' was to centre on a consideration of the relative merits of development and/or 'adjustment'.

The objective of the research phase is to identify the main problems and potentials of the area and to settle on a broad strategy for adjustment and/or development (Poetschke 1971: 273).

Most of the projects formulated under this program contained some attempt at population centralization (*Ibid.*: 274–80).

In 1968 regional development in Canada moved from the economic to the political arena. As part of his campaign for leadership of the Liberal Party and the position of Prime Minister of Canada, Pierre Elliott Trudeau turned regional development into a national issue. He argued that regional disparity had the same divisive potential as the more publicized French–English cleavage (Phidd 1974: 174) and promised that, if elected, he would make an effort to rectify regional economic differences. After his victory, he undertook to make this promise good by establishing a Department of Regional Economic Expansion (DREE) in 1969. This new department has encouraged regional development in Canada through interrelated programs of (1) industrial incentives, (2) infrastructure assistance and (3) social adjustment (Francis & Pillai 1972: 46). All three activities take place primarily within 'special areas' selected by the Department in cooperation with the provinces (*Ibid.*: 54–5).

The unique feature of DREE has been its focus on industrial incentives as the key to regional underdevelopment. It would appear that underlying this program is the assumption that economic growth will not take place in underdeveloped areas without industries being established there. Thus large financial 'incentives' are offered industries to entice them into slow-growth areas.

This focus on industrialization is paralleled by a program of assistance to the 'special areas' within each of the underdeveloped regions of the country. Basic to this strategy is the belief that these selected centres will offer particular attractions to industry, once 'substantial improvements have been made to the infrastructure and social services currently available to them' (*Ibid.*: 54). Thus 'selected urban centres' (Phidd 1974: 179) have been given additional large sums 'to provide the utilities and services that *industry requires*' as well as 'adequate social capital facilities to meet the needs of the growing population' (Francis & Pillai 1972: 55 – emphasis mine).

The focus on industrialization and urbanization completely changed the thrust of Canadian regional development. Indeed, many of the FRED programs were cancelled by DREE before they could proceed beyond the research phase. Some ARDA programmes, particularly of a self-help type, still exist and have been made part of DREE's 'social adjustment' activity, but there would appear to be little emphasis on rural development in DREE. There is some evidence that the Department is beginning to realize that population resettlement is more likely to move unemployment from rural to urban areas than to solve problems of regional under-development. There is a new emphasis on manpower retraining:

An induced process of economic expansion has little likelihood of success so long as the capacity of the people to participate actively in the process of economic growth and social change is limited by reasons of inadequate education, lack of enterprise, and socio-economic circumstances generally (*Ibid.*: 73).

However, here again the focus seems to be on training people for urban rather than revitalized rural occupations.[2]

This new thrust in regional development strategy has not been without its political and economic critics. The Liberal Party has been accused of rewarding industries for their political support (*Ibid.*: 187–8), and DREE has frequently been accused of paying industries to close down old plants in industrialized areas and open new ones in underdeveloped areas so that there is no net gain in jobs. Both criticisms were incorporated into an attack by the socialist New Democratic Party which questioned the economic rationale for using public funds to develop private industry (Lewis, D., 1972). My own criticism rests on still other grounds.

It is ironic that Canadian programs for rural and regional development are built on strategies of urbanization and intensified industrialization. For all its large land area, nearly 80 per cent of Canada's population lives in only fifteen major centres. Yet all rural development programs now seem to revolve around the 'adjustment' of rural depopulation.

Between 1945 and 1965, Canada's farm population was cut in half; it continues to shrink by 10,000 farms a year. The federal government expects that by the end of the century, two-thirds of Canada's farms will have vanished and those that are left will be corporations (Robertson 1973: 95–6).

Much the same future seems to be in store for the rural fishermen of Canada's east coast, and particularly Newfoundland.

Lack of concern for these effects may be attributed to the 'growth centre' approach to regional development (Perroux 1955; Thomas 1972: 53–4). Planning strategy is based on the assumption that economic growth is propelled by centres or poles within a particular 'economic space'. Hence large-scale propulsive industries, being linked to regional suppliers and extra-regional distributors, are expected to spawn a network of related industries within the region and accelerate the process of development overall.

The shift in Canadian regional development policy from rural development to urbanization and industrialization appears to be a direct result of this expectation, although the men responsible for much of Canada's recent regional development policy have indicated that their approach is not fully coincident with a growth point or growth pole strategy.

The 'special area' concept, although it draws in part on the 'growth point' idea, does not imply that the areas themselves are all growth points. . . with clearly delineated 'growth areas'. . . nor does it imply that the general strategy of the present federal regional development policy rests entirely on the growth point concept (Francis & Pillai 1972: 63).

Certainly, the Atlantic Provinces Economic Council, an organization of eastern Canadian industrialists and businessmen, in a recent review of the growth centre strategy of development, called on the federal government to intensify its use of this approach in the Atlantic region (A.P.E.C. 1972). Without entering into the reasons for its appeal, this brief description of growth-centre theory provides a context for the new direction of Canadian regional development. But the description has a second purpose: it indicates the commitment of recent regional planning to economic growth and its failure to consider social factors. The specific effect of the model is apparent in communities left behind in the process.

The Other Side of Planning

Most planners are committed to their plans; they tend to accentuate the positive and overlook the negative effects that their plans may have. True to form, the brochure circulated by the Newfoundland government to 'explain' its resettlement program listed only the advantages to be gained by moving. It even concluded that resettlement 'tends to offer a wider scope for the development of better citizens' (Iverson & Matthews 1968: 146). The same emphasis occurs in Canada's overall regional development strategy: in their efforts to better the economic situation of poor people, economic planners have developed a model which makes economic sense, but which fails to take into consideration the social costs involved.

At the other extreme, it is often those whom a plan is supposed to help who are most upset by planning policies. It is they who are most likely to focus on what is happening besides development in development programs, and it is they who often see quite clearly what they are losing through development.

I became particularly aware of this in the study of communities which had refused to succumb to the pressures to resettle. Indeed, it was their perceptions of development which led me to begin questioning current Canadian regional policies. A more detailed analysis of these communities appears elsewhere (Matthews 1976), but a brief synopsis of findings from two of them illustrates the extent of their commitment to rural community life and the need for more socially oriented approaches to planning.

Small Harbour[3] (1971 population 200) is located on an offshore island on Newfoundland's east coast. The decline of fish stocks in the area has left this community almost devoid of an economic base. As a result, most workers are forced to go outside the community. Though there has been some migration out of the community, most of those who left permanently have been single men and women: of the several family men who moved away, most have settled in nearby villages on the Newfoundland mainland. However, well over half of the remaining men of the community work away from their homes but leave their wives and families there. They either commute back on weekends throughout the months of the year when weather and ice conditions permit, or they work away at seasonal summer jobs and return to spend the winter months with their families. The men who remain in the community year-round are the elderly, the two village shop-keepers, those who are permanently in receipt of welfare assistance, and a handful of household heads who are still able to make a living from fishing combined with gardening, brief periods of 'road-work', and a variety of other activities.

Small Harbour is just one of a dozen such communities scattered around a small archipelago in this area. Indeed, two other small communities are nestled on the opposite side of this particular island approximately seven miles away. Though some of these communities are larger than Small

Harbour, all are suffering the effect of the decline of the inshore fishing. Indeed, by almost any economic standard, Small Harbour and many of her neighbours must be considered non-viable. Their household heads must go away to find sustaining work, and almost all their children tend to leave in search of a better future.

Under normal circumstances such a pattern of employment might be assumed to indicate a total breakdown in community life. Although there has been an obvious decline in some community activities, Small Harbour residents show a remarkable *commitment to their community*. Indeed, their level of commitment was so strong that they are the only community in Newfoundland to issue a public announcement, broadcast over all radio and television stations in the province, protesting a statement by a federal government minister that they were slated for resettlement. Their statement read in part:

It is hard to believe that our government could have so little regard for human beings and reach such a deplorable decision. This decision by our Government to strip us of our birthright and deny us of our freedom of choice is only the same as the Russians did in Czechoslovakia in 1968. Since 98 per cent of the people of our community are opposed to the Centralization Programme, we are proud to announce that we are here to stay. Therefore it is time for the government to abandon their attempt to force the people to move by denying them public services, and make a speedy decision to give our community the public services we are requesting but have long been denied.

Sometime before this manifesto all the communities on the island had banded together and formed a community council, apparently despairing over their declining economic situation and almost total lack of services. One of its early acts was to petition both federal and provincial governments for more facilities. The federal minister made the mistake of replying that no services could be provided as Small Harbour was on a provincial list of settlements to be resettled. The community council reacted to this with the public outburst which in turn created a political furore: government officials had continuously claimed that resettlement was a local community decision and had denied that there was any list of communities to be removed. They began to shower Small Harbour with services to 'prove' to the people that the Minister's statement was not true. In the words of a council member.

So we started right off the bat then. It's been eighteen months now and you can see what we've accomplished. We got $200,000 worth of electricity last year, and we got a beginning of the road [across the island]. We're guaranteed a $24,000 Post Office and telephones this fall.

Most residents saw a bright future for the community in these acquisitions.

She was going down for eight years or so, and now she's just picking up again.

Perhaps as a result of these developments, there was no real interest in resettlement and the households with whom we talked denied that they intended to move. It is common for rural Newfoundlanders to deny that they intend to move almost up to the day that they do so, for to do otherwise would virtually have them ostracized as traitors to the community. Small Harbour residents differ from others in that many did admit that they had once considered moving. They had a wide range of reasons for not going. Most emphasized that it was cheaper to live on the island than anywhere else, for they owned their house and had few expenses. Others felt that they were more 'self-sufficient' there. Some also felt that the people just seemed 'more contented' than elsewhere. There can be no doubt that those who remained have a high level of commitment to the community and its way of life.

The same can be said of those who migrate away to work but leave their families in Small Harbour. For many of these people the *goal* is to live in the community with their families year round. As this is not possible, they work outside the community for part of the year so that their families can live the 'good life' on a year round basis. The values and orientations of almost all these people are directed toward rural living rather than urban life.[4]

There is a certain desperation in the desire of the people of Small Harbour to remain in their community. Their belief that recent government investment in services marks a major change in the prospects of the community has many of the qualities of a drowning man clutching at straws. Most detatched observers would probably conclude that, despite this considerable recent investment, there is little real change in the community's economic viability. Though living may now be easier than before, there are no new sources of employment in the community. The only government planning strategies which affect Small Harbour are those aimed at the 'social adjustment' of the population into growth centres. The people still have to leave in order to find work, no matter how strong their commitment to the community and to rural life.

But does commitment to a community constitute social vitality? Our investigation of the community has led us to conclude that there is certainly a strong relationship between the two. Commitment might well be described as the *informal level of community social vitality*. Without the involvement and commitment of its members, the institutions of a community could not and would not function. Particularly in a community such as Small Harbour whose economic viability has all but disappeared, it is often only the commitment of the community members which maintains the community.

But there is also a more *formal level of community social vitality*. These are the institutions which formalize ongoing daily activity and structure social life. They include the institutions of socialization and the institutions of social control (Martindale 1962, 1963, 1966). In a small rural community the institutions of socialization are usually represented by the family, the school and the church, while the institutions of social control can extend from informal gossip to a formalized community council. It is at this more formal level that the social vitality of Small Harbour shows the most signs of distress.

The community has had chronic difficulty in obtaining a resident clergyman and frustration over this has historically led many community members to abandon their traditional faiths for new ones which purported to serve them better. As a result many community members have switched from Church of England, to United Church, to Salvation Army, and the community now has a mixture of religious faiths. But at the time of fieldwork none of the three denominations had sent a clergyman to the community for many months. This meant that community members could not perform such basic sacraments as marriage and baptism, and the absence of regular religious services was considered a major loss by most community residents. But even in this sphere things could be said to be 'picking up': the Pentecostal Church had stationed a resident clergyman in the community just prior to our visit and many members were considering converting to it.

I think that church is going to take everybody. The other churches will go down and if we're going to church we got no choice. . . If people are going to church at all, we got to go there.

The educational situation does not appear as promising. Most of the island's pupils attend one-room schools in their home village, though there is also a two-room school on the island. These schools, however, take only the junior grades and children have to travel to the nearby mainland for high school. There they board during the week with local families and return home only on those weekends during the school year when weather conditions permit access to the island. In effect, many children are wrenched from their families during their early teenage years and there is resentment and concern over this in the community. As if this were not bad enough, declining school enrolment brought about by emigration from the community jeopardizes even these school facilities which exist on the island. Department of Education regulations require that there be a minimum number of students per classroom before they are willing to support a teacher: if enrolments fall so do the number of available classrooms and teachers. In Small Harbour this had reached the critical point where, as one schoolboard member put it, 'If we'd have lost one more pupil this year, we'd have lost a room. So if one big family went, the schooling would get bad enough right there. We'd have to move.' The social vitality of the community seems to hang on its ability to provide school facilities for its children. But the preservation of these formal institutions rests on the continued commitment of community members. In a community as small as Small Harbour virtually everyone must remain committed if the community is to remain socially vital.

The interrelationship between formal and informal factors is also apparent in the changes which have taken place in the sphere of social control. The basis of social control has recently switched from an informal leadership pattern dominated by the merchant, to a formalized elected community council. Because the people of Small Harbour were committed to their community they formed a council in an attempt to organize their resistance

to governmental neglect. This body has been instrumental (albeit fortui-
tously) in ending some of that neglect. At the same time it has served to
integrate community life and give the residents a renewed sense of purpose
and commitment.

Whether Small Harbour can continue to survive remains to be seen. At
the present time it lacks any real economic base, and unless one is provided,
its survival depends almost completely on its social vitality. Up to now this
has been enough to maintain the commitment of those who remain, though
many others have left to seek both '*a living*' and '*a way of life*' elsewhere.
The appearance of a new church and the formation of a community council
are encouraging signs that the formal level of social vitality may be reestablished. Much hinges on the development of better school facilities. If this
formal requirement is not met, it is likely that the commitment of families
with children will not be strong enough to hold them in the community.

A very different picture emerges from Pebble Cove, a larger (1971 population 700) fishing village on Newfoundland's west coast. Outsiders and welfare
officials report a high rate of welfare assistance in Pebble Cove, and generally
describe it as a 'typical welfare ghetto'. However, from our own investigation of the community it would appear to have a much sounder economic
base than Small Harbour. Residents talk incessantly of the vast quantities
of fish caught in recent years by the small-boat fishermen and these stories
are confirmed by the records of the fish buyers to whom they sell their catch.
These large catches were also used by the residents as an indication of their
own industry, and were an obvious source of community pride. But in
addition to fishing, the community has other sources of income. It is located
in a fertile valley at the base of a mountain range. Many residents maintain
kitchen gardens; a number of families raise beef cattle and sheep which
provide additional income; the nearby slopes abound with timber and there
is sporadic lumbering activity in the area. As a result most household heads,
when asked to indicate what they 'like best' about the community, referred
to the ease with which they could make a living:

This is the easiest place to make a living off of fishing.

I'd sooner be here than anywhere else in the world. It's lovely scenery here, and
there are a lot of fishermen here. Three quarters of them makes their living at it and
gets a very good price.

I'd say they lives better here on accounts you got all your fresh fish and meats and
butter, milk and cream. Most people here have their own vegetables.

It's a nice quiet spot and you can also make a good living...

From the viewpoint of many of its residents, Pebble Cove seems to be
an idyllic paradise, and few of those with whom I talked show any indication
of wanting to leave. Of a sample of twenty-six families, fully fifteen household heads had never lived anywhere else than Pebble Cove, while five others
had been away to work for only short periods on boats, in lumber camps,

or in nearby towns. Only six had lived and worked outside the community for longer than a year at any one time. They included three men stationed in Europe during the World Wars, two who had worked in other Newfoundland centres, and one man who had worked in Ontario for a year. The extensive pattern of commuting and working away from home which I found in Small Harbour simply did not occur among the household heads in this community.

However, migration from the community has taken place. Most of our sample had more siblings living away from their birthplace than in it, and there is some evidence that a number of children of these household heads have already migrated. A favourite location in recent years appears to be the industrial city of Brampton, Ontario. One respondent exclaimed enthusiastically, 'Half of Brampton is Pebble Cove'. However, even though some children are leaving, the rate of emigration in Pebble Cove is approximately half what it is in Small Harbour. Pebble Cove appears to have a relatively strong economic base, and a people generally committed to its way of life.

Nevertheless, at the time of our study the community was also under threat of resettlement. After many years of negotiation, the federal and provincial governments had announced plans for a major national park in the area. According to reports published by the provincial government, one of the federal conditions of that agreement was that Pebble Cove must be 'removed' from the area of the proposed park – but the provincial document which announced this also claimed that this 'removal' was still 'under negotiation'.

The government's proposal for the park had been widely circulated through the area, and news of it had been frequently broadcast over radio and television. Most respondents in Pebble Cove indicated that they knew of the tentative decision. The announcements appear to have provoked a flurry of discussion in the community and to have become embellished in the process: 'I've read that here and down the coast are supposed to be reserved as old time fishing settlements.' One of the community leaders had been approached by both federal and provincial officials to sound out the extent of his (and others) opposition to the proposal. One or two residents were emphatic in their condemnation of the proposed resettlement and of the park in general:

The park is no good for we people. I'm a fisherman. When I can't fish I cuts logs. How am I going to do that with the park here?

If the park come here you wouldn't be able to fish...

But most people seemed unconcerned about their future in the light of the park proposal:

People aren't concerned because I don't think they are going to resettle anywhere but the cemetery. You can make a good living here.

I heard sketches of it this spring that they was going to close it down and shift the people out...I haven't heard talk of it since the spring...

Conversations about the subject had all but died out. Most residents of Pebble Cove simply refused to take the government's proposal seriously. Though some felt that resettlement 'is O.K. for little small outport places', they obviously felt that their community was too big to move, that there was nowhere else where they could get as good a living, and that they would definitely never consider living in any of the nearby communities. Their own words bear this out.

No sir-e-bob. That's what we don't [think that removal is a good idea]. Not now and not ever. At least we've got a living here. We're a cent above a beggar, but take us where we can't get a job and what would we do. The first man that comes here and suggests it is going in the water.

In a place like this I say it's a bad idea. Because what is the government going to offer seven hundred people out of here, regard to work. If they got no work here they got none in Newfoundland. It wouldn't be nice.

Where in the name of God are they going to shift them at? They can't come and force seven hundred people away. To force seven hundred people out of Pebble Cove is a big thing to talk about. They got to have someone to catch the fish, and this is a good fishing port.

The economic viability, size and social stability of their community led them to regard resettlement as a foolish idea.

The government must have ultimately agreed with this opinion: approximately three months after our study ended they withdrew their proposal for the removal of the community. As a result Pebble Cove's future is probably more secure than ever before. Though they may have to give up some of their traditional fishing and timber rights (for federal parks tend to limit both activities), these sources of income will be replaced by the park itself as a source of employment.

Our analysis to this point enables us to make two important conclusions about the stability and structure of Pebble Cove. First the community is economically sufficiently viable to satisfy the majority of its residents. Second it also appears to have an extremely high level of commitment from its residents, and thus has the informal ingredient of social vitality. It only remains for us to demonstrate the community has also considerable strength in its social structure as well.

Because of its size, it has none of the problems with its formal institutions that plagued Small Harbour. It is well served by clergy from three denominations, one of whom lives in the community while the others visit there 'on circuit' at least every two weeks. It has excellent schools, including a large high school for the pupils from all the small sectarian primary schools. In the sphere of social control, the community has recently organized a community council, to which both traditional and younger leaders have been elected. In short, Pebble Cove gives every indication of a stable, complete and consistent pattern of formal social institutions.

It is important to realize that both the economic viability and the social vitality of Pebble Cove remain outside most government planning programs. Although the national park may ultimately provide some employment, it was obviously not designed for the residents of this particular community: any benefits to them are unintended consequences of policy.

Pebble Cove, Small Harbour, and communities like them are left out of the development process, dismissed out-of-hand as economically non-viable.

Present and future tasks

This paper had three objectives. First, I have attempted to show the definite bias in regional development planning, as it is practiced in Canada. In doing so I have argued that most approaches to regional and rural development judge rural life almost solely in terms of its economic viability without ever considering its social vitality. As a consequence they usually overlook the attitudes, values, and goals of the people who will be affected by their programs.

My second task has been to trace the changing direction of Canadian regional development policy from a focus on rural development to one on urbanization and industrialization under the impetus of the 'growth centre' approach. I have argued that, even though these new directions may make 'economic sense', they often fail to make 'social sense' because of their neglect of social considerations.

My third task has been to demonstrate some of these ideas with data drawn from my research on Newfoundland communities which have actually resisted programs aimed at moving them into urban areas and into 'the manpower stream of Canada'. I have tried to present those aspects of community life which best demonstrate the social vitality of rural communities. These I have divided into *informal components of social vitality* based on the commitment of individuals to their community, and the more *formal components of social vitality*, the structure of institutions of socialization and social control within the community.

Throughout I have tried to demonstrate the way in which current approaches to regional development in Canada almost totally neglect those persons who value and are committed to rural life. Implicit in this is my belief that development planning should take into account the perceptions and goals of those for whom the plans are presumably being made and should incorporate them into the plans as far as possible. Indeed, it would appear that it is only this which separates 'planning' from intimidation and force. Also implicit here is my belief that it is time to end the programs which force more and more Canadians into urban areas and industrialized jobs. Instead, our concern should be with defining and fostering a variety of ways of living.

10

Like the previous paper, this one is concerned with the local repercussions of a national development plan. In this case the contrast is drawn between 'normative' and 'efficiency' criteria of planning. It is illustrated by an analysis of housing 'development' in Zambia in which it is shown that economic dimensions are not in reality separable from the socio-political dimensions of a 'development' situation, however neatly they may be distinguished in planning theory. Unlike the government of Malta (Ch. 6) the Zambian government of the time neglected to discover and to reconcile the various priorities for growth: the way 'ahead' was neither debated nor agreed. The plans themselves therefore exacerbated the political difficulties of a post-independence period. The inference drawn can be generalised: where 'efficiency' in the form of economic growth undermines the 'normative structure' or group values of a particular society, only popular participation in its planning can reconcile the separate needs of 'autonomy' and 'development'. This formula worked in the smaller scale contexts of 'Eagle Bay' (Ch. 3) and Olowo (Ch. 2) in which no direct contact with government planners occurred. It works comparably, however, in the two cases following this one.

'A house should have a ceiling': unintended consequences of development planning in Zambia

PETER HARRIES-JONES

Economic development in Africa during the course of the 1960s was characterized by the importance new states attached to national development plans. The 'national plan' was not only a focus for determining economic priorities, but one of the strongest political resources of new governments.[1] Nevertheless, subsequent rise and fall of African governments have borne only a partial relationship to successes or failures in national development planning. The dynamics of *coup*-making in Africa seem to have resulted more from the emergence of new élites, than from the ability of the first batch of government ministers to manage the complexity of economic forecasting. In this respect African political experience during the decade 1960–70 was very different from that of Europe.

Despite the partial relationship between development plans and the coming to power of alternative élites, this paper will argue that details in national development plans often have greater socio-political effect than is generally realized. More specifically, the details of development planning affect the public's evaluation of political standards. Thus, while a plan may bring economic benefits, the political cost of such benefits can be a loss of organization, or possibility of governance. The net effect of this is to put government in a worse position *vis-à-vis* its electorate than when the plan was inaugurated. Moreover, the dynamics of this loss of governance may send the whole planning exercise out of control.

The usefulness of national development planning in the African context may be compared to the usefulness of the Westminster model of parliamentary democracy. African governments soon came to realize that the success or failure of the Westminster model depended to large measure upon the institutionalization of negotiated gaming-procedures as a means for conflict resolution. Such gaming-procedures, though by no means unknown in African societies, are mostly confined to certain sectors of urban society (like that of industry) or to procedures in local level politics. The Colonial experience had inhibited negotiated gaming on a national level, and it is hardly surprising therefore that new African governments were unable to utilize this procedure as the basis of political control.

The inappropriateness of national development planning in African states as the main means for allocation of scarce resources has provoked far less debate. The comparative absence of monitoring bodies in the economies of the new states has meant that there has been a time-lag between the introduction of an economic plan, and the full assessment of its effects. Moreover, a major inhibition to open debate has been the slow awareness of western practitioners of national planning that some of the most cherished assumptions of the whole exercise are questionable. Until recently, development planners in the West failed to realize that outcomes of development plans are as much political and social as they are 'economic', and that the 'economic' component of the plan cannot be separated from its socio-political framework. Hence it is possible for development plans to introduce growth in the 'economic' sense and the negation of growth in the political sense, both at the same time.

The elucidation of the 'counter-intuitive effects' of planning – causing constraint where relaxation was needed, and 'runaway' where constraint ought to have been an outcome – stems from the late 1960s (Forrester 1969: 107). More recently, the argument that 'growth' must involve step-by-step goal-setting has been criticized and the anomaly of 'optimizing' in the planning process explored (Vickers 1972). It is argued instead that the reduction of multiple objectives to a single goal, and the acceptance of *effectiveness* as the single criterion by which governments choose between alternative operations 'dehumanize the high human function of government'. The proper function of government is not to optimize on a simple trajectory of costs against benefits, but rather to optimize 'the realization of many conflicting situations without wrecking the system in the process'. Equating goals with growth has introduced into Western economics highly unstable sets of relationships which, interacting with each other, push economic systems into increasingly more unstable phases. The same dynamic operates with even greater force in low-technology countries, yet the West's lack of insight into its own economic instability has been exported to developing countries (*Ibid.*: 116ff).

The major point is that a government which wishes to be in control of its own affairs has to pay more attention to *normative* conflict in development planning. All governments have to cope as much with rapid change in the electorate's standards of evaluation, as with rapid change in monetary flows. The real-life context of decision-taking cannot proceed as if all decisions could be made on a comparison of costs and benefits. 'Costs' and 'benefits' in a complex economy cannot be precisely determined; instead the notions of 'goodness of fit' stem from an inexhaustible series of viewpoints and multiple valuations, in a context of uncertainty. The human context of decision-taking is an attempt to bring order into multiple evaluations and multiple viewpoints. Analysis of the optimizing behaviour of an intellectual abstraction called 'economic man', is, by contrast, a bogus exercise (Vickers 1972: 140).

This argument has particular relevance to Africa. In those countries which had reached independence through the activity of mass political mobilization, decision-taking procedures reflected procedures of norm setting in conditions of great uncertainty. These procedures were of the 'town hall' variety in which government leaders transmitted ideas to the party's local bodies and leaders were able to listen to the ideas of the people (Wallerstein 1961: 1960). The object of such meetings was often to determine what sort of policies, or what sort of standards, people wanted, rather than announcing what sort of goals the government expected to obtain. Meetings were interactive and aimed at definition of tasks – not the expounding of effectiveness of government performance.

Much of this decision-making procedure changed in the era of national planning. The national development plan offered leaders a greater feeling of certainty, authority and 'efficiency' in their decision-taking. In effect, decision-taking through reference to the national plan cut short the intensive normative debate on definitions of the acceptable or unacceptable among interest groups. It inculcated an arbitrary definition of 'growth' as the normative and pragmatic measurement of future policies, rather than attempting to create a common understanding of the values of independence.

This paper sets out to explore the rapid cut-off in normative debate during a period in which development planning was accepted as a definition of political and economic well-being. It deals with the case of planning for urban housing in Zambia. From 1962 to October 1964, Zambia's officially proclaimed date of independence, condition of houses and amenities of urban living were inflammatory local issues bound up with expectations of rapidly improving standards as the new state moved away from colonial influence.

Housing Policy and Colonial Rule

Urban administration in pre-independent Zambia provides both similarities and contrasts to that of the Republic of South Africa. While the latter instituted legislation to maintain Africans as aliens within urban areas, the position in pre-independent Zambia was to grant Africans a type of 'temporary citizenship' in town. This 'temporary citizenship' was dependent on an African having a specific job, enough income to pay rent, and – if he wished to avoid a barrack-like existence – a validated marriage.

Until as late as 1963 the daily farce of assessors at Urban Native Courts was the hearing of 'unauthorized residence' cases; indeed approximately one quarter of all 'criminal' cases handled by this court were infringements of statutory law relating to residence (Clifford 1960: 8). Residence regulations in urban areas were enforced by the mining companies' or municipalities' police. These private police forces both investigated cases of alleged 'unauthorized residence', and carried out evictions of those unfortunates unable to pay rentals.

Outside African townships, housing patterns developed along lines of social segregation, though regulations delimiting housing according to racial group were not so explicit as in South Africa. For example, the mining companies had their own housing areas for white employees; government, too, assigned grade of housing to grade of job. Municipal housing rentals were classified in such a way that there was a separation between low-density housing areas for skilled (usually white) employees and medium-density housing for artisans – who were usually Eurafrican. Indians, many of whom could have afforded to live in white housing areas, chose to live between the medium-density (Eurafricans) and low-density (white) housing areas.

The level of wages offered African employees aggravated, rather than reduced, their condition as 'temporary residents'. Though the mining companies had decided in the 1930s that migrant labour was unsuitable, and that a policy of 'stabilization' was the only effective means for training a workforce, the companies were extremely reluctant to provide an appropriate industrial wage. A 'stabilized' work force would need a wage conducive to staying on in town, but the copper companies were quite prepared to adopt the South African practice of pegging mine wages at levels corresponding to those of rural farm workers. As late as 1953 copper companies paid 1s.10d. a shift to all grades of unskilled labour – the vast majority of their African mineworking force.

The advent of an industrial wage was prompted by the success of the Northern Rhodesia African Mineworkers Union (now The Mineworkers Union of Zambia) in declaring industrial disputes and threatening strike action. Throughout the era of Federation, 1953–64, wages increased progressively, upgrading 1s.10d. to 12s. 6d. per shift for the majority of underground workers. A minority of Africans got considerably higher rates of pay, and about 50 miners even achieved European wage levels and conditions. During this decade union bargaining also improved paid leave provisions, medical facilities, and leisure-time amenities. The corresponding effect was a dramatic reduction in labour turnover from 50% per annum in 1953, to less than 8% per annum in 1965 – a true measure of stabilization. As might be anticipated, such domestic improvement also brought a considerable increase in copper-output per African employee. From 1953 to 1965 this increased by as much as 70% (Edgren & Harries-Jones 1964).

In effect, by 1965, the 'temporary resident' employed by the copper mining companies in Zambia had become a 'permanent townsman'. The standard of pay and provision prevalent on the copper mines had filtered down to secondary industry in Zambia, so that unskilled and semi-skilled labour on the mines and in industrial employment on the Copperbelt were in a position much superior to the migrant recruited from Barotseland to the South African gold mines.

While wages and conditions of service gave evidence of this gradual transfer of status of the urban worker from 'temporary resident' to 'permanent townsmen', housing standards continued to reflect the position of their tenants in the earlier period of urban growth. The vast majority of African housing, both in mine and in municipal townships, was of a distinctively outmoded style. Some so-called 'houses' constructed for single men were nothing short of deplorable. For example, Roan Antelope Township, then the major mine township in Luanshya, still had 2,400 houses built in circular 'rondavel' style of extremely elementary construction – one large circular room with an iron roof and white plastered walls over Kimberley brick. Another 400 houses were scarcely 'improved', having only one-room with communal water and ablution facilities; while 3,600 'two-roomed' houses, the major housing type in the township, were of no better standard (Edgren & Harries-Jones 1964: Appendix B).

In fact the vast majority of urban dwellings at Roan Antelope were in sharp contrast to the few that the mine company had built since 1960 consisting of four-rooms with proper kitchens, power circuits for electrical appliances, individually supplied water, indoor toilets and car ports. These houses of 698 sq. feet, nearly all of which had a small garden attached, were symbolic of a permanent urban worker status. On the other hand those who still had to live in a 15ft. diameter rondavel, were housed in structures reminiscent of urban-squatters' quarters.

Municipal housing of the pre-independence period was scarcely better in quality. The municipalities' single-roomed 'bachelor quarters' were little more than 'garden sheds'. The majority of municipal housing was of the two-roomed or three-roomed variety, with individual pit latrines, but having communal water taps, and no electric light. In Mikomfwa muncipal township in Luanshya, only the very newest type of housing had provision for powered electrical circuits, or was in any way comparable in square footage to that of the four-roomed housing in the mine townships. The occupants of the 30–40 houses having such amenities were known throughout the township as 'abakupuka', the fortunate ones, that is those who had attained élite status through successful business, or through senior jobs in government service.

Financing and administration of municipal townships had been based on the findings of the Eccles Commission in 1944 and implemented through the Urban African Housing Ordinance (Cap. 234 of the Laws of Northern Rhodesia). The Commission took the view that good housing conditions for Africans in urban areas could only come about when Africans had sufficiently high wages to buy or hire them, and to maintain for themselves and their families a reasonable standard of living. Such conditions, the Commission noted, had to await minimum wage legislation and the prospects of such provisions in 1944, it acknowledged, was exceedingly unlikely.

The Eccles Report came to the conclusion that while 'subsidization' of African urban housing was fundamentally unsound, there was little option but to recommend it as a 'temporary measure'. The Report stated that loans be made to local authorities at rates of interest well below market rates, each loan repayment being based on a conservatively estimated life of the housing assets so acquired. The heaviest proportion of housing should be of the 'married quarters' type, since at that time the law did not force employers to make appropriate housing provision for married employees.

As one of its final recommendations, the Commission turned to the question of 'canteen funds' or profits from beerhalls. It noted that a number of witnesses before the Commission, many of them African, had suggested canteen profits should be used for the provision of good housing on the grounds that it was illogical to provide expensive recreational facilities for people who lived in hovels. The Commission felt it was quite wrong to use canteen funds to relieve the employer of his responsibilities to provide adequate married housing. Hence, it argued, canteen funds should continue to be used for recreational facilities including the provision and maintenance of parks, open spaces gardens and trees, which were insufficient in most townships, if provided at all.[2] The Commission's recommendations, while rationalizing housing standards, tied the development of local authority housing projects to very narrow guidelines. 'Interesting' or 'substantial' housing provided by local authorities could only be built when economic rentals could be charged. In the interim, an accounting formula which made income from rents equal to cost of loan capital suffered from the fact that for more than a decade after the report wages were not paid on an all-cash basis. Until the mid-1950s wage payment was made on a cash plus 'allowance' for accommodation, plus allowance for rations.

The relation of wages to adequate housing facilities thus continued to revolve in a vicious circle. Employers were responsible under the terms of the Employment of Natives Ordinance (Cap. 171) for paying employees' rent. A wage was a combination of a market rate for labour plus a standard housing allowance. Since any move to increase rents for better housing fell upon employers, rather than upon employees, plans for improved accommodation met strong resistance. At the same time, local authorities encouraged the establishment of new industries within municipalities by attempting to reduce to a minimum the cost to employers of all municipal services. The most prominent of all municipal costs was services for housing. Thus local authorities were in neither a monetary nor a moral position to call upon employers for higher rent payments in order to erect better quality housing.

So long as the narrow guidelines laid down by the Eccles Report remained part of colonial administration, the topics of rental charges and housing standards were all but removed from the political process. Even when the copper boom in the mid-1950s raised wages to a point where the all-inclusive wage became a preferred method of payment, African residents had no significant municipal vote to question the validity of the Eccles formula. In 1956–7, a Committee appointed 'to examine and recommend wages and means by which Africans resident in Municipal and Township areas should be enabled to take an appropriate part in the administration of these areas' opposed direct participation by Africans in decision-making processes at a local level. The Committee members considered direct representation on Municipal Councils 'would not be in the best interests of the Africans'. The Committee concluded that 'until such time as Africans had had experience, and proved themselves capable in positions of executive responsibility', other measures were needed to 'establish a system of administration for people who have yet to comprehend the complexities of urban problems' (Lusaka Government Printer, Brown Committee Report 1957: para. 28 (1)).

Nevertheless, the Committee's report initiated a cautious move in the direction of African policy-making at a municipal level. It created Area Boards in African townships, and Boards were permitted to elect two of their members to the African Affairs Committee of the respective Municipal councils. Area Boards were given some financial and executive responsibilities, including action on the provision of parks, bus shelters, street lighting, the tarring of roads, playing fields and improvement of beerhall amenities. All activities under Area Board control were to be financed from profits derived from the sale of beer; they fell outside the main area of funding represented in municipal accounts.

The appearance of Area Boards was a considerable advance beyond the wholly negative attitude of the mining companies towards African employee participation in management of mine townships. In the mid-1950s the mines established a series of 'Advisory Committees' which it hoped would inform management on issues relating to 'general maintenance, roads, designs, playing fields, planting and landscaping, road safety measures, market and township regulations, health, sanitation, housing and services'.[3] Yet African membership to the Advisory Committee was confined to two representatives nominated by the mine companies, who soon came to be seen as 'political stooges' by the miners themselves. In addition, the Advisory Committees were supposed to include representatives of the two major trade associations, the Miners African Staff Association and the Northern Rhodesia African Mineworkers Union. While the former co-operated, the latter union was never in favour of the activity of the Advisory Committees, and throughout their existence relied on obtaining improvements and amenities through industrial bargaining processes. Not until the very eve of independence was there any concerted move by the mines to delegate responsibility for township affairs to the residents of townships. Even then, the copper companies tried to remove all question of housing standards from the consideration of the proposed mine township boards.

Before the mine-township boards took up their administrative duties, the companies attempted – successfully as it turned out – to convince the Zambian government that mine housing was now a municipal affair, and should be subject to the appropriate Ministry of the new nation-state. The financial question of the companies handing over to the municipal government a dilapidated stock of housing, whose benefits lay more in tax depreciation than in the amenities provided, was never satisfactorily resolved.[4]

The housing question in its local context

Promises of amelioration of existing housing conditions were an integral part of the United National Independence Party's popularity in the urban townships. Upon coming to power in 1962, UNIP devised a two point programme to relieve the frustration of poor living conditions. First the party aimed at securing a political majority in local government in order that urban residents have decision-making powers they had been denied for so long. Second, UNIP began to address itself to a full-scale reform of housing amenities including the launching of an extensive building programme to provide housing for those it anticipated would attempt to move into towns from rural areas.

The implementation of the first part of UNIP's programme was comparatively easy. The municipal electorate was enlarged and municipal electoral boundaries redrawn, enabling African township residents to elect their municipal representatives for the first time. The composition of the municipal council moved in a series of steps from a council reflecting dominant white interests, to a transitional phase of parity representative between white and African-interests, to a multi-racial, but predominantly black municipal council.

The second part of the programme, that of reform, proved to be a more formidable task. The complexity of the issue of reform in urban townships involved not only a question of finances, but also the standards of urban amenities which residents expected in a newly independent state.

In Luanshya, the ensuing debate between government and local party organizers cannot be understood unless it is realized that the argument was conducted at two contradictory levels of meaning. For the local level organization of the party in Luanshya, any aspect of reform of urban housing and amenities was normative – in the dual sense of that term. It was normative in that reform must fulfill expectations of higher standards than those existing for the urban population. It was also normative in that higher expectations were defined in relation to the values of freedom from colonial rule. Expectations of freedom and the good life inferred expectations of better housing conditions and *vice versa*.

Within the Ministry of Housing and Social Development in Lusaka, the national capital, housing questions were defined in terms of a specific number of new units which could be completed. That, in turn, related to an overall framework of economic growth, as defined by Zambia's national development plan. The fundamental issue for the Ministry was finance, and this was tied to the amount of money which employers would continue to pay as 'housing allowance'. Indeed, to encourage 'efficiencies', the Ministry proposed that municipalities should compete with one another on the international market in order to attract new industry to their area. From the Ministry's point of view, if housing cost less in one municipality than another, this would be passed on as a benefit to the prospective employer.

In Luanshya, the UNIP-supported state of councillors representing the South Ward (a combination of Mikomfwa and the second-class or Indian trading area) presented a lengthy motion in 1963 calling, *inter alia*, for every dwelling in the African township of Mikomfwa to be provided with waterborne sewage, individual water supplies, and electric lights. The motion proposed that open spaces in all areas of Mikomfwa be converted into parks and playing fields, while additional housing of an 'improved' type be built to accommodate those on the waiting list. The Municipal Council agreed to send a delegation to the capital to meet with the Ministry and to arrange finances for the proposed projects. However, the delegation had an unsatisfactory meeting with the Ministry and later learned that no decision would be taken on its proposal before the government held a conference to outline a national housing policy.

By February 1964 municipal councillors reported back to Council that they were under heavy pressure from Mikomfwa residents to 'show results' in improving housing and other amenities. Yet the cost of the improvements, taken together with a proposal to erect 250 new houses in Mikomfwa was estimated at £225,000, and such a programme could not be financed through increased rentals alone. It could only be carried out with a massive loan or grant-in-aid from the central government (*Minute* 783: 27 December 1964).

The type of housing that the sub-committee had requested in its meeting with the Ministry was equivalent to the best that Mikomfwa had available. Houses would include indoor water-taps, showers and lavatories, metered electricity and ceilings. Therefore, it was with much concern that sub-committee heard in June 1964 that the national policy of the Minister of Housing and Social Development was one of rapid building, in order to relieve 15,000 inhabitants in urban areas without proper accommodation. In short it was a policy of 'as many roofs over as many heads as possible', regardless of housing standards. The Ministry proposed to build a vast number of simple 'shells', which could later be enlarged and improved. This, the Minister said, would provide a place for a family to live in good condition until money became available to improve plumbing, increase the number of rooms, 'and provide internal doors, ceilings, fly screens and other amenities'. (*Northern News*, 24 June 1964).

The Minister argued that there would be little point in putting up houses if people could not afford them. The government would have to avoid excessive expenditure on individual houses and use that money to build extra houses. Since the Ministry had only limited funds available, it had to spread that money as far as possible. People who wanted bigger and better houses would simply have to wait until the greatest demand had been met.

This statement committed the Ministry to a housing design equivalent to the two- or three-roomed dwellings of the colonial period, without the amenities of internal electricity and waterborne sewage. The shock that the local organization of UNIP received with the Ministry's announcement resulted in total confusion as to how best to proceed. In effect the Minister had destroyed the local platform of the party with a single blow. So confident had both the party and the municipal councillors been prior to the Ministry's statement, that they had invited the public in to view a model of the new 'improved' houses that were to be built in Luanshya, and had requested the public to participate in designing final modifications.

The only possible course of action the local party leaders could follow was to take the issue back to the people again, and ask them what to do. Clearly, if the municipal councillors did a *volte face* and agreed with the Ministry's position, or, alternatively, tried to persuade residents of the virtues of the Minister's plan, they would lose all support for their own position. If, on the other hand, they continued to press for their own housing model against the Minister's, it appeared that Luanshya would get no new housing at all.

The Meeting

A meeting held in July 1964 taking the issue back to the people reflected patterns of power brokerage in Luanshya at the time. During the course of the meeting, which lasted for two hours, there were some 19 speakers in addition to the formal explications made by South Ward Councillors. Of the speakers from the floor, three held positions in the Constituency Office of UNIP, six were UNIP Branch officials and five held positions at the very base of party organization, the 'sections' or political cells.[5] One speaker was a representative of the UNIP's female auxiliary, the Women's League; and one a representative of UNIP's male auxiliary, the Zambia Workers. Another three speakers represented the Rentpayers Association, a municipal organization under UNIP's auspices which had campaigned for urban improvement during the colonial period. Only one speaker held no political connection: he was a market trader. Excerpts from the meeting show how debate sharpened, but finally produced no clear decision at all:

KATIMBA [Constituency Secretary, and Municipal Councillor]: The first proposal on housing for Luanshya was the erection of shelters with one bedroom.
CROWD: One bedroom, with children? *Ya chabe.* [It's useless].
KATIMBA: We councillors turned this plan down because we wanted houses with plenty of bedrooms and submitted our recommendations to the Minister. But the Minister said that the first priority was for the waiting list in Luanshya to be eliminated. The rent for the houses the Councillors proposed was too high, he said. Shelters were far more flexible, since they could start off with one bedroom and as more people got better pay and were able to afford higher rent, the shelters could be extended.

We councillors, on the other hand were interested in good housing, with a proper ceiling, supplied electricity and modern equipment.

The two things now need to be resolved, and we call upon you people of Mikomfwa, to agree to a change, or to call up a Minister to come to talk to you.
CHILONGO [Section and Councillors' Advisory Committee official]:[6] I have heard about the plan and I would like you to be very careful. If I am unemployed and yet have a good house, I will have to pay £8 per month. As a 'loafer' [*mulofwa*] what I want to do first is to get a job and then manage to help my children. I am not interested in getting an expensive house. But a house should have a ceiling. The Government should supply at least a house with a ceiling.
MOLOBEKA [Constituency Trustee]: UNIP promised good housing. But we have no jobs, so trouble is still with us. Be warned – if Government says that we shall have improved housing in a short time, it is saying the same thing as the Mining Companies have always said. When they say that they are putting up a particular type of house for a few years, and then improve upon it, they mean 50 years. How much rent will you Councillors charge for the good housing you have proposed?

KATIMBA: Rent would be between £4 and £5.

CROWD: Four to five pounds!

MALAMA [Market Trader]: I hear from Katimba that these shelters will have no ceiling and no electricity. Thus there is nothing to interest the tenant. A house should have a separate room for the children. As for these improved houses you Councillors propose, we have no jobs. We don't get enough money to pay for those houses.

KATIMBA: My opening speech was that we had three models of improved housing which we showed to you people at Hindu Hall some time ago. At that time we chose the model we preferred and forwarded it to the Minister in Lusaka. After the Minister considered how much he was going to spend on houses and after finding out how much the Council would have to charge, the Minister rejected our model because it was too expensive and he advised us to have shelters, which, as I said early on, can be extended.

CHATUPA [Rentpayers' Association]: I was present when the model was chosen in Hindu Hall and we chose the model that we wanted. Today we are told that the Minister has turned it down. It we have preached on the anthill[7] that the rent will be cheap *and* that we will provide people with decent houses, what will happen now the Minister has turned this down. I say to you all that we must stand by our decisions. Houses should be cheaper because we promised cheaper houses; they should be better because we promised better houses.

CROWD: Sense, Sense, Sense.

CHIMBWA [Section official]: It is a mistake that we are blaming the Government for turning down this model. I hope you will agree with me that the Government would like to give you a better and a cheaper house. Now, because the Government has no money and everyone would like to have a house, we should have a cheaper type of a house so that everyone is accommodated. And I hope that you all know the Welensky's gone with all our money. So let us agree with the Minister.[8]

CHATUPA [Rentpayers Association]: Houses like the model the Councillors have proposed are too expensive. No one will shift to that type of house.

MOLOBEKA: I am told that here we have a waiting list of 800 people. House rents should be £2.11s. only because we can't afford to pay higher than that. It's true we have no jobs. Why should we pay higher rents. We should tell the Minister that the rents should be £2.11s. *E pela* [That's all].

CHILONGO [Section official]: As I am speaking here today, I am not talking as I would on the anthill. That was different. First, what we want is good jobs. Houses will come later on. The unemployed would be happier if they had good jobs now.

LUPUPA [Section and Councillor's Advisory Committee Official]: The model for improved houses is good. Those who would like to shift to good houses should do so if they can afford it. To those who cannot afford to shift to good houses, I say they should be given cheaper houses.

MUSHIBWE [Branch official]: We are all made differently. It looks as though we will never solve this problem. What we want now is good housing with an extension for our children, houses with ceilings and electricity.

STAN [Section official]: What we want now is to ask the Government to provide us with good houses and a cheaper rent. If this is turned down we should ask the Minister himself to come and explain why they should not charge less for houses.

CLLR PHIRI: Demand for better housing is not very great. The economic rent for good housing is £5. But those who can't manage to pay £5 are at the moment able to afford £2.2s. You say 'What we want is a cheaper house' and 'build houses for those who have no houses now.' But your call for ceiling fittings and the installation of electricity in all houses is the problem.

KAMBATIKA [Rentpayers Association]: Your speech is too long and full of rubbish!

KAPALALUBULI [Branch Treasurer]: We want to know the exact amount the Minister says he is going to charge for the shelters. If you can't tell us, then we must ask the Minister to come and tell us. You said the Minister wants housing with cheap rents. What sort of housing?

PHIRI: The Minister's houses will be built in Kimberley bricks, as are most houses in the township.

CROWD: *Ata tetitwikalemo* [Rubbish, we won't stay there].

PHIRI: Government will be giving loans every year for the extension of these cheap houses. Next year we will be given £20,000 to repair and to extend old houses. That will be done yearly so that we will be extending our houses any time you approve. After extension, houses also will be of the same type as those in the European area of town. This will discourage those who would like to shift from Mikomfwa to the town centre.

MUKOKWA [Constituency Secretary]: We have no jobs. Next time you Councillors think up a housing scheme you will want to build it in Mikomfwa dam!

KATIMBA: We have not decided where and when we shall build this improved type housing.

MAMBWE [Rentpayers Association]: My suggestion is that we have the Minister's model with electricity and with ceilings.

PHIRI: His model cannot have ceilings and electricity.

KABANDA [Branch official]: That is no good then. Nor is the model you Councillors propose any good. Whites in town don't have that type of housing. Latrines are too near the sitting room. Our children don't know how to use toilet rooms properly. Our present houses are also rubbish. We don't want those either.

DOKOWE [Section official]: We want to know how much the loan from the Government will be and how many houses we can build in Mikomfwa.

CROWD: One hundred thousand pound loan.

DOKOWE: What we want now is to have about 10 houses with ceilings and electricity, about 174 without ceilings and electricity, and the rest should be cheap to meet the 1100 on the waiting list. What is the point of having very expensive houses with electricity and ceilings with such a big waiting list. So, Mr. Chairman, let us have cheap houses to combat the waiting list.

MOLOBOKA: Cheap house, cheap rent. If a Minister is coming, we must have the Councillor's model at £2.11s. only.

MBAZA [Branch official]: The Minister is going to give us improved houses at £2.11s. That will be all right.

CHATUPA: We want cheap rent on old houses too!

LABAN [Zambia Workers]: What we must decide on are two things: whether we are going to have improved houses and whether we invite the Minister to come and address us. Let us decide now instead of worrying your Councillors.

SANTIMA [Branch official]: We don't want very expensive houses.

MUSONDA [Branch Chairman]: It seems we cannot resolve the issue. Close the meeting, Mr Chairman.

[The public meeting was then closed. The Chairman asked the Advisory Committee to the Councillors to remain.]

KATIMBA: Let us now sit down and do business properly. You are composed of very reasonable people and you were chosen to advise the Councillors. Because you are here, I hope we will be able to come to a compromise, but please do remember that to attract investors to come to Luanshya we should be in the position to provide housing for their domestic servants and others who are employed in the various firms. When they inquire about putting up business in Luanshya, they also inquire about the availability housing. If they are going to find that we have one million on the waiting list then they will go to Kitwe or Ndola. This will never solve unemployment in Luanshya.

CHITAMBALA [Constituency official]: Now gentlemen, what we want is the Minister to give us as many shelters as possible. For those who can afford good houses and have got money to pay, I propose that some should be set aside for them. Therefore my suggestion is three-quarters cheap housing and one-quarter good housing.

CHILONGO: I agree with the previous speaker. We should follow our Minister. We must have cheaper houses first.

MOLOBEKA: The improved house is good but they definitely must be less than £5 per month.

LUPUPA: We must not only try to get rid of the waiting list, we must also ask the Minister to lower the rent.

PHIRI: What we want is more investors to come forward and put their businesses here in Luanshya. This will solve unemployment. I agree that we should do away with the waiting list by giving houses to people on the waiting list in Luanshya. Then we shall ask the branch officials to explain to the people from the anthill about the problem of housing we have in Mikomfwa, forcing us to build cheap houses.

CHILONGO: We must have half of this improved model and half of the Minister's semi-detached houses.

KABANDA: I agree that we must have two-roomed shelters only, so that we give a house to everyone on the waiting list.

SANTIMA: And we want electricity in our houses.

CHITAMBALA: No, three-quarters cheap housing, one-quarter good housing.

KATIMBA: We are now going to vote on whether we are going to have three-quarters cheap semi-detached as those that are being built in Kitwe and one-quarter of the improved model; or all cheap housing.

From this outline of the meeting, it is clear that its most remarkable feature came following the ending of public debate. The meeting agreed to have problems raised in public discussion brought to a decision of the Councillors' Advisory Committee, a Committee predominantly of section representatives who were duly appointed to 'advise' South Ward Councillors on the opinion of the 'people of Mikomfwa'. The ostensible purpose of the Advisory Committee was to make known Branch and section views (that is, the base of the party organization) direct to elected Municipal Councillors, and thus avoid situations in which Councillors acted on a policy directly contrary to decisions made in Sections. When the Councillors' Advisory Committee convened itself around the table on which the model of the improved type housing sat, the atmosphere of public indecision quickly vanished. One Advisory Committee member, Molobeka, in complete contrast to his 'public' speeches demanding good quality housing with cheap rents, informed the Committee that the only solution was to support the Minister's proposal. He stressed to the Advisory Committee that 'We are the leaders, we must decide what we are going to have in Mikomfwa...'

Cr Katimba whose chairing of the meeting had suggested that he favoured high-standard housing, asked the Advisory Committee to abandon these plans. The major need, he said, was to put Luanshya in a position competitive with other Copperbelt towns by provision of cheap and plentiful housing. Another Advisory Committee member put a compromise proposal authoritatively: three-quarters of the houses should be of cheap 'shelter type' variety and one-quarter of high standard housing. Section representatives to the Advisory Committee, Chilongo and Lupupa, maintained a view consistent with that they put in the public meeting, that the majority of the houses must have cheap rentals. Only Branch officials were still convinced of the necessity of providing cheap houses with amenities better than those already existing in Mikomfwa. Within ten minutes, by a vote of 10–4, the Committee had agreed to the proposal that three-quarters of new houses should be 'shelter type' and one-quarter should be of high standard.

As an exercise in decision-making of the 'town-hall' participatory variety, the compromise vote of one quarter high-standard housing and three-quarter 'shelter-type' housing might look to be a successful outcome. In fact, the vote was not a compromise at all, but rather an outcome reflecting a desire to avoid political confrontation with the new Minister. The real issues from the viewpoints of urban residents surrounded expectations of political independence and the standards which would be adopted in a new political era. At several points during the meeting leaders referred to promises made 'on the anthill' to the public of Mikomfwa as compared with the position in which they now found themselves. Housing was an issue on which most Mikomfwa residents had an opinion and was an important issue through which residents could match their own expectations of amelioration of poverty to the new government's interpretation of freedom from colonial rule. The whole indecisiveness of the public meeting stemmed from a 'mismatch' in expectations as a result of the housing policy proposed by the Ministry. In this situation it was unlikely that this or any public meeting could come to a firm conclusion on the issues involved. A clear decision on options available could only come when normative expectations on the part of the electorate began once again to match government capability.

In terms of this analysis Government's next moves ought to have been concerned with the normative implications of their decision. Instead the national development plan became, in government's eyes, the justification for political action.

Conclusion

Throughout the colonial period, basic urban amenities such as four-roomed housing, electric light, and water had been the privilege of only those few Africans holding the top posts available to Africans in the mining companies or the Civil Service. The rest of the urban population had to accept the employers' and colonial government's evaluation of his status as a 'temporary

6

resident' in town. The most conspicuous example of such evaluation was a strict correspondence between wage levels and style of housing. Since pay packets only began to increase progressively from 1953, a majority of the stock of housing in the urban townships reflected an equivalence that mining companies and colonial authorities had made between the rural and the urban worker.

At independence urban residents clearly wanted to break the complicated legislative knots that had tied entry to town to availability of jobs, and tied low-wage earning levels to poor standards of accommodation. Urban residents expected a minimum standard of good housing that would define them as 'townsmen'; equally, they expected clear government support in attaining this status. Instead they were asked to accept proposals to house more urban newcomers at the sub-standard levels of accommodation typical of colonial times. The new government told them good standards of housing could wait until the crisis of the urban waiting-lists for housing could be overcome. As in colonial times, the Ministry had decided that adequate availability of housing at cheap rents would foster 'national development', a policy which related stock of housing to employment opportunity at prevailing market conditions. Industrial growth and full employment could only be accomplished if housing were competitively priced.

On the basis of strict accounting procedures to yield growth of seven per cent per annum, the Ministry's proposals had much to recommend them. On the other hand, the unintended consequences of this exercise in national planning were to call into question reciprocal expectations between national leadership and the base of the party organization. The Ministry was gaining a housing policy integrated to the rationality of growth. Yet it was losing a revolution of expectations associated with unclear, but strongly felt, values of 'freedom'. 'Growth' could be defined with certainty; a suitable definition of 'freedom' on the other hand could only emerge through substantial agreement of a vast number of individual viewpoints. Such an agreement could only come about if government positively sought to create it.

To return to the point stressed by Vickers (p. 139 above), policy making in government is in error if it attempts to collapse a series of multi-level normative issues into a goal-setting formula for 'development'. In order to govern, rather than simply announce proposals for growth, government has to establish a complex of interdependent expectations between officials and people – between the 'doers and the done-by' so that the values and standards of both 'doers' and 'the done-by' are reasonably clearly defined. Once this context is created, then new policy communications can be compared in relation to sets of common standards. The resulting match or mismatch of data to commonly appreciated values or standards enables both the 'doers' and the 'done-by' to identify options available (Vickers 1972: 182ff).

If, on the other hand, the debate on the values or the standards involved in the decision is never undertaken; or if the policy defines outcomes only in terms of efficiency criteria of the market place, then the possibilities for governing are considerably reduced. The likely result is the production of a policy in which the aims and objects of the system of which that policy is a part becomes completely divorced from the human context out of which the policy originally sprang. In effect, policy becomes part and parcel of a self-exciting system, which in generating its own goals rapidly creates a dynamic of decision-taking going 'out of control'.

It could be argued that nowhere was there greater need for 'control' – in the sense of interpreting and matching information to a set of values and standards – than at the outset of independence in Africa. Zambia was one of the few countries in Africa which had the means available, through the prior achievement of mass political organization, to undertake the process of normative 'stock-taking' that this process involved. In that UNIP's organization penetrated both neighbourhoods in urban areas and villages in rural areas, it also had the decision-making structure available for a flexible response to changing patterns of norms. Hence the party was in a good position to undertake the policy adjustments this might entail.

The case study presented here suggests that UNIP's strong political identifications with national development planning produced an effect quite opposite to its intentions, for it began to undermine the very organization which had brought it to power. The decision-making structure which the party was beginning to introduce was also beginning to reflect the administrative priorities of the colonial organization which had preceeded it. Yet at the outset, nothing could have been further from UNIP's policies. As a party UNIP was dedicated to the elimination of racism and the promotion of social welfare for all inhabitants of Zambia. Industrial growth and the elimination of unemployment in urban areas seemed to be congruent with these aims. So did a policy of 'housing for all'. What the Party had not anticipated was that the promotion of rationality and growth in the economic sphere would undermine its own success in the sphere of politics proper.

11

This paper is also concerned with housing. It compares and contrasts the official and unofficial systems of urban 'redevelopment' in Montreal. Like the author of the piece on Newfoundland (Ch. 9), these writers insist that systems of organisation and criteria of development that are not economic in the narrow sense may nonetheless pay economic dividends. What they have called 'the other economy' – the one which resident houseowners organise quite apart from city planners – in fact enhances residential and monetary values for the downtown city areas as a whole. Their analysis of the two economies in relation to perceptions of redevelopment typical of home owners, small investors and professional investors respectively shows economic efficiency to vary directly with the sense of autonomous participation in the development process. It also indicates the advantages of a small scale operation in which people may share a sense of common purpose and identity.

Perceptions of redevelopment:
a conflict of social economies in Montreal

MARILYN MANZER AND ROGER KROHN

In the past decade much public attention has focussed on the continuing
shortage of good low-rent housing in Canadian and American cities. The
issues have often been raised by local citizens groups struggling to preserve
their neighborhoods. A large (six square blocks) development project in the
Quartier Ste-Famille in downtown Montreal provoked a citizens' committee
in the late sixties to try to prevent what they saw as the destruction of their
neighborhood. Initially, we studied the tangled issues in this conflict between
Concordia Estates Holdings Limited and the Milton Park Citizens Committee. They made contradictory assertions about, but neither seemed to
understand, how the old housing was operated and its economic viability.
Since new construction could not possibly replace the old with new low-rent
housing, we began to study the actual operation of the houses and the effects
of nearby developments, to understand what steps might be taken to preserve
it. We believe we found out why new development is so destructive to
existing housing and neighborhoods, far beyond the buildings immediately
affected.

Redevelopment, both present and planned, can be seen to affect the
neighborhood at three levels. First, the direct effects of developments on
owners are revealed in their sharply divided opinions about it. The larger
professional investors seemed to favor both the present individual highrises,
and the new large development. However, the smaller investors and home
owners differentiated between the existing individual highrise apartment
buildings, which they linked with their management and neighborhood problems, and the new Concordia project, which they saw as having possible
advantages – adding commercial facilities, and having a positive effect on the
social quality and economic value of their neighborhood. Second, more
indirect effects accumulated at the neighborhood level. For example, speculative investors bought properties for potential land value, then reduced
tenant services and maintenance, and rented to more 'undesirable' tenants.
This impinged most on the owners with the greatest stakes in the area. And
the worsening of physical and social conditions, once begun, is difficult to
reverse. Third, City Hall, seeing and encouraging the growth of the central
business district, relaxed zoning regulations and raised assessments. Both
these local and municipal responses to development undercut the viability
of the small owners and their property.

We examine these dynamics of change set underway by development, or even its promise, and their different effects for *home owners, small investors,* and *professional investors.* We find that the various owners not only have particular goals and resources, but participate in different socio-economic systems. The *home owners* and the *small investors* operate in what we have come to call 'the other economy' and the *professional investors* operate in the national capital economy (Krohn & Fleming 1972; Krohn & Duff 1973). We have found that good low-rent housing is peculiar to the other economy, whose amateur owners do not achieve and often do not even seek competitive returns to capital. Because they borrow as little capital as possible, avoid when they can the high wages and fees of the organized occupations, and maintain their properties themselves, they can keep their rents low. This in turn leads to positive, stable landlord–tenant relations, and to a stable neighborhood. We will show how the entrance into the neighborhood of professional investors who have large capital resources and seek short term economic gain, erodes and eventually defeats the peculiar productivity of 'the other economy'.

In short, redevelopment does not simply dislodge a few individuals, but can set in train events which attack the bases and dynamics of 'the other economy'. This system requires a good residential neighborhood, reliable tenants, and minimum cash and capital outlays by owners. If the owners are to continue to provide good housing for low rents and to contribute to integrated neighborhoods, their contributions must at least be accounted in the urban political and planning process.

The Quartier Ste-Famille

The Quartier Ste-Famille is a heterogenous 24 square block residential area immediately to the east of McGill University, south of Mount Royal Park, and ten minutes walk from Montreal's downtown shopping and financial districts. It both contains and borders upon French and English educational institutions, hospitals, and many smaller agencies, schools, churches, and stores. It is this location and these amenities that have attracted new economic development.

The area was built largely before 1900 with large two and three storey stone houses. The western part was single family houses for the upper-middle class. and the eastern part contained duplexes and triplexes (*Service d'urbanisme,* 1968). The majority of houses are still structurally solid, useful dwellings. Some large four-storey walk-up apartment buildings with three and four room apartments were built in the 1930s. Since before 1940 the single-family houses have been gradually converted into rooming houses and small apartments, and here is now a negligible number of single-family dwellings. The duplexes and triplexes remain as family occupied residences. Between 1956 and 1970 scattered groups of old houses were demolished for the construction of two dozen new highrise apartment buildings. Others gave way to parking lots. Already by 1961, 55% of the housing units in the Quartier had one and two rooms. (This reflects the small units in new construction as well as conversions.) Another 26% contained three or four rooms (*Service d'urbanisme* 1968: 17). Aside from the new construction and sub-division, there was a small amount of extensive renovation being done in older buildings.

As would be expected, relatively few of the Quartier's 13,000 people are families with children. Forty-five percent are young adults, and 57% over 15 years of age are single people as compared to 25% and 36% for the city of Montreal (Statistics Canada 1971). Between 1951 and 1971 the number of families decreased by 42%, and there is a trend towards shorter periods of residence in the Quartier (64% of the population had lived in their dwelling longer than three years in 1951 compared to 44% in 1961 and 37% in 1971). The area is ethnically mixed with 40% of the 1961 population having been born outside Canada and 24% in 1971 having a mother tongue other than English. The most common language is English, with only about half (33.5%) as many francophones as the city of Montreal (67%). The eastern part of the Quartier is especially European with many languages spoken.

In the mid 1950s the Quartier began to be seen as highly desirable and as presenting new opportunities for profit by developers and speculators, mostly wealthy private individuals. Since then 21 highrise apartment buildings over 10 storeys in height have been built. They contain between 50 and 300 units each and range in value from $85,000 (Canadian) to over $3,000,000 (Canadian) . A few new four or five storey apartment buildings, each replacing one old house and containing 15 to 20 units, have also been built. The new units are small, most having less than three rooms.

A large developer, Concordia Estates Holdings Ltd, has since 1958 bought 97% of the privately-owned properties in six square blocks in the centre of the Quartier, intending to demolish existing housing and construct a complex of highrise residential, commercial, office, and recreational space called '*Cité Concordia*'. At the time of this research 255 dwelling units had been demolished, vacating a large section of land in the centre of the Quartier.

These developments and rising prices have been accompanied by apparent speculative buying. Many properties were sold several times between 1955 and 1965 at substantially higher prices each time. The City of Montreal subsequently raised assessments to match the peak selling prices of 1965 and 1967. However, since 1967 prices have been declining until some property assessments are now higher than selling prices, placing an unfair tax burden on old buildings. The city also introduced – in 1967 – a construction limit for floor area equal to twelve times the area of the site. This high ratio allows developers to build at high densities, neglecting the need for open spaces and community facilities, and ignoring problems of population density.

We will examine how these changes in building types, land prices, assessments, zoning regulations and population composition set into motion by the entrance of the national professional economy weaken the basis of 'the other economy' and of its good low-rent housing.

The other economy

Although we cannot yet identify its exact boundaries, we take 'the other economy' to include particularly the older, smaller, low-rental buildings. The owners typically make large labor inputs in relation to their capital investment. They own the buildings for a variety of reasons – to control and improve their family residence, for future financial security, and to try to increase their assets through their own efforts and skills.[1] They often rent to family or to friends, so protecting their investment and allowing social as well as economic exchanges as part of the rental relation. They develop managerial skills primarily through personal experience, or learn from relatives and fellow ethnics. The owners always deal with tenants face to face, and often do most of their own maintenance. This self-management is possible because they have manual skills, often being blue collar-workers and skilled craftsmen. And because their tenants are working class much like themselves, there is no stigma attached to the personal service involved in managing small buildings. Finally, the 'rational' side of real-property ownership, such as the calculation of the return to equity, of the consequences of financing for 'cash flow' and tax planning is completely missing.

Owners in 'the other economy' also operate without the aid of the legal and political institutions. They cannot use legal enforcement of their rental contracts because the costs are too high and they do not understand the complexities. They seek instead to self-enforce contracts via complex social relations and personal sanctions. Nor do they belong to real estate associations or have other political access, not even at the municipal level. Typically, they are not conscious of the effects of government housing policies until the effects are at their doorstep – a tax increase, an expropriation notice, the demolition of neighboring buildings, etc.

The other economy in Quartier Ste-Famille

The above model has been developed from four studies done in Montreal, including this one.[2] It also fits certain data gathering under quite different frameworks by other investigators (Sternlieb 1966; Coons and Glaze 1963). While the Montreal studies have shown that owner types vary across the older areas of the city, resident owners of rental housing and some local small investors consistently show the same orientation while the larger absentee investors behave on quite different bases.

To examine the social and economic participation of owners in the Quartier Ste-Famille, we classified owners as *home owners, small investors*, or *professional investors* on the basis of their reasons for buying property and their scale of operations. Home owners wanted to settle in the neighborhood and saw rental property as an inexpensive means to ownership. Small investors were part-time owners who sought a current return by maximizing the present use of the buildings through renovation and careful choice of tenants.

The full-time professional investors were also interested in current returns, but most of them anticipated capital gains by resale of the property. There were many more of these larger absentee investors in the Quartier than in the other low-rent areas studied.

In brief, from interviews with 33 owners we found the *home owners* to be participating in the other economy and the *professional investors* in the national capital economy. The *small investors* represented something of a mixed case, seeking good current returns, yet by and large they were amateurs operating in a fashion specific to the 'other economy', contributing to a viable neighborhood by conscientious self-maintenance and by the finding and keeping of reliable tenants.

Most of the *home owners* are immigrants who bought only in their middle years, after they had saved enough cash for a down payment. They typically bought duplexes or buildings with larger apartments. They are long-term owners who bought for security and comfort. Three of the twelve home owners in our sample had moved to other areas when their economic status improved, but they kept the former home as an investment, their only rental property, and continued to care for it as a home.

Renovation and the investment of personal energy into management and maintenance are the key strategies of these small owners. The home owners in our sample average a return (in relation to assessed value) of 5.6%; it is obvious that this return is not the primary reason for ownership. Three-quarters of the home owners are satisfied, in spite of low returns, because 'It is better to invest in real property; it doesn't disappear.' The dissatisfied home owners were those who have moved to new houses, and now find management to be more difficult and costly. As long as income exceeds expenses, home owners do not focus on economic returns; neither do they calculate annual 'net returns', nor 'return to (equity) capital'.

Small investors own from one to three rental properties, usually small apartments, to supplement other income. Some are sophisticated managers, but many are not. They are upwardly-mobile people, who embark into rental housing knowing very little about the techniques required for success. They often work on their buildings to improve them and to increase their capital assets at little cash cost. One small investor said,

We bought to make money – as an investment. We won't make money now, but maybe in five or ten years. We want to renovate old houses; they are good houses, strong, and good to live in. When we get the mortgage paid we will own a valuable piece of property.

Another said,

We thought this neighborhood was a good place to invest in property because of appreciating land value and because it is our own neighborhood. I have personal relations with my tenants – I have coffee with them and chat about all kinds of things. They are my friends. I choose my tenants very carefully. I interview them and if they are still interested, I check their age to make sure they are over 21 and check their previous place of residence if possible by talking to the landlord or going to see how they keep their apartment. In 14 years I have had trouble with only four or five tenants. I completely redecorate and paint the apartments after each tenant leaves to get it ready for the next one.

These small owners, then, view property ownership as a security and a convenience, and as a means of turning their spare time and labor into future economic assets. Three-quarters of the small investors and home owners had done major renovations at some time during their ownership, and all of them expressed interest in proper maintenance and in making minor renovations as they could afford them.

The national professional housing economy in the Quartier Ste-Famille[3]

The *professional real estate investors* contrast with both home owners and small investors. They own or have owned many properties and make their living from them. They evaluate a building's operation in terms of its return to equity capital, and are sophisticated about finances and management. All ten we interviewed were absentee owners. Some participate in running their properties by telephoning janitors and tenants, or going to check up. But most spend little time on any one property, and leave day to day management to employees. This is a professional investor's description of himself and another who owns near him.

I have owned many properties in my time. When I got rid of my business many years ago, I went full-time into real estate speculation. I always figured that the return must be at least 25% clear in order to make it worthwhile. Now I own only these two rooming houses. I have liquidated all the rest. I now clear only 10% on these houses, but don't quote me on that, because I don't want the income tax people to know that. But I figure you can't lose on centre-city land. Some day this land has to be worth a lot more, with all the redevelopment that is going on around. So I am content to hold them until I get my price. They aren't profitable, but they do O.K.

I will sell to a developer. Mme —— and Mme —— and Mrs —— who own next to me will sell with me, so we can sell the whole lot together. Do you know Mme ——? She is an old bear. She is 86 now and she really knows the business. She had 14 rooming houses at one time. And what a dirty rotten mess they were! She never did even the most minor repairs. The one she owned on Hutchison was so full of bugs that you hated to walk in the door. I don't know how anybody could live in there. But she always owned properties in the areas which were about to be demolished, so she made a lot of money. I have known her very well for a long time and I know she will sell with me.

Nearly half the professional investors said they had bought primarily for speculation on rising land values. Another half bought because of good income from renting small units to students and hospital workers. None indicated any ties to or preference for the neighborhood.

Only one professional investor does more than minimum maintenance. He had owned his properties for 25 years and renovated them extensively just prior to *Expo*, Montreal's World's Fair, in 1967. They appeared to be kept in excellent condition still. This owner wants a good return on his rooming houses. He is an example of the multi-parcel owner who has a 'strong rental policy', substantial equity, good maintenance practices, and careful tenant selection (Sternlieb 1966: 178). Only two of the nine other professionals had done renovations. Both bought between 1965 and 1967 when *Expo* was on the horizon. They bought large houses with small apartments and rooms and made extensive renovations. But at present (1972) both buildings look dingy and the owners give no indication of recent repairs. Both have vacancy problems. The other seven professionals have never done any renovation. They all complained about the repairs. One said,

We do as much repairs as is necessary to keep the buildings from falling down. One big problem is that the city imposes a lot of renovations on the property owners, having to do with fire escapes and electrical wiring and things like that which are expensive. This is underhanded and unfair of the city because it raises the taxes on the property. On one building we were forced to put in all new wiring, and we are still paying off a debt to Hydro Quebec for that!

Another said,

I can't do too many repairs. The building won't pay for it. I only do repairs if I am forced to – like a new hot water heater.

Another said her tenants were justified in complaining about a lack of hot water, but she was not prepared to put money into such an old building.

To obtain an estimate of the current rates of return realized by the professional investors is most difficult. The problem is complex and data are sparse. Only one of the ten professional investors gave details of his income and expenses. Although his potential return rate (based on assessed value) was 18% if he had no vacancies, vacancies in fact reduced it to nearly zero. The professional quoted earlier felt that a 10% return justified his holding the properties until he could sell to a developer. Another said that she could hold on with 8 to 8½%. In short, the inference is that current returns to professional owners are modest.[4] For them, management in the form of janitors and service people is also an expense, so even modest returns can be achieved only by allowing the buildings to deteriorate.

Management problems loom large for professional investors. Unlike the small investors and the home owners who were selective about tenants, most (5 of 9) professionals were not. These non-selective owners were all speculating on rising land value. The professionals who did choose tenants carefully sought to obtain a good long-term return on the present buildings. But even the latter often find tenants to be destructive, irresponsible and dishonest. Janitors often steal the rent money, or are lackadaisical about filling vacancies. Non-resident small investors had similar but lesser problems.

At present, prices are going down because of a lull in development. Many speculators find themselves locked into the neighborhood, unable to sell at a profit and unwilling to accept a loss. Many of them bought 10 to 15 years ago, and, being older now, are more inclined to see the area as just one big headache and not worth any effort at improvement. The problems these investors have with tenants and janitors, their lack of maintenance, and the high prices they often paid all work against the social and economic viability of the neighborhood. They undermine the bases of 'the other economy', which requires a satisfying residential environment, long-term tenants, a high investment of personal time and energy, and low prices and expenses.

The conflict of the local and the national economies

As outlined in the introduction, we can see the impact of the national professional economy on the residential neighborhood at three levels: on individual owners and residents, on the neighborhood process, and on the policies of City Hall. Our treatment is not exhaustive at any of the three levels. This is only a useful way to group our data and to analyse neighborhood conflict and change.

In their reactions to the growing number of individual highrise apartment buildings, both home owners and small investors differ from the large professional investors. Twelve of the 19 small owners thought the highrises to be detrimental: they are not well built; they bring in too many strangers; the dwelling units are too small and noisy; people in them are immoral; and they have big dogs which mess up the neighborhood. The large owners (7 of 9) were more favorably inclined: they more often felt that the highrises improved the area, they got rid of old dirty ugly buildings and replaced them with modern clean ones, and brought in better tenants. Underlying this division is economic interest. Most professional investors bought for immediate or eventual resale to developers, while the interest of the small investors and home owners who bought to use the existing buildings and to live in the area is both economic *and* social. The latter see highrises as having a bad effect on their buildings and on their neighborhood in ways which do not concern most professionals.

Interestingly enough, the categories of owner reacted differently to the proposed Concordia project. First, half (5) of the *professionals* preferred not to express an opinion on the project, perhaps because they did not want to discuss or be drawn into the then current controversy. But four of the five who did express an opinion favored it. Second, half of the *home owners* had no opinion or had never heard of the Concordia project, and the seven who had opinions were divided for and against. Resident owners thought it would be nice to have a beautiful shopping centre so handy, but they also were annoyed that the houses had been closed for so long and that the project would exaggerate the low-rent housing shortage. Those in the east end of the Quartier did not feel that the project would affect them economically in any way, or have any direct effect on their neighborhood.

Most important, nearly all of the *small investors* expressed opinions (7 of 8) and were most strongly in favor (5 of 7) of the project. They felt it would make the area more beautiful, raise the land values and bring in better tenants. For example:

There is a future for small owners in the district and the Concordia project will bring them a better class of tenant and the district will pick up its former character. It will uplift the prestige of the district and drive these hippies out.

We will see later that the small investors are under the greatest pressure, caught between rising expenses and more stable rental incomes.

A good part of the difference of opinion among investors is attributable to their location in the neighborhood. The two investors in the east end were both opposed to the project. As one said: 'They shouldn't do that because all those people need a place to live and when they move they will have to pay more rent and they can't afford it.' These investment owners could identify with the present tenants rather than with Concordia because they did not see the project as affecting them directly. West end investors, if they felt such sympathies, tended to favor the project anyway because they thought they stood to gain by it.

I think the project is unfortunate, but that sort of thing is coming, and there is not much one can do about it. It will affect the value of the land, but that is not a bad thing because it will make properties like mine more valuable, both for sale and for housing, as people will want older, larger units.

Thus, even small owners, including a number of home owners, when they had formed and expressed an opinion, often favored the Concordia project as benefitting the social quality and economic value of their neighborhood, in spite of the low-rent housing shortage and congestion. And investors did not necessarily support the project, as one might expect. Its perceived effect on investment was more important to an owner's attitude than his investment orientation.

The earlier phase of highrise development had brought about a much stronger and broader worry and discomfort to all Quartier owners (except those professionals interested only in land prices), than had the proposed large Concordia project. Although it would remove low-rent housing, it was also seen to have redeeming advantages. Yet the opposition to development by the MPCC[5] was in response to the Concordia project. Before dealing with that question, we will look briefly at the neighborhood and city level effects of development.

Change and conflict in the neighborhood

The first sign and most important factor in the coming changes was increasing real estate prices. Prices rose about 15% per year in the west part of the Quartier between 1946 and 1953, about 6–7% until the mid-sixties when they again increased by 13–14% per year. Old houses (with 4–10 units)[6] are now selling at from $30,000 (Canadian) to $60,000 (Canadian) in the west part of the Quartier, and no new home owners are buying. Increasing numbers of *investors* with low maintenance policies have affected the appearance of the neighborhood. Buildings have less paint, more broken stairways, and more pigeons on the balconies. The *home owners* complain:

(A) Too many owners are just owning to make money and because they don't live here they don't care what goes on or what kind of tenants they get. Mr —— owns two buildings here and lives in Montreal North. He doesn't care who he rents to. He just tells his janitor to rent to anybody that comes along and then we get all these hippies around here.

(B) The owner next door is a real slumlord. She won't do any repairs on her building and she causes me a lot of trouble. She does not clear snow and ice from her roof and it leaks like a sieve. Her rotten roof affects and deteriorates mine; and not only that, but the water leaks down through the walls between the two buildings clear down to the first floor. There is water in between all the walls in her building and where her building adjoins mine; my walls are beginning to rot. I have complained to the health department several times. They say they have written her a letter, but still nothing is done. It makes me very angry.

These represent 'spot problems', involving one, or two or three contiguous buildings owned by professionals. The entire six square blocks owned by Concordia have suffered visible deterioration to the point where surrounding home owners favor redevelopment because it will get rid of all those 'dirty old houses'.

Local owners also face problems finding and keeping good tenants which are indispensable to successful low-rent housing management. All except two of fourteen *small investors* and *home owners* required good references and made sure that prospective tenants fit their criteria of responsible people. Buildings of more than two or three units necessitated a unified 'atmosphere'. Three owners wanted single, stable, quiet working people, and would not rent to any other types. Another said his tenants were all young people, and he would not rent to an old lady, for instance, because there would be too much noise and loud music for her. Three liked to rent to students. Four others would not rent to students, either because they move in the summer or because they have too many visitors late at night.

The ability of these owners to find stable dependable tenants is being undermined by the population changes in the neighborhood. Most of the owners felt the neighborhood was deteriorating socially and several were particularly upset about the 'new breed' of tenants with whom they had had bad experiences:

(C) On a Friday some Americans came looking for a place. They rented a one and a half and paid me two weeks rent. I moved a sofa from my apartment and put it in theirs. I put the money in the bank. Then on Saturday they came and told me they had found another place and they would like their money back. I told them I didn't have it because I had put it in the bank, and that if they wanted to move, they could, and to come and see me on Monday and we would come to some arrangement about the money. Well they moved out that day. They took the new double mattress that was in the sofa, and left an old beat up one from the back of their station wagon in its place. They turned the fridge upside down and then sprinkled candies all over the apartment and then crushed them and then swept up a little pile of crushed candy and buried the key in the middle of it. Needless to say, they never came back for the money.

(D) In the summer the janitor rented the apartment to a middle-aged man, and five to six hippy boys moved in. They never had money to pay the rent and it didn't get paid. When they left at the end of the summer the apartment was wrecked. They had confiscated all the doors. They plugged up the plumbing. They put big holes in the walls. They painted the bathtub red. The apartment has been vacant for five months now because we haven't got the money to make the necessary repairs.

Over the two years that this research was done, the increase in social pathology was noticeable. A research report of the Urban Social Redevelopment Project (Prince 1966) says serious crime as measured by the number of adult arrests was negligible in this area. But in six tenant interviews conducted on one street seven years later we heard of five killings, several robberies and countless incidents of 'insane' behavior, fighting, and property destruction on the street, all within the last six months. One resident small investor said:

Crime has got much worse in the last three years... a lot of drugs, pushers knifing each other. I was cutting the grass in front of the house one day last summer and a guy came running out of the house next door shouting. A man standing in the street grabbed him, and my wife shouted at me from the balcony, 'Look, he has a knife!' Then a lot of other people started shouting and looking, and the man let go of him and put the knife away. Then there was that pusher that got his throat cut across the street... and the millionaire that got stabbed in front of the Playboy Club...

There is generally agreed to be an exploding drug problem, with hard-drug pushers living in the area and an increasing number of addicts. Such occurrences are rare in the buildings of resident landlords and conscientious small investors, but their presence in the neighborhood affects their ability to find good tenants and increases the risks with any tenant they might accept.

The only organized neighborhood response to the encroaching development has been made by the Milton Park Citizens Committee. This group, sparked by social workers and young professionals in the Quartier, began in 1968 to organize other residents to examine and eventually to oppose the Concordia project. The MPCC opposed the destruction of scarce low-rent housing and of a socially viable neighborhood in favor of a prestigious commercial and residential complex of small high-priced units. In brief, through various common tactics – community organization, demonstration, and publicity – they were able to inconvenience and perhaps delay but not to halt either the project or the decline of the neighborhood.

Two points out of this complex story are of interest here. First, because the Concordia project involved a six block area and was a multi-million dollar project it gave a better organizational base and was a more prominent public issue than the previous individual highrises. But unknown to the MPCC, it was not seen by owners, even the home owners, as problematic for them or for the area. And second, the MPCC tended to view all property owners as 'capitalists' making huge profits by turning their neighborhood into a slum. They believed that a non-profit corporation should buy up the houses and operate them so that the profits being 'raked off' could be put back into renovation. Had the committee actually bought properties, it would have found itself in the same difficult position as the large investors with high overhead costs and high debt service.

This demonstrates a misunderstanding of the economics of the area's housing which is common both to those who wish it well and to those who propose to displace it – even though they place opposite social and moral evaluations upon it. The City can be seen also to share and to have an interest in a purely economic interpretation of the area.

The City's response to neighborhood change

The City administration has apparently decided that the entire Quartier is capable of commercial development, and has raised assessments accordingly. Although assessments on the houses are low ($3,000–$15,000), the land assessments are higher, sometimes six or more times that on the buildings. The latter range from $5 per sq. ft. in the east to $17 in the west.[7] They were increased sharply between 1964 and 1969, sometimes doubled and tripled. Owners are becoming disillusioned:

It's better to own your own home. We could afford it. But now we are finding out how much it really costs with taxes, etc. We bought in this area because we thought it was going to be cheaper. We didn't know the taxes would rise so much every year. When we pay the mortgage, then we will sell. It is very hard to keep this building. The rents are low here but the expenses are high.

With assessments equalling the peak selling prices of 1965–7, it appears that the City, in effect if not by intention, is encouraging development by weakening the position of the small owners.

Nor has the City made other efforts to alleviate the burden on small owners or to maintain the physical and social structure of the area. Owners applying for municipal renovation subsidies are told that these do not apply to their area. One owner, after having been refused what she regarded as a reasonable rent increase by the Rental Control Board, was told by the Assessment Department; 'The land is too expensive there for that old house; you should tear it down and build a highrise.' Comprehensive zoning bylaws have never been written for the Quartier and, according to one City Planning Department official, directives had come from City Hall not to initiate any changes in zoning for the Quartier Ste-Famille until after Concordia had started construction. It becomes clear, then, that the City is placing more importance on higher economic revenue from new construction than on the comfortable low-cost housing the area now provides.

Summary

In the Quartier Ste-Famille, residential and other *small owners* supply better housing to tenants at lower rents than *professional investors*. In effect they subsidize the housing economy with their labor and capital, investing far more in their properties than they will ever receive in monetary return. They can do this because they will work in their leisure time or use otherwise unemployed labor to manage and maintain their houses. They convert 'non-market resources' into personal security, the social stability inherent in home ownership, or even a modest economic return in increased rentals or resale value of an improved building. In short, there are both implicit resources and implicit returns in local small scale housing which financial accounting cannot tally.

The *small owners*, who can operate the low-rent housing within 'the other economy' are edged out and weakened with the entrance of *professional investors*, whether developers or speculators. Land values, both real and assumed by the City, have allowed it to double and triple taxes within a few years. Rental incomes have lagged behind. Small owners are unable to raise rents and to keep the good tenants essential to their method of operation.[8] They are unsettled by the number of strangers around and the increasing difficulty of finding reliable tenants. They worry that neighbors might sell to developers and wonder when they themselves might be forced to sell. They find that many resident owners and families have left the area and that new ones are not entering.

It is therefore not so much the direct effects of new development – the buildings themselves and their tenants – that create problems for small owners, as it is the indirect effects. These include speculative owners with their building neglect and poor tenant-selection, increased taxes, and lack of new home owners.

However, the *home owners* still represent a point of stability for the area; they have owned for the longest time, and nearly half still express no desire to sell, even in the long term. No resident home owner wishes to sell immediately. It is the *small investors* who want to sell immediately. High taxes and interest rates and increased tenant instability are defeating their attempt to maximize income from present land use. They cannot take risks or sustain losses in the hope of future gains. Nor are they psychologically attuned to permitting deterioration in order to increase profits. The small investor, key to the economic and social vitality of the area, is hardest hit by these contradictory pressures, and is at present the most unstable type of owner. And it is he who looks with the most hope on the Concordia project.

Because of these linked processes, redevelopment conflicts with low-rent housing not only by removing some buildings, but also by destroying the social and economic basis of many more: it saps the resources and weakens the rewards of participants in 'the other economy'. Because of these indirect and systematic effects, the decline of low-rent neighborhoods may be far advanced before the problem is recognized, when there are too few committed locals to try to reverse it. Further, local owners are rarely organized to protect their interests, nor even to understand the problematic process until it has gone too far and many are already discouraged. This dynamic of the Quartier Ste-Famille would seem likely to be found in other areas under redevelopment or designated for urban renewal.

Once we see the actual basis of the operation of good low-rent housing – the personal attention and high equity of thousands of small owners – we can understand why large-scale ownership, whether private or public, cannot produce an equivalent product. As things now operate, when professional investors are attracted to a neighborhood because of redevelopment, the old housing will no longer be viable.

Because new construction is increasingly uneconomic even for middle-income groups, without public subsidy, older multi-unit buildings represent an irreplaceable source of low-rent housing. And it seems apparent that at least the smaller buildings are only viable in the hands of small owners and in terms of 'the other economy'.

We have begun here to establish the case that the over-taxing, in terms of current use, of wide areas of the central city assumed ready for redevelopment may expose far more housing to deterioration and destruction of value than could ever be gained for the city in increased revenue and new construction.

12

This last example covers the whole range of perceptions of 'development' and 'autonomy' evoked by a single hydro-electricity project in Quebec – 'the project of the century'. The complexity of the case inheres in the number and variety of people who felt themselves to be directly involved in the case and who expected to gain and/or to lose massively by its outcome; and it is compounded by the fact that the perceptions and expectations of these various groups changed through the period of discussion and negotiation. The analysis therefore takes up many of the themes dealt with individually or in combination in previous papers. It is shown that more involvement in and information about the perceptions and expectations of others allow the better – perhaps the more 'efficient' – formulation of one's own position. In such circumstances there is at least the possibility that 'development' will be achieved without jeopardy to the 'autonomy' of any of those party to the process.

A prism of perceptions:
the James Bay hydro-electricity project[1]

RICHARD SALISBURY

In April 1971 Premier Bourassa of Quebec announced that a $6 billion hydroelectric project would be begun, to develop the James Bay region of the Province's boreal forest. It would involve the diversion of waters from five river basins, draining into James Bay, to flow through a single set of dams, and would constitute 'the project of the century'. This paper describes the range of reactions to that announcement, and the events which followed, in terms of the perceptions of development held by different groups.

Our research group had been working in the area concerned for about seven years, particularly with the 6,000 Cree Indians who still hunted and trapped over the area much as they had done since the Hudson's Bay Company established a trading post at Rupert's House in 1670. We had studied the small but growing impact of the mining and pulp and paper enterprises that had been established on the southern fringes of the region during the 1950s and early 1960s. We immediately protested to the Government that no research had been done on social or ecological impacts, and that there had been no consultation with the Cree. The Government and the James Bay Development Corporation (JBDC) then asked us to undertake research on the social impact, and in the course of so doing we became involved in discussions with – I believe – every different interest group concerned with the Project, government, industrial, or private, Indian or white. The recognition that each group had a stereotypic perception of what 'development' was, and then interpreted what it learned about this project in the light of that perception, is the starting point of this paper.

We had initially thought that establishing and communicating 'facts' would create attitudes and permit communication between people with different attitudes. We soon found that facts were ignored unless they confirmed prior perceptions, while non-facts were accepted if they were in confirmation of perceptions; that attitudes too reflected perceptions; and that communication between people with different perceptions was almost impossible. Among the Cree we encountered an additional problem. At least at the moment of announcement, the set of activities we categorise as 'development' was not perceived as a specific set, but only as part of the general category 'white men's activities'. Attitudes toward this category were pragmatic – positive if they helped, but mainly non-commital – while the project provoked fear. This ambivalence towards white men's activities does appear to have become resolved during the period 1972–4, as a distinctive perception of 'development' has emerged. This permits unambiguously structured attitudes towards both the project and other local attitudes. In addition to merely documenting a variety of perceptions as they relate to a single project, this paper will indicate some of the processes by which perceptions can change, or become culturally structured.

White views of development

(a) 'Development as heroism'

This perception, indicated by the phrase 'project of the century', and stressed by the Quebec Government, has been spelled out at length by Premier Bourassa[2] himself in a book (1973). 'Development' means making Quebec 'an economically powerful modern state (p. 8)' (though it is recognised that 'intense economic and commercial activity' (p. 9) accompanied and preceded the 'eras richest in cultural development'). Available energy is one key to industrial development; natural resources are another. Both together need finance to put them to work, and manpower for the work. Development is an heroic process – 'a fascinating challenge. . . the conquest of Northern Quebec, its rushing spectacular rivers, its lakes so immense that they are veritable inland seas, its forest of coniferous trees concealing fabulous mineral resources of all kinds. . . The whole history of Quebec must be rewritten. Our ancestors' courage will and must live again' (p. 10). The appeal of such a vision to a political audience is clear, and the book was issued with the approval stamp of the Liberal Party agent to clarify its status as a political document issued during an election campaign. That M. Bourassa was overwhelmingly re-elected in 1973 however, indicates how widely this perception of development is reflected in Quebec society.

Of as much interest for the present paper is the way actions derived from the perception. In deciding on the project all that had been considered were engineering and stream-flow data which showed that the project was technically feasible; financial studies and negotiations to indicate that capital was available; and assumptions about the exponential growth of power needs in Quebec and the northeastern United States. Its immense size was a positive, not a negative, feature. Social, ecological, cultural, national or moral considerations were not entirely ignored in the original decision; it was merely assumed that they could all be dealt with after the project was in progress, and that since development was by definition good, the consequences of development could not possibly be bad.

(b) 'Development as national self-realization'

The perception of *development as heroism* was not inconsistent with this second perception, held by several sub-groups in Quebec with somewhat divergent views. The technocrats were one such group. When the Liberal party was returned to power in Quebec in 1960 after 25 years of more conservative administration it ushered in what has been called 'the Quiet Revolution'. Where previously the church, medicine, politics and the law had been the major avenues for upward mobility among francophone Quebeckers, and anglophone Quebeckers had stressed business, engineering, science and finance, the Quiet Revolution aimed at secularising francophone education, training engineers, scientists, and businessmen in French, and establishing francophone pre-eminence in those fields where anglophones had dominated. The James Bay project had first been studied in the 1950s by Shawinigan Power Company (an outgrowth of aluminium and pulp and paper interests) and nationalising this Company had been one of the first acts of the new Government in the 1960s. The resulting Crown corporation, *Hydroquébec*, continued the studies while initiating another massive hydro-electric project at Manicouagan–Outardes. Its boast, and the boast of the francophone engineers who graduated in the 1960s, was that 'Manic' had demonstrated what francophones could do – '*Québec sait faire*' (Quebec knows how). Quebec separatism, riots by upwardly-mobile college students demanding the jobs of anglophones in business (cf. Breton 1973), and the emergence of a philosophy of 'rational' central planning in state-directed enterprises (Léveillé 1971) have been other elements of this movement.

Development as national self-realisation, a sub-theme in Bourassa's book, was a major perception among the engineers and the bureaucrats with whom we talked. Insofar as these people were respected by others – junior college-students, and white-collar workers particularly – their stance was more widely accepted without question. *Hydroquébec*, this view presumed, had decided after years of rational planning that the project was desirable; *Hydroquébec* had played a major role in national self-realisation in Quebec; it stood for rationality and the use of French; the project would expand Quebec sovereignty over territories not currently occupied by French speakers; we are *for* the project. It became, in fact, a symbol of Quebec nationalism among a very influential group of upper-middle-class franco-phones, many of whom supported the separatist Parti Québecois.

This perception became strengthened as controversy over the project developed, particularly as opposition to the project became defined as 'English'. All the Indian bands in the area have since 1670 had English as their second language (after Cree). The area from 1670 to 1870 was part of Rupertsland, administered by the Hudson's Bay Company and was trans-ferred to the Dominion of Canada in 1870. Even when the Dominion Govern-ment gave the area to Quebec in 1898 and 1912 (subject to negotiation of Indian claims) the major white agencies in the area remained the HBC (the economy), the Royal Canadian Mounted Police and the (Federal) Indian Affairs Branch (the government) and the Anglican Church (religion and education). If francophone technocrats initially ignored the existence of Indians in the area, when Indian protests emerged they were dismissed because they were anglophone. Three comments were typical; 'Why should 6,000 Indians stand in the way of 6,000,000 Québecois?' 'Indian protests are made because white anglophones are putting them up to it', and 'The project will integrate Indians into [francophone] Québec.' The second comment was an incorrect reflection of fact – Indian protests were first reported by our group at McGill University, but they were not incited by it. They were subsequently taken up in press campaigns by the *Montreal Star*'s Boyce Richardson. His public opposition drew in the ecology movement across anglophone North America – the Sierra Club published his book (Richardson 1972); radical anglophone groups across Canada took up the cry that the project was simply to export energy to the USA (Sykes 1973). In response the nationalists argued that an anglophone conspiracy was under way, to give Ontario an edge over Quebec in power generation in Canada (Ontario's nuclear programme had just then been aided by the diversion of heavy water from the single Quebec plant) and so to preserve Ontario's growing industrial superiority. Confrontation in this way ensured that facts which were dissonant from a perception got ignored, as believers preferred to strengthen their own stereotype: language became a critical issue when 'development' was viewed as 'national self-realization' as it is by many francophone Quebeckers.

(c) 'Development as jobs'

A second Quebec view appealed to by Bourassa was held by most workers. For them development has traditionally meant industrial employment. Historically one can go back to the nineteenth century, when junior sons of large farm families had to migrate from their farms. Some sought new farm land at the northern and western frontier, but a majority went to the burgeoning textile plants and heavy industries of Quebec and New England (Hughes 1943). *This was 'development' – industry and jobs.* It was a process that had stalled with the 1930 depression, and with the movement of industry away from the east coast and into Ontario and the U.S. Middle West, but high unemployment rates in 1968 confirmed the view that what was needed was 'development'. Bourassa's promise of 100,000 jobs in his campaign of 1969 was a major factor in his re-election, and the James Bay Project was announced as a fulfilment of the promise. Construction alone would employ over 12,000 workers at the peak; the employment generated in Quebec industry – building generators, fabricating transmission lines, producing concrete – would be more than four times as large. 'Expert consultants' alone would number several hundreds. Revelations at inquiries into the construction industry in Quebec (the Cliche Commission of 1974) show how organised labour also viewed the project as a source of jobs, patronage and funding at all levels, including private profit by union personnel. This stereotypic view has been a mainspring of action.

Again the record shows how discrepant facts were ignored. The optimistic Bourassa view of *development as heroism* had been challenged, as mentioned, by many anglophone socialists in Canada, who saw it as a sellout of Canadian resources to feed U.S. capitalism while preserving Canadians as hewers of wood and drawers of water. Some sorts of jobs might not be 'development'. The left-wing of Quebec nationalists accepted this position, and tried to brand the project as merely a political football proposed by an élite subservient to U.S. interests. They tried to make opposition to James Bay a major plank of the *Parti Québecois* election campaign of 1973. But as can be appreciated from the previous analysis, other nationalist segments, both technocrats and workers, saw the project as consistent with their goals. After the first 'trial balloons' the issue was dropped from the nationalist campaign; the uncomfortable facts about jobs that agreed with neither positive or negative stereotype were avoided and never received public discussion. The only issue on which a united front emerged was opposition to awarding a management contract to a U.S. firm – Bechtel.

(d) 'Development as civilisation'

This view is a traditional one from Quebec's missionary and fur trade history and for residents of Quebec's middle north. The boreal forest was the eighteenth-century hinterland to which the *coureurs des bois* went to seek their fortunes away from the family farms of southern Quebec, or where in the nineteenth century prospective farmers could cut down forest to clear land. The early twentieth century also saw a movement of colonisation, sponsored by religious groups, into the forest areas (Verdon 1974), facilitated by the building of northern railroads. Some of the settlements around Lake St John and Val d'Or have remained agricultural, but most farming was marginal, abandoned after years of dire poverty and hard labour, with the *colons* being absorbed in the mining and forestry enterprises that later grew up. The self image of northerners as the tough hard workers who lived through difficulties, but who have conquered them, and made the north their own, the true heirs of the *voyageurs*, is important. Politically, it is marked by support of the Créditiste Party, the party of the little guy, the independent frontiersman, fighting against the big business interests of the south. Ideologically it involves the perception of *development as civilisation* moving back the frontier, of Indians as the *sauvages* who appear out of the forest to trade, and of an almost religious mission of development to clear the forest, so that the Indians either move back deeper into the forest, or 'become civilised'.

The early 1960s (Chance *et al.* 1968) saw the opening up of roads and mines at Chibougamau, Chapais, Matagami and Joutel on the Southern fringes of the James Bay Area, and the building of a huge pulp and paper complex at Quévillon. The next step northward would be into the roadless back yard of these northerners – into James Bay. They were enthusiastic that government supported their 'development'.

(e) 'Development as disaster'

Among anglophone Quebeckers many of the same perceptions existed as among francophones. The anglophone business community, sharing the perception of *development as heroism*, differed only in not being so confident that the project itself was economically justified. It recognised and accepted the francophone view of *development as national realisation*, even if it did not agree with the brand of nationalism. Development as industry and employment was accepted also. In this view Indian objection to the project was seen in terms of 'how could Indians stand in the way of such a large project' – but their opposition was seen as entirely reasonable as a tactic for negotiating the largest possible amount of compensation. In effect the anglophone business community stood aside from the project, considering it as a legitimate, but poorly conceived and executed example of development as they perceived development. Anglophone workers, particularly those whom I talked to in the engineering and construction industries, shared the francophone view of *development as employment*, but differed in being sceptical of who would be employed if the project was used as political patronage.

Anglophone intellectuals, however, took a distinctive view and joined fervently in an attack on the whole project. Different aspects offended different sub-groups, but all were united in seeing 'Development as disaster'. For ecologists the 1972 study by Meadows *et al.* '*Limits to Growth*' was still newly released, reinforcing the movement that had surged earlier after Rachel Carson's *Silent Spring*. The effects of the Peace River Dam in Alberta on the downstream marshes, and of the Aswan Dam on salination of downstream croplands were fresh in people's minds. Any big project was anathema, and the need for ecological assessment was becoming a hot issue. Techniques of ecological assessment were still being worked out, and the Federal Provincial Task Force on James Bay ecology that was hastily assembled in late 1971 was one of the first assessment groups to report – even if its January 1972 report was so sparsely documented it was immediately labelled a 'whitewash'. 'Stop the Project until full ecological analyses are in', became a rallying cry, attracting ecologists and people who were unaware of the differences between Aswan and James Bay, or who saw 'development' as 'spoliation of virgin lands' that should be kept intact for all time, not recognising the 3,000 years of human occupation of the area, and the pressures of present human needs.

Another group, also perceiving *development as disaster*, stressed the imposition of white-man's ways upon the Indians of the region. The lack of involvement of Indians in the project at its announcement was undeniable, while the efforts by the JBDC to consult Indians during 1972 were mainly ineffectual if well-meant. But the perception of many people of this group equated 'development' with the evils of modern industrial society – consumerism, frenzied rush, artificiality, domination by powerful élites.

These latter were being forced on a people who lived quiet frugal lives in a natural environment, where every man was his own master, at peace with himself. Opposing the project was in this view striking a blow against modernity and its stresses, against powerful élites, and in favour of 'natural man'. The romantic and paternalistic aspects of this perception appear constantly in the portrayal of all Indians as hunters and as wantiog to continue an unchanged 'traditional' life. But the reality of Indian usage of a highly industrialised hunting technology (snowmobiles, rifles, radios, airplanes) based on settlements with department stores and, increasingly, indoor plumbing and electricity, suggests that Indians want to use modern techniques even while remaining distinctively Indian. Boyce Richardson's work, in newspaper articles, in films and in his 1972 book was perhaps the most effective appeal to this view of development across North America. The support of people with this view was greatly appreciated by Indians, although the Cree themselves had much less romantic perceptions. The Indian readiness to negotiate about the project, and their coming to an agreement in principle with the Quebec Government and the JBDC, in November 1974, profoundly shocked people with this perception. They felt that Indians had 'sold out' and betrayed their supporters. They persistently failed to notice that the Indians had, since 1971 *always* said that they were not *necessarily* against the Project, provided that Indian rights were respected, damages avoided, and full negotiations entered into; initial adamant opposition by Indians had been because none of these provisos seemed at all likely to be observed.

A third hostile view of development, that in some ways overlapped with the previous one, was the radical view that development is capitalist exploitation (even when conducted by a government agency). From this viewpoint all the participants in the James Bay affair could be fitted into pre-existing scenario roles. The Indians were an exploited under-class (regardless of their own view of themselves as a superior category of independent individual workers); the Liberal government, elected and re-elected with a massive majority, were alternatively a capitalist élite or a bourgeois group, deceived by the multinational or U.S. industrialists; the beneficiaries of the project were seen to be entirely the U.S. capitalists who might receive some power from the project during its early years, and the Quebec élite who would make a profit from the sell-out of the natural resource of hydro-electric power. Sykes (1973) provides a graphic portrayal of this viewpoint, linking James Bay with Columbia River electricity, mining and paper developments, the Canadian oil and natural gas industry as a 'sellout' to U.S. capitalism. In talking to groups with this perception of the project across Canada I found amazement when I indicated the various Quebec francophone views that James Bay was to benefit Quebeckers, using the project and its power to create industrial jobs for Quebec, that few benefits of power or jobs would go outside Quebec, and that Quebec could borrow finance without strings in both Europe and the U.S.A. Conspiracy by a self-seeking élite who perhaps did not understand the nature of their sellout and who managed to deceive most of the population, was how this support was reconciled with the 'sellout to capitalism' view of development.

Discussion of white views

Thus far the discussion has been of attitudes to the project that will strike most readers as 'understandable'. These attitudes, which I have described as deriving from more general perceptions of what 'development' means, could be interpreted in many other ways. For example, political party affiliations of right or left could be taken as basic and the 'perceptions of development', as I have described them, could be seen as the working out of the party ideologies in regard to this specific issue. Alternatively, the views described could be seen as those of particular interest groups – of urban industrial labour, of small independent farmers and businessmen, of large business, of francophone nationalists, etc. What I have described as 'perceptions' could be interpreted as the selective emphasis of particular aspects of the project that would benefit (in the short-run at any rate) each particular interest group. I have no quarrel with these political or sociological interpretations of events; I merely feel that both are improved by a perceptual analysis.

Particularly is this true insofar as I was repeatedly struck, in my role of talking to all sides, by the failures of communication between the various groups. It was as though people were talking about different projects. My own involvement had begun initially with somewhat of an anglophone intellectual pro-Indian viewpoint, illuminated by long experience with native peoples in New Guinea, the Caribbean and elsewhere who want increasing affluence. This made me sceptical of assertions that native people opposed all development. I had to learn the various francophone views and the different premises they took for granted in order to interact effectively with officials as I studied the 'facts'. As an anthropologist I started with an assumption that there were culturally distinct Indian views which I would have to learn. Subsequently in trying to communicate my experiences to colleagues, neighbours, and a variety of audiences in Canada and the U.S. I realised the variety of stereotypic views that were held, and the problems of communicating about a reality which did not fit precisely with any of the expectations of my audiences.

Implicit in an 'interest group' interpretation of the data presented is the notion that people know what 'the real facts' are, and then choose to emphasise only those which fit their own interests. If this were the case, then in an argument two conflicting groups could presumably agree on the facts, and then negotiate about how much of each side's 'interest' can be traded-off for some of the other side's interest. By contrast what has been striking in the James Bay case has been a repeated failure to agree on 'facts', heated accusations that the other parties were deliberately falsifying facts, and a constant reiteration with every appearance of sincerity of 'facts' which our research indicated as being non-facts. The adversary process of courts of law did little to clarify this non-communication, for lawyers could argue (and produce witnesses) only in relation to issues on which judges could decide – the terms of the 1763 proclamation by King George III regarding Indian land claims, or the monetary costs of delaying a major construction project – and not on issues that the concerned parties saw as crucial – the way of preserving a distinctive Indian way of life in a modern world, or the future of the Quebec economy. Long negotiation in private, with intensive research and discussion of 'facts' by both sides, and much consultation back from negotiators to the parties concerned, has eventually produced grounds for agreement in principle (in November 1974). Even so there remains much further negotiation to be done, and it is still unclear whether both primary parties fully recognise the differing assumptions held by the other side.

Indian views of development

It will be noted that throughout the preceding discussion of discrepant white views of development, nothing has been said about Indian views. Anthropologists, as I indicated for myself, are pre-disposed to accept the view that different cultural groups have different perceptions and thus would take it as nothing unusual if I had merely described an Indian view which differed from a white view. A range of contrasting white views has been deliberately presented first, before considering Indian views, in order to strengthen my argument that interpretations of events and even the percep-tion of facts, are strongly influenced by pre-existing cognitive structures. A knowledge of such pre-existing structures was as valuable in predicting people's reactions, as a knowledge of the 'real' parameters of plans and facts.

But in the case of Indian reactions predictions were very difficult to make. 'Pre-existing cognitive structures' as described in literature available were not discussed in terms that would have been relevant to hydro-electric development. Several possible explanations exist for this. Researchers pre-viously may simply not have asked about Indian views of development; there may have been so little Indian experience with 'development' that views of it were not organised into 'structures'; or Indians categorised the experiences of previous 'development' under other headings, and did not have a concept translating the white term 'development' as such, which could serve as a 'pre-existing cognitive structure' through which to interpret their experience of the James Bay Project. Our description of Indian reactions to the project will indicate some elements of all these explanations. But as Indian familiarity with the project increased, Indian perceptions of 'development' crystallised dramatically. From being inarticulate, attitudes became articulate. In accor-dance with the argument that attitudes are best described as deriving from more basic cognitive structures, I will focus now on Indian cognitive structures, the concepts and terms used, and their organisation around issues and symbols. These have permitted subsequent position-taking by local Indians about the James Bay Project in particular and about development in general.

Before 1971 James Bay Indians had experience of various things which we would include under the heading 'development'. Starting with the Hudson's Bay Company opening stores and trading manufactured goods for furs, the Anglican church settling missionaries near HBC posts and building churches, a long procession of white settlers have been known. All said that they had come for the good of the local people, 'to help them'. And to be sure, acquiescing in what they wanted done had usually provided practical advantages to Indians – better tools, clothing, education, etc. But the logic behind the white people's actions was often very obscure to local Cree. Agents chose sites for posts that sometimes were understandable, at good fishing sites, or protected from the wind, but at other times the site was ridiculous in local perspectives of good camp sites. Sometimes agents and ministers behaved like friends, sharing with local people and participating as though they wished to live there and stay for ever, but sometimes they were unsympathetic, orienting themselves to things outside (such as prices set in London) that were locally meaningless. For the sake of the practical advantages of co-operation it was best to go along passively with incomprehensible things that white men suggested doing, just ignoring them or forgetting about them when more urgent local matters, like seasonal goose-hunting, arose.

When the era of social welfare legislation began after 1947 a succession of new 'developmental' activities began, again without any clear logic being visible: – family allowances for children, provision of boarding schools and insistence on children going to school, procedures for elections of band councillors and for the recording of minutes and transmission of motions to the Department of Indian Affairs, funding to build sawmills but then no purchasing of the wood cut in them or encouragement of local housing using local lumber, occasional jobs guiding tourists fishing, or cutting lines through the forest for mining surveys. Undoubtedly most of these activities made life easier in some ways – tools and food could be bought without having to rely on the HBC manager advancing credit – and most of them could be undertaken at very little cost. They could be fitted into slack periods of one's ordinary life without having to give up anything important. But *why* white people came into the Indian land to do these things and insisted on Indians doing them, that was not easily explicable. Education, being irrelevant to the north, seemed to lead nowhere. The whites, for all their apparent pursuit of wealth and possessions, were not seen to get wealthy in the north. Development amounted only to *white men's activities that have no logic*.

The surveyors who, from the late fifties on, began measuring stream flows, collecting rocks, or drilling holes were noted by Indians and put down as incomprehensible. They were working for Shawinigan Power, the precursor of the nationalised *Hydroquébec*, and the fact that this activity was possibly connected with building dams, flooding, and occupation of the land by whites was the subject of widespread rumours and general knowledge. No public announcements were made, no precise knowledge was available, and over the years before 1971 the undercurrent of rumours gradually subsided as no project materialised. It was another inexplicable white activity. Like all the other things white men did, there was no sense in opposing it as it would happen any way; if it was passively accepted it could probably be endured, and would go away eventually. It did give a sense of insecurity however. The cognitive structure of 'white activities/Indian activities', had a transform where 'Indian' meant predictable and secure, and 'white' unpredictable and insecurity-provoking, but the two categories were not mutually incompatible or inevitably 'good' and 'bad'.

Ignatius LaRusic, a member of our research team, was in the area when the first definite statement about the James Bay Project reached the area and has described what happened (LaRusic 1971). The premier's announcement stated in general terms that a project would be undertaken. It appeared in the newspapers, abbreviated because of the limited knowledge of northern geography possessed by Montreal and Quebec reporters. Cree Indians read few newspapers, especially those from Montreal, and only second-hand comments reached them from whites who had read the newspapers. Again these were abbreviated and varied. No information was available on where dams were proposed, or what areas were to be flooded (it transpired that decisions had not actually been made), but raising the level of Lake Mistassini and of a chain of lakes in the Waswanipi area was clearly implied. M. Bourassa had talked about plans to move villages that would be flooded. Flooding was a main concern. Boyce Richardson later subtitled his volume 'the Plot to Drown the North Woods' and this was clearly the major aspect that Indians focused on in the initial stages, fed by insecurity and rumours. Well-wishers, our own team included, desperately tried to get accurate information to pass on but for months were unable to do so. Rumours spread, and were probably encouraged by the effort to allay them.

In my talks with Indians the refrain of flooding and its consequences was constant and consistent – '*all the animals will be killed, all the burial places of ancestors will be flooded, we shall all be destroyed, there will be nothing for our children; the white man is doing this, and we do not understand why*'. The consistency of this listing of priorities of concern indicated the cognitive structure into which the project had to be fitted. The animals are of course, the main source of subsistence food, and as Feit (1973) has shown are seen as a highly predictable resource – provided one treats them respectfully, killing only enough for food, and using every part of the animals, while also giving thanks to the spiritual Master of the Animals. If the animals are offended by over-hunting or waste they will cease to provide, and humans would be unable to live in the area. Supernatural statements of this conservational ideology abound in Cree myths and ritual. So too the ancestors symbolise continuity, and predictability; 'drowning' them would offend them and break the chain between the past and the future. Not merely would presently-living people be destroyed, but more significantly there would be nothing for children and descendants in the future. The whole world of Indian activities, Indian beliefs, and Indian goals would be upset, and this by white men, acting for inexplicable reasons. Incompatibility of 'white' and 'Indian' activities had emerged.

The catchwords *destruction of the Indian way of life* were used only by whites: local people did not have a set of explicit concepts about 'way of life' or 'culture', but utilised symbols which meant the same thing to them. 'White activities' had now become antithetical to Indian activities, not tolerable alongside them. Yet the symbolic phrases were often misinterpreted by whites as practical objections to be solved by wildlife resettlement schemes, reinterment of human remains, or investment of money for descendants. Failures of communication multiplied.

The attempts made by the JBDC during 1971 and early 1972 to consult with the Cree and to communicate information to them often fed into the mutual misunderstanding. It further crystallised the Indian view of white behaviour as inconsistent and inexplicable, yet gave no indications of ways out of the impasse. A paper prepared by a Federal–Provincial Task Force on Ecology and circulated among local Indian bands was so superficial (detailed documentation was in working papers) that it offended Indians; and the errors it contained, because of the very limited amount of available scientific research on boreal forest ecology, confirmed how ignorant whites were. It was ceremonially burned at Rupert's House. The change of plans that the Ecology Report stimulated – the deferral of any damming of rivers in relatively more populated southerly areas in favour of the more northerly and even less well known Fort George River – did little to change the impression that flooding was a main aim and that it was decided on capriciously. The report also contained information about possibilities of dams breaking, or suffering seepage, when built on the fine impervious glacial clay of the southern region. It talked of the smaller risk with dams in the older rocks of the northern region. Indian cognitive structures perceived only the warning that dams might break.

Indian communications workers – local Indians in their mid-twenties with at least a high-school education appointed by the Indians of Quebec Association but paid by the JBDC – did bring back accurate information to the various bands with maps and specifics about dams, stream flows, years of construction, and numbers of workers. They fed into the impression of this as a truly immense project, one that indeed nothing could be done about. In the early days of the project local people would say 'They will never cancel such a huge project as this because they have already brought in a whole plane-load of fuel drums' – more than had ever been seen at one time in many small settlements. Every additional item of information made the project seem bigger than ever – more inevitable and less comprehensible. The behaviour of survey teams which discarded empty drums, threw away equipment, carelessly left garbage, or pointlessly damaged stream banks or trees gave further evidence of lack of concern for the environment or possessions, and of the vastness of the project.

Always the items fitted into a picture of approaching apocalypse. Information that communication workers received that the Development Corporation accepted the desirability (if it were economically feasible) of cutting and removing trees in areas to be flooded, was tied in with other information about the use of defoliants and the dangers of these if consumed by humans: a rumour that the project would make breast milk poisonous to children in Fort George greeted one set of white visitors. The planned location of one dam (LG-1) was the main spawning area for white fish on the Fort George River – 'the First Rapids'. Our research indicated it would destroy 5% of the local annual food supply. But the fear of this dam went far beyond the food loss, and was phrased in terms of flooding if the dam broke. Scientific evaluation reinforced Indian fears. Governors' Island, the site of the settlement of Fort George, is made of sand, and shifts in the river flow have in living memory caused erosion. It could easily be washed away entirely by altered stream flow (though equally, planned channel diversions could protect it).

In August 1972 all these apocalyptic aspects were repeated over and over to us in the form already given – destruction of the animals, drowning of the ancestors, destruction of humans, and nothing for posterity – at the same time as we collected empirical evidence for the Indians of Quebec Association of the potential damage, and as the Association mustered cross-Canada support for stopping the project. But local Cree also said 'there is nothing we can do about it', and they carried on, with little overt antagonism to local whites, participating in plans for a five year housing project, for relocating the axis of the airstrip, and for expanding kindergarten and elementary-school facilities in outlying settlements while creating a secondary school at Fort George.

Though the project was categorised as 'a white-man's project', intensely fear-provoking, unpredictable and specifically opposed, there was not a rejection of *all* 'white-men's activities' – too many were already accepted as beneficial. The words used in IQA press releases were that the Cree were 'not categorically opposed to the James Bay Development as such, but opposed those features of the project which pre-empted Indian rights or harmed the Indian way of life'. Yet Cree did not see any change of these specific features as possible, and withdrew from negotiations six weeks after their being started in earnest in September 1972. Lawyers, white friends of the Indian people, and Indian politicians of many groups took up the cry of confrontation to 'stop James Bay'. The northern Cree readily went along. This was one thing they did want.

Yet the inconsistency between desire for *some* white activities and a rejection of the project was also uncomfortable. Many local people worked for the project in various capacities, including a team clearing trees at the projected shore line of the major reservoir. Television reception via Anik satellite had been proposed for the area in 1973, and Indian politicians from outside the area predicted to us that the large dish antennae that was erected would be destroyed to symbolise rejection of this propaganda for white ways. In fact the antennae were not destroyed, and the eventual delay in receiving service (caused by other factors) was complained about loudly by Cree. The desirable features of television, as explained to us by educated Cree who had been outside the local area, were that it would enable older people to understand what the younger people were talking about, when they discussed white goods and customs. In this way it would remove the 'generation gap' that was being felt in the North, and restore the older people to their position as the wise counsellors of the young, which they were now unable to hold since they were ignorant of white society. People overtly discussed the continuity of Indian society but also the use of any features of white society that seemed advantageous. When I was asked by whites what the Cree Indians wanted (expecting a simple answer, 'a maintenance of the traditional way of life') I could only reply: 'I don't know. They have conflicting wants.'

The development of autonomy

A resolution of this conflict has emerged in the two years since August 1972. Phrased in terms of perceptions, the activities subsumed under the English term 'development' have begun to be categorised by many people not as 'white activities' but rather as 'activities where we Indians plan for our own future', to ensure that there will be something in the North for posterity. The terms of the agreement in principle between the Quebec Government and the Grand Council of the Cree indicate the concern with Indian planning. Although the cash settlement, of $150 million over a ten year period, received the most mention in the white press, the features that the Indian negotiators held out for and which local people stress are the other aspects. For the people of Fort George the moving of the dam at LG-1 twenty miles upstream is seen as a major gain, though not as desirable as removing the dam altogether. Indians proudly say that the JBDC offered to add another $100 million to the cash settlement if the dam was allowed to remain, and that this sum was refused. Two thirds of the total region was designated as land over which only Indians would have hunting rights, and exclusive rights to outfit white sport hunters (though the Government's rights to subsurface minerals were confirmed). All the dam and diversion projects on the third of the land area under JBDC control were explicitly agreed not to harm any Indian areas downstream, guaranteeing in future 'equal catches from equal effort'. Native corporations to provide for both native communities, and to contract for supplying services to the development Corporation are encouraged. Although the mechanisms are not fully spelled out and will be subject to further negotiation, it is envisaged that local people will staff, administer and police the various organisations that will spring up.

This legalistic formula was not something worked out by white lawyers alone. It has involved constant discussion between the Indian negotiators and the Cree bands. Even if not ideal, it met most Indian wishes and was accepted by the Cree as the best that could be achieved.

The perception of development as *planning for one's own future* is now manifest in many other areas of Cree activity. In 1972 co-operative stores had largely been ventures suggested by white economic development officers that eked out a struggling existence, supported by band funds but little local enthusiasm, stocked with a limited range of slow-selling goods and much overshadowed by the Bay stores which had a great variety and rapid turnover of attractively displayed goods. Increased local cash incomes have been reflected in similar increases in the turnover of the Bay, but in tenfold increases in the turnover of co-operatives. While the variety of the Bay stock makes it the place to buy specialty products, the Co-op – run by local people – has established a niche for itself in staple clothing and foodstuffs. Greater turnover has meant that the Co-op stores have been able to improve the efficiency of operations and their attractiveness as well.

In the field of housing the federal programme that made bands decide in 1971 and 1972 how many houses they would need over ten years, and then granted subsidies to permit a proportion of these to be built each year, has begun to pay off. Where most of the planning was done by the advisers at the start, with many skilled white workers doing the building, and bands involved mainly in the allocation of the houses, bands have now become much more involved in the planning. House rentals received by the bands form a fund for additional building construction; the local employment created by house-building has been recognised, and imported skilled workers are becoming much fewer in number. Suitable housing for everyone is now seen as an attainable goal, so that houses can be allocated with longer-term considerations in mind and not just to solve immediate crises. Community facilities like electric generators and sewage disposal are discussed as things to be provided locally, not as something that should be provided by whites in Ottawa. Development now implies *local social evolution*.

How did this critical restructuring of perceptions of development occur? Although it is a restructuring that our social impact report (Salisbury *et al.* 1972) called for as desirable, and for which it tried to provide planning data, I do not think that the report had much effect in Indian settlements, although it may have had some effect in making the Quebec government more receptive to Indian wishes. It was a long technical document, written for a white audience. The causes I would credit would be firstly a political awakening of Cree nationalism, and secondly the fact that research was conducted.

The Cree nationalism awakening is understandable when one realises the extreme parochialism of small bands – 200 people – separated into dozens of smaller micro-bands for months of the year and covering a territory of about 10,000 square miles. The administrative grouping of several former bands at the posts of Mistassini and Fort George to form settlements of over 1,000 people produced factionalism rather than cohesion, as reasons for settlement collaboration were non-existent. Poor communications led mainly outwards to the bigger white centres of Moosonee, Val d'Or, or Chibougamau, and were minimal between bands. In 1971, except among young people who had been at boarding school together, there was little awareness of other Cree Indian people outside the band territory and its immediate neighbours. Remembrance of the pre-1914 days of long-distance travel in canoe-brigades organised by the HBC[3] to transport supplies inland was remote. Attempts to combat parochialism by the educated Cree communications workers and officials of the Indians of Quebec Association met with great problems – meetings where no-one turned up, inability of workers to explain white concepts in Cree for older people who had not been outside, confusion when successive visitors talked about different ranges of issues to audiences which changed from one meeting to the next, transport problems which meant that too little time could be spent in any one settlement, and that people in one settlement did not hear views from other settlements.

The crisis of fear of 1971–2 increased the flow of communication between settlements immeasurably, culminating in the presence of research teams in the area in August 1972, and in the flying out of Cree witnesses to the injunction proceedings in Montreal in November, 1972 and January, 1973. The common interests throughout the area became obvious to everyone.

The main agents in the information flow were the educated communications workers, who became known in all settlements with their constant visits. They could understand Cree, and listened to what local people said, even though they came, like white administrators, to speak to meetings. While officials of the Indians of Quebec Association and whites urging 'stop James Bay' had perforce to behave like administrators lecturing in English, the communications workers were Cree, but with the status of administrators. Use of Cree became normal in meetings even when non-members of the band were present, and communications workers were seen as members of communities rather than as 'foreigners' coming in from 'outside'.

This acceptance was not achieved without costs to the workers. They had to spend much time in Montreal and Quebec, and on the move between settlements; visits to wives and children – and most were newly married with one or two children – were widely spaced, and many arrangements were tried to permit more family life, with the moving of the family to Montreal being the worst alternative. To some extent the communications workers were explicit in their ideology that they were working 'for the Indian people', and were deliberately choosing, at personal inconvenience, to remain with their own people rather than 'sell out' for the expense-account existence in cities. To some extent they talked in these ideological terms to local communities, but more generally they became examples of how Cree-speakers could run their own affairs, and be responsive to the wishes of the settlements. They were not simply mouthpieces for a wider pan-Indian ideology. Not so the more urbanised Indians of the Quebec Association who seemed unresponsive to local wishes, yet expressed more clearly the pan-Indian ideology; by local agreement in August 1974 the Cree decided to set themselves up as the Grand Council of the James Bay Cree and to negotiate on their own behalf.

I have already described the local planning activities that permitted this expanded political consciousness to express itself at the local level. Indian Affairs officials had long claimed that their activities were only to set up a structure and to operate it on behalf of Indians until the Indians themselves were ready to do so. Now that bands said that they wanted to run things the officials accepted this (though often with mixed feelings). Management of local affairs became more readily accepted by locals as it proved effective. In the wider field united political action by Indians received an even stronger universal acceptance when in November 1973, Judge Malouf granted the Cree an interim injunction against the project.

But if political unity fed on a sense of crisis, better communications, an informed and interacting elite, and successful action on practical issues, the idea of planning, I believe, came from an awareness of issues, created by research.

Initial research in 1972 focussed almost exclusively on project impacts on hunting. Empirically there had been a slight but continuing decline in the numbers of full-time hunters, particularly in northern areas, over two decades. The small absolute decline had been accentuated by the increasing population size. At the same time greater cash income, the increase of settlement facilities, and the advent of snowmobiles had altered the pattern of hunting, away from a predominance of isolated hunting groups living several months in the bush away from settlements, to a predominance of short hunting trips within a radius of forty miles of the settlement. Young people spending their winters at school had little opportunity to learn the knowledge that is taught during winters in isolated bush locations (*cf.* Sindell 1968). Families had begun to see education as a choice of bringing up children as 'white' or as 'Indian', with no synthesis option; children brought up 'white' were uninterested in learning bush-knowledge, even if they could fish and drive snowmobiles. Old people seemed resigned to the disappearance of traditional knowledge.

When research started on sizes of catches, uses of hunting territories, long-term historical changes in flora or fauna, etc. the reaction by high-school students or educated young adults who worked as interviewers was one of amazement and interest. Here was a fund of knowledge among older residents about which they had never previously inquired, and which covered types of hunting that they did not even know by repute. It made sense, and was also respected as making sense by the white professional researchers. It was the basis of evidence in the court hearings. It could be phrased in the language learned in school, and the scientists did rephrase it in this way, but clearly Indians had better knowledge than white scientists and could express that knowledge more simply.

But this collation of data also made clear how hunting techniques were changing – how little use was made of distant territories, and how much increased dependence there was on ptarmigan and hares rather than bigger game. The legal case also made it clear that if territories were not used they might well be lost. A major growth has occurred of interest in hunting by the young adults, and in the use of distant territories. The possibility of a synthesis, of a white-educated person living and working in a settlement, and being 'an Indian' has become available for the first time. It has required both a growth of white-collar employment in settlements, and a recognition and awareness of what portion of the Indian heritage was in danger of becoming lost.

An initial concern for hunting, during the research, has become a more general concern, as settlement negotiations have proceeded, with asking what activities of all kinds were crucial to settlements, what feelings were about white sport hunting, where roads were desirable, what areas were needed as reserves for residential purposes, what offered terms of settlement might be acceptable. The Cree negotiators were clearly in charge, using white professionals to do technical jobs of compiling figures or maps; the questions were practical ones that local people could comment on meaningfully; for once it appeared that local people really could influence their own future. The new kindergartens and primary schools in all settlements use Cree as a first language; research teams (again mainly composed of local assistants) have collected local materials for use in textbooks. Development viewed as *planning for our own future*, is an activity that is no longer 'white' and 'unpredictable' but has become part of 'predictable' behaviour. The dichotomy 'Indian/white' has been restructured.

Epilogue

The last few paragraphs may suggest that a united Cree Indian society is now engaged in successfully planning its future. This is erroneous. A realist would immediately question how far any local planning among a group of 7,000 people, even if it is for an area of 60,000 square miles, can be effective; it must be dependent on the wider forces and politics that affect Quebec, Canada, or the whole world in its energy crisis; any assumption of local autonomy is short-sighted. On the individual level, too, Cree react to their own specific circumstances in practical direct ways that have little to do with *local planning for the future.*

Yet a definition of the situation as one where 'conscious future planning by Cree, for Cree' is possible, alters the choices one makes. Empirically in a situation of confrontation with white workers viewing development as *employment*, or Quebec technocrats seeing development as *heroism*, the 7,000 Cree may well be swept aside by the greater resources of their opponents and their perception may be entirely rejected. Alternatively their perception may be accepted by others, and they may be allowed to plan for themselves in a ghetto-like reserve. In the second case the perception may lead them to stagnation, while in the first case by recognising their own goals and the different perceptions of other parties the Cree may be able to negotiate to the best advantage, as seen in their own perceptions.

In short what this paper has tried to suggest is that cognitive 'perceptions of development' for Cree, as for other Quebeckers, become ideologies orienting attitudes and guiding future activities. A knowledge of the perceptions held by other people provides a useful tool for predicting their actions. A realisation that they are acting from assumptions other than one's own helps to avoid communication failures. At the same time perceptions are not irrevocably fixed. They change at times of crisis and frightened insecurity, when relying on existing perceptions leads to ambivalence and inconsistency. Wallace (1970) has discussed massive restructurings of whole cultures as 'mazeway reformulations', has stressed the 'revitalization' of cultures, and has indicated the role of the charismatic leader in this process. Our data suggest that essentially similar reformulations can also occur in particular aspects of culture, by similar processes, but not necessarily involving charisma. They do involve feelings of political unity, the availability of new sources of information, and the opening of new channels for information flow.

Notes

Chapter 1

1 This essay presents a facet of material to appear in monograph form under the title *Sometime Kin: the perception and management of resources in an alpine settlement.*

2 For these and other socio-linguistic observations, I am indebted to Dr G. L. Clivio of the University of Toronto and of the Centro Studi Piemontesi, Turin.

3 Each household must necessarily (see note 5) keep at least one cow. The largest holding is fifteen. For some years the number of cattle in the *comune* has been exactly equal to the number of fulltime residents.

4 Bellino seems to suffer a rain-shadow effect. Several times during the summer of 1973 outside work was stopped by rain for more than a week at a time.

5 So to some extent are the people. Their relationship with their cows is explicitly symbiotic. Throughout the winter even those with modernised houses depend on the heat of a breathing cow.

6 *lit.* 'large shoes' in reference to the mountain boots they wear.

Chapter 2

1 This paper is taken from *The Rise and Fall of an African Utopia*, now submitted for publication. A version of it appears in *Administration for Development in Nigeria* ed. Collins (University of Ibadan Press). I am grateful for the support of The Wenner-Gren Foundation and a Canada Council doctoral fellowship during the initial field trip; a Research Advisory Board Grant from the University of Guelph during the second field trip; and a Canada Council Research Fellowship and Research Grant which allowed me to take a leave of absence from the University of Guelph during 1973–4 for further field research.

2 For an analysis of the role of *oba* among the Yoruba, see Lloyd (1954 and 1960).

3 Talika joined Olowo in a political union in 1969. Olowo made the adoption of communalism a precondition of the union, which Talika accepted in principle, hoping to become wealthy like Olowo. However, not only was communalism rejected by Talika people, but within three years the union had fallen apart.

4 There were 137 and 156 houses respectively in the male and female sectors. The figures on occupations were derived from a questionnaire administered to all of the residents in the male sector and the residents of 76 of the 156 houses in the female sector (or 49%), consisting of 429 and 197 adult men and women.

5 Talika was also divided into male and female sectors, consisting of 40 large and 121 small houses respectively. The figures on occupations were derived from a systematic sample of 50% of the houses in the male sector, containing 175 people, of which 81 were adults, and a combination of a systematic and judgement sample of 17% of the houses of the female sector, containing 96 people, of which 38 were adults.

6   Olowo was a closed community and people who were disillusioned were not allowed to leave, but had to 'escape' – the term used by the people themselves. I have data for 46 defectors between 1947 and 1972, which is probably an underestimate. After 1972 the rate of defection accelerated: at least 67 people departed during 1973 and 1974. Offsetting these defections was the recruitment of outsiders, which amounted to 129 women and one man from 1970 to 1974; 35 of these women as well as the man only remained in Olowo for a few months. I have written about conflict and defection in *The World is at Peace: Stratification, Conflict and Control in an African Utopia* now submitted for publication.

Chapter 3

1   Assumed names have been used for all persons and places, in order to avoid embarrassment to individuals.
2   Banton suggests (1968: 203–4) that high social density leads to a high level of social control and to a high degree of resistance to change. At Eagle Bay there is a high level of informal social control, but the resulting consensus and homogeneity operates in favor of economic change.
3   Important historical sources are Hudson's Bay Company, fur trade records (Ontario Archives).

Chapter 4

1   The research on which this paper is based was conducted between June 1969 and January 1973. Funds were provided by a National Science Foundation Dissertation Improvement Grant and a Woodrow Wilson Dissertation Fellowship. A portion of the fieldwork was supported by the National Institute of Mental Health grant number 1 RO3 MH 26528–01.
2   The dates for these two periods reflect the conditions and attitudes of Molokai. Similar periods occurred on the other islands in the state but varying with conditions such as the nature and rate of economic development. The 1959 dividing line coincides with Hawaiian statehood and the introduction of the jet plane. The remarks in this paper can be fully attributed only to members of *Ierusalema Pomaikai*, and only partially extended to all Hawaiians.
3   A true story circulating on Molokai that seemed to be on its way to becoming a legend was about a family from California who, while vacationing in Hawaii, had come to Molokai for a day-long visit. When they were to leave the island they found themselves stranded at the airport (either having missed the plane or their flight had been cancelled, depending on the version). A Hawaiian who happened to be at the airport invited the family home for the evening, and they stayed three weeks. Not only did they stay for three weeks, but they came back in succeeding years. This story is told to contrast the way things used to be on Molokai with present circumstances.
4   For example: numerous people come to Molokai to hunt and go hiking in the isolated valleys at the east end of the island. Those without experience can easily get lost or stranded. In the past Molokai residents would gladly volunteer to join rescue parties when an individual got into such difficulty. But when incidents began to occur with increasing regularity local people were less willing to expose themselves to danger to rescue careless strangers.
5   The presence of the immigrant labour groups did affect social life of the island, but their influence is best considered elsewhere. While the introduction of family

farming and later pineapple production produced heavy silting on the coral reef around the island, most of the silting took place on the west end of the island; the more traditional Hawaiians use the oceans in the east.

6   'Hawaiian culture' is what members interpret or re-interpret Hawaiian culture to be and does not necessarily have anything to do with traditional ethnographic Hawaiian culture. Hawaiian music of today for example is influenced by country and western music, but can be claimed as Hawaiian in terms of its content and form.

7   This was first pointed out to me by Michael Mays, a fellow student of contemporary Hawaii.

Chapter 5

1   The term 'tribe' is used here in the sense that colonial governments used it, without regard for internal political structure as in Service's definition (1971: 99ff). It is intended only to convey the emphasis placed on common descent – the political implications of which were heightened by British policy, and on group identity which was also encouraged by British policy.

2   It was formally a Trusteeship Territory, but the Cameroons was administered as part of Nigeria and for all but diplomatic purposes was treated as a colony (Ardener 1967; Rubin 1971).

3   According to the A.D.O., Harry Vaux, the arresting officer, the charge was 'offences in connection with tax money'. Ntoko's suicide was taken as proof of his guilt. The baKosi version is that Ntoko was persuaded to cross the Munto River to discuss a bridge building project with Vaux. Only out of baKosi did the A.D.O. dare arrest Ntoko. His suicide is interpreted as the expression of his great humiliation (Ejedepang-Koge 1971: 121–5).

Chapter 6

1   I am grateful to Josef Bonnici, Mark Miceli-Farrugia, Edward Scicluna and Denise Vella for many helpful discussions and researcher assistance, and to Ot van den Muijzenberg for helpful criticism on an earlier draft. The research in 1973 and 1974 on which this discussion is largely based was made possible by a grant from the University of Amsterdam. The Department of Economics of the Royal University of Malta provided important research facilities.

2   *Third Development Plan for the Maltese Islands 1969–974. Revised October 1970.* Valletta: Office of the Prime Minister, 1970.

3   *The Development Plan for Malta 1973–980.* Valletta: Office of the Prime Minister, October 1974.

Chapter 7

1   This paper appeared first in the *Journal of Development Studies* 8:2, 1972. The ethnographic data are taken from Wallman 1969.

2   I am uncertain whether this no-emigration bind is peculiar to Lesotho and/or of the extent to which it is thereby disqualified from comparison with otherwise similar regions.

3   This geographic dependence is exaggerated by the fact that Lesotho (with Swaziland and Botswana) has been party to a Customs' Union with South Africa since

1910. This allows the country no independent foreign trade, but guarantees it a fixed annual income from Customs revenues. It was revised somewhat in 1969 (Turner 1971).

4   Because time could always be differently allocated (present usage being sanctioned only by habit and custom), its expenditure has obvious ideological components. But this is true of any resource and I have chosen to isolate the most glaring shortages together, as economic facts of equivalent weight.

5   I find it significant that this man, who is the only person in the village who really makes money out of individualistic enterprise in Lesotho, has never been a migrant or worked in South Africa.

6   The facts of poverty combined with figures showing twice as many married as unmarried migrants (Table 2) suggest that the initiatory function of migration is not predominant (cf. Schapera 1956).

7   Migrants may bring or post money home, or make arrangements through the Native Recruiting Corporation (N.R.C.) to have payment deferred until they return to Lesotho. It is officially estimated that about 9 per cent of wages comes through in this way. For a sample of household incomes and expenditures see Wallman 1969: 69–74.

8   Particularly by sections of the South African public: as e.g., newspaper reports of the severe freeze-up and famine of the winter of July 1964, and the comments of South African border guards seeing Basuto tenacity for the first time.

9   This negative reaction is normally referred to as 'demonstration effect' (Nurkse 1953: 68–70). 'Aspiration effect' seems to be a revision of this model. See Bauer and Yamey (1957: 137–42).

10 A situation said to be 'among the curiosa of economic development or economic history' (Bauer & Yamey 1957: 42).

11 I must re-emphasise that this self-deprecation is economic. The pride of the Basuto in the beauty of their country and the glory of its history is striking (cf. Wallman 1969: 25,34,155–6 and Ch. 8 below).

Chapter 8

1   A version of this paper was first presented at a joint meeting of the Canadian Association of African Studies and the School of International Affairs at Carleton University, Ottawa, in February 1973. The title of the conference was *Dependence and Development in Africa*. The paper was published as a note in the *Journal of Southern African Studies* Vol. 3, No. 1 (1976).

Chapter 9

1   I am indebted to my wife, Anne Martin Matthews, for her help in formulating the conceptual framework used in this paper.

2   This urban and industrial focus of DREE shows in the changing pattern of government spending on regional development between 1966 and 1971. In 1966, all industrial incentives programs amounted to only 2% of federal regional assistance; by 1971 the proportion was nearly 40%. In that same period infrastructural development totals declined from 66.9% to 38.4%, and the percentage spent on all regional programs of development *and* social adjustment fell from 31.1% to 21.9% (Phidd 1974: 184–5). It should be emphasized that federal expenditure on regional development rose from $57 million to $271 million during the same period; expenditure in all three areas actually rose considerably.

3   The names of these two communities are altered here to protect the anonymity of informants.
4   This is also the case for those who move to nearby communities on the mainland. Such communities offer them the best of all possible worlds: their children can be bussed to better schools than those on the island, and can yet remain in a rural setting. Similarly the household heads can move out to work and yet return home on weekends all year round. The goal is invariably to live as much as possible in the rural environment.

Chapter 10

1   In Zambia, for example, the ruling United National Independence Party began to introduce legislation in support of its first development plan before the release of the official document. In the field of industrial relations, the national plan's goals relating projected productivity to projected wage levels became the main guideline for undermining trade unions. The Party attempted to isolate the unions claiming that they were special interest groups whose policies ran counter to the development of national unity.
2   *Report of the Commission* appointed to inquire into the Administration and Finances of Native Locations in Urban Areas, 1954: Paras 120, 121.
3   Letter to General Managers from Chamber of Mines Oct. 17, 1955.
4   *The Commission of Inquiry into the Mining Industry* of 1966 did raise the whole question of administration of mine company housing, but only to emphasize that arrangements then current could not continue.
5   For a further discussion of UNIP's local organization see Harries-Jones 1975, esp. chapters 2, 3.
6   The Councillors Advisory Committee was formed in order to keep the municipal councillors informed as to the feelings of members of the party in neighbourhood cells, without transmitting reports up through the Branch and Constituency. It was, in effect, a communication short-cut to the most volatile element in the party.
7   *The anthill*: a reference to a public platform from which local and national leaders addressed their followers. In rural areas, and sometimes in town, an anthill was used in the construction of the platform.
8   *Welensky*: a reference to Sir Roy Welensky, former Prime Minister of the Federation of Rhodesia and Nyasaland.

Chapter 11

1   See Krohn and Duff 1973 for a description of the most developed and productive example of small owner housing in an area of self-renewal sparked by Portuguese immigrants.
2   The first study was reported in Roger G. Krohn & Ralph Tiller 1969. The second and third are cited above.
3   Note that here we discuss only owners of old houses.
4   This is supported by more complete data given by a large real estate company on its buildings in the St Louis Square area in our study of that area.
5   MPCC: Milton Park Citizens Committee.
6   The houses are roughly equivalent in size, but some have been further subdivided.

7   Compare this with a maximum of $2 per sq. ft. in lower N.D.G., a middle to working class residential area, and $2–3 in middle Westmount, a middle and upper-middle income area. Assessments in the central business district of Montreal reach higher than $70 per sq. ft.

8   There is also rent control, which has applied only to buildings built before 1951 and renting for under $125 per month.

Chapter 12

1   The field research from which this paper springs has been spread over many years and has been supported by the Government of Canada (ARDA, DIAND, DOC), by the Government of Quebec (JBDC) and by the Indians of Quebec Association. Current support for preparation of this paper is from the Quebec Ministry of Education (FCAC programme) and from a Canada Council Leave Fellowship to the author. I would wish gratefully to acknowledge long discussions of this paper with Bob Schneider, Iggy LaRusic, Harvey Feit, and Nathan Elberg.

2   I would also point out the imprecise equivalence between French and English terms. *Développement* is an even vaguer general term than its cognate in English. *Planification* is more commonly used to discuss future-oriented activities than its cognate in English, and *aménagement* is used to refer to ongoing, reasoned, but not necessarily expansionist 'development'. *Exploitation* has more of the traditional meaning of the term and less connotations of evil in French than in English. I cite the authorised English text of Bourassa (1973).

3   HBC: Hudsons' Bay Company.

References

Adelman, I., & Morris, C. T. (1973). *Economic Growth and Social Equity in Developing Countries.* Stanford Calif.,: University Press.

Ames, D. (1963). 'Wolof Co-operative Work Groups', in *Continuity and Change in African Cultures,* W. Bascom and M. Herskovits, eds, pp. 224–37. Chicago: University Press.

Amin, Samir (1973). *Neo-colonialism in West Africa (trans.* Francis McDonagh). Harmondsworth: Penguin.

Anon. (1957). 'Aiyetoro', *Nigeria Magazine.*

A.P.E.C. (Atlantic Provinces Economic Council) (1972). *The Atlantic Economy: Sixth Annual Review.* Halifax N.S.: Atlantic Provinces Economic Council.

Apter, D. E. (1965). *The Politics of Modernization.* Chicago: University Press.

Ardener, E. W. (1967). 'The nature of the re-unification of Cameroon', in *African Integration and Disintegration,* A. Hazelwood, ed, pp. 285–338. London: Oxford University Press.

Ardener, E. W., Ardener, S. & Warmington, W. A. (1960). *Plantation and Village in the Cameroons.* London: Oxford University Press.

Aron, R. & Hoselitz, B. (eds) (1965). *Le Développement social.* Paris: Mouton.

Arthur, O. R. (1937). *Re-assessment report on the Bakosi, Eluny and Native Court Areas,* Kumba Division, Cameroons Province.

Ashton, H. (1952). *The Basuto.* Oxford: International African Institute.

Bailey, F. G. (1957). *Caste and the Economic Frontier.* Manchester: University Press.

(1971). 'The Peasant View of the Bad Life' in *Peasants and Peasant Societies,* ed. T. Shanin, pp. 229–321. Harmondsworth: Penguin.

Bailey, F. G. (ed.) (1973). *Debate and Compromise: The politics of innovation.* Oxford: Basil Blackwell.

Banfield, E. R. (1958). *The Moral Basis of a Backward Society.* New York: The Free Press.

Banton, M. (1968). *Roles: An Introduction to the Study of Social Relations.* London: Tavistock.

Barrett, S. (1974). *Two Villages on Stilts.* New York: Chandler.

Barth, F. (1963). *The Role of the Entrepreneur in Northern Norway.* Oslo: Scandinavian University Books.

(1966). 'Models of Social Organization', Royal Anthropological Institute Occasional Papers no. 23.

(1967). 'Economic Spheres in Darfur', in *Themes in Economic Anthropology,* R. Firth ed. Association of Social Anthropologists Monograph no. 6. London: Tavistock.

(1969). *Ethnic Groups and Boundaries.* Boston: Little, Brown.

Batten, T. R. (1968). *Communities and their Development: an introductory study with special reference to the tropics.* London: Oxford University Press.

Bauer, P. T. & Yamey, B. S. (1957). *The Economics of Underdeveloped Countries.* Cambridge Economic Handbooks, No. 1. Welwyn: Nisbet.

Bennet, J. (1967). *Hutterian Brethren: the Agricultural Economy and Social Organi-sation of a Communal People*. Stanford Calif.: University Press.

Berger, P. L. (1974). *Pyramids of Sacrifice*. New York: Basic Books.

Bourassa, R. (1973). *James Bay*. Montreal: Harvest House.

Brenner, Y. S. (1966). *Theories of Economic Development and Growth*. London: Allen & Unwin.

Breton, R. (1972). 'The Socio-political Dynamics of the October Events', *Canadian Review of Sociology and Anthropology* 9, pp. 33–56.

Brewis, T. N. (1969). *Regional Economic Policies in Canada*. Toronto: Macmillan of Canada.

Brokensha, D. & Erasmus, C. (1969). 'African "Peasants" and Community Develop-ment', in *The Anthropology of Development in Sub-Saharan Africa*, D. Brokensha and M. Pearsall, eds. Lexington, Kentucky: Society for Applied Anthropology (Monograph no. 10).

Buckley, H. & Tihanyi, E. (1967). *Canadian Policies for Rural Adjustment: A Study of the Economic Impact of ARDA, PERA and MMRA*. Ottawa, Special Study Number 7, Economic Council of Canada.

Bury, J. B. (1955). *The Idea of Progress*. New York: Dover Publications.

Canada, Parliament (Various dates, 1870–1910). *Sessional papers*.

Carson, R. (1962). *The Silent Spring*. Boston: Houghton Mifflin.

Chance, N. A. (ed.) (1968). *Conflict in Culture*. Ottawa: Canadian Research Centre for Anthropology.

Chenery, H. *et al.* (1974). *Redistribution with Growth*. London: Oxford University Press.

Clifford, W. (1960). *Criminal Cases in the Urban Native Courts*. Lusaka: Government Printer.

Cohen, Yehudi. (1969). 'Social Boundary Systems', *Current Anthropology* 10, pp. 103–17.

Cole, H. S. D., Freeman, C., Jahoda, M. & Pavitt, K. L. R. (1974). *Thinking about the Future: a critique of The Limits to Growth*. London: Chatto & Windus for Sussex University Press.

Coons, A. E. & Glaze, B. T. (1963). *Housing Market Analysis and the Growth of Home Ownership*. Columbus, Ohio: Ohio State University Press.

Copes, P. (1972). *The Resettlement of Fishing Communities in Newfoundland*. Ottawa: Canadian Council on Rural Development.

Cranston, M. (1954). *Freedom: A New Analysis*. London: Longmans.

Critchfield, R. (1974). *The Golden Bowl be Broken: Peasant Life in Four Cultures*. Bloomington, Indiana: Indiana University Press.

Daneel, M. L. (1971). *Old and New in Southern Independent Churches*, Vol. I: *Background and Rise of the Major Movements*. The Hague: Mouton.

Dalton, G. (ed.) (1971). *Economic Development and Social Change: The Modernisa-tion of Village Communities*. New York: Natural History Press.

Davis, J. (1969). 'Town and Country', *Anthropological Quarterly* 42, pp. 171–85.

De Kadt, E. (1974). 'Introduction' to *Sociology and Development*, E. De Kadt & G. Williams, eds. pp. 1–19. London: Tavistock.

De Kiewiet, C. W. (1941). *A History of South Africa*. London: Oxford University Press.

Deloria, V. Jnr. (1969). *Custer Died for Your Sins: an Indian Manifesto*. New York: Avon Books.

Duckworth, E. H. (1951). 'A Visit to the Apostles and the Town of Aiyetoro', *Nigeria Magazine*, No. 36.

Du Sautoy, P. (1958). *Community Development in Ghana*. London: Oxford University Press.

Edgren, G. & Harries-Jones, P. (1964). *Wages and Conditions of Employment at Zambian Mines*. Kampala: I.C.F.T.U. African Labour College (Contract Survey No. 3).

Eisenstadt, S. N. (1964). 'Breakdowns of Modernisations', *Economic Development and Culture Change* 12, pp. 345–67.

(1966). *Modernisation, Protest and Change*. Englewood Cliffs: Prentice-Hall.

Ejedepang-Koge, S. N. (1971). 'The Tradition of a People: Bakossi, Yaounde', *Mimeo*: Government of Cameroon.

Elkan, W. E. (1963). *Employment and Manpower in the Economic Development of Basutoland*. Report for International Labour Organization (unpublished).

Epstein, Scarlett (1962). *Economic Development and Social Change in South India*. Manchester: University Press.

Evans-Pritchard, Sir E. E. (1937). *Witchcraft, Oracles and Magic among the Azande*. Oxford: Clarendon Press.

(1940). *The Nuer*. Oxford: Clarendon Press.

Fanon, F. (1967). *Black Skin, White Masks*. New York: Grove Press.

Feit, H. A. (1973). 'The Ethnoecology of the Waswanipi Indians', in *Cultural Ecology*, B. Cox, ed. Toronto: McClelland Stewart.

Firestone, O. J. (1974). 'Regional Economic and Social Disparity', in *Regional Economic Development*, O. J. Firestone, ed. pp. 205–67. Ottawa: Editions de l'Université d'Ottawa.

Firth, Sir R. (1939). *Primitive Polynesian Economy*. London: George Routledge.

(1951). *Elements of Social Organisation*. London: Watts.

(1964). 'Structural and Moral Changes produced in modern society by scientific and technological advance', in *Essays in Social Organization and Values*. LSE Monographs on Social Anthropology. London: Athlone.

(1967). 'Themes in Economic Anthropology' in *Themes in Economic Anthropology*. Association of Social Anthropologists Monograph No. 6. London: Tavistock.

(1972). 'The Sceptical Anthropologist?: Social Anthropology and Marxist Views on Society', *Proceedings of the British Academy* LVIII. London: Oxford University Press.

Firth, Sir R. & Yamey, B. S. (1963). *Capital, Saving and Credit in Peasant Societies*. London: Allen & Unwin.

Forrester, J. W. (1969). *Urban Dynamics*. Cambridge, Mass: M.I.T. Press.

Fortin, G. (1972). *La fin d'un regne*. Montreal: H.M.H.

Foster, G. M. (1965). 'Peasant Society and the image of the limited good', *American Anthropologist* 67, pp. 293–315.

(1973). *Traditional Societies and Technological Change*. New York: Harper & Row.

Foster-Carter, A. (1974). 'Neo-Marxist Approaches to Development and Underdevelopment', in *Sociology and Development*, ed. De Kadt and Williams. London: Tavistock.

Francis, J. P. & Pillai, N. G. (1972). *Regional Development and Regional Policy: Some Issues and Canadian Recent Experience*. Ottawa: Department of Regional Economic Expansion of Canada.

Frank, Andre Gundar (1969). *Latin America: Under-development or Revolution?* New York: Monthly Review Press.

(1971). *The Sociology of Development and the Under-development of Sociology*. London: Pluto Press.

Galbraith, J. K. (1962). *The Affluent Society*. Harmondsworth: Penguin.

Gallimore, R. & Howard, A. (eds.) (1968). *Studies in a Hawaiian Community: Na Makamaka O Nankuli.* Honolulu: The Bernice P. Bishop Museum.

Galtung, Johan (1973a). *The European Community: A Superpower in the Making.* London: Allen & Unwin.

(1973b). 'The Limits to Growth and Class Politics', *Journal Peace Research* (Oslo).

Gellner, Ernest (1964). *Thought and Change.* London: Weidenfeld & Nicolson.

(1973). 'Concepts and Society' in *Cause and Meaning in the Social Sciences*, I. C. Jarvie and J. Agassi, eds. London: Routledge & Kegan Paul.

Gill & Duffus (1968 Oct.) *Cocoa Statistics* London: Gill and Duffus Ltd.

Goffman, Erving (1959). *The Presentation of Self in Everyday Life.* New York: Doubleday.

(1975). *Frame Analysis.* Harmondsworth: Penguin.

Gonzales, N. (1961). 'Family Organization in Five Types of Migratory Wage Labour'. *American Anthropologist* 63.

Goodenough, W. E. (1963). *Co-operation in Change.* New York: Russell Sage Foundation.

Goody, J. (1958). *The Developmental Cycle in Domestic Groups.* Cambridge Papers in Social Anthropology No. 1. Cambridge: Cambridge University Press.

Hailey, Lord W. (1953). *Native Administration in the British African Territories* (Part V). London: HMSO.

Halpern, J. (1965). *South Africa's Hostages.* Harmondsworth: Penguin.

Harries-Jones, P. (1975). *Freedom and Labour: Mobilization and Political Control on Zambian Copperbelt.* Oxford: Basil Blackwell.

Heilbronner, R. L. (1974). 'The Human Prospect', *New York Review* 24 January 1974.

Hesse, H. *Steppenwolf*, Various editions.

Hill, P. (1963). *The Migrant Cocoa Farmers of Southern Ghana: A Study in Rural Capitalism.* Cambridge: Cambridge University Press.

Homans, G. C. (1950). *The Human Group.* New York: Harcourt, Brace and World.

(1961). *Social Behaviour: its elementary forms.* New York: Harcourt, Brace and World.

(1964a). 'Bringing Men Back', *American Sociological Review* 29, pp. 809–18.

(1964b). 'Social Behaviour as Exchange', in *Interpersonal Dynamics: Essay and Readings on Human Interaction*, W. G. Bennis ed. Homewood, Illinois, Dorsey Press.

Hughes, E. C. (1943). *French Canada in Transition.* Chicago: University of Chicago Press.

Inglis, G. B. (1970). *The Canadian Indian Reserve: Community, Population and Social System.* Ph.D. Dissertation, University of British Columbia, Vancouver.

Iverson, N. & Matthews, R. (1968). *Communities in Decline: An Examination of Household Re-settlement in Newfoundland.* Newfoundland Social and Economic Studies, Number 6, Institute of Social and Economic Research. St John's: Memorial University of Newfoundland.

(1970). 'Anderson's Cove', in *Poverty and Social Policy in Canada*, W. E. Mann ed., pp. 239–50. Toronto: Copp-Clark.

(1973). 'The Fate of the Outport Newfoundlander', in: *The Political Economy of Newfoundland*, P. Neary ed. pp. 233–40. Toronto: Copp-Clark.

Jahoda, Marie (1974). 'Postscript on Social Change' in *Thinking about the Future* eds. H. S. D. Cole *et al.* London: Chatto & Windus for Sussex University Press.

Jarvie, I. C. (1972). *Concepts and Society.* London: Routledge & Kegan Paul.

Joffe, N. F. (1962). 'The Fox of Iowa', in *Acculturation in Seven American Indian Tribes*, R. Linton ed., Gloucester, Mass.: P. Smith.

Jones, G. I. (1951). *Report on Basutoland Medicine Murder*. London: HMSO, Cmd 8209.

Krohn, R. & Duff, H. D. (1973). 'The Other Housing Economy: Self-renewal in a central Montreal neighbourhood' (mimeo.). Montreal: McGill University.

Krohn, R. & Fleming, E. B. (1972). *The other Economy and the Urban Housing Problem: a Study of Older Rental Neighbourhoods in Montreal*. Working Paper No. II. Cambridge, Mass.: Joint Center for Urban Studies of MIT and Harvard University.

Krohn, R. & Tiller, R. (1969). 'Landlord-Tenant Relations in a Declining Montreal Neighbourhood', *The Sociological Review* Monograph No. 14. Sociological Studies in Economics and Administration. University of Keele, Staffs.

La Rusic, I. (1971). 'Comment les Indiens de Waswanipi ont appris les nouvelles du Project', *Recherches Amérindiennes au Quèbec*.

Lerner, D. (1958). *The Passing of Traditional Society: modernising the Middle East*. New York: The Free Press.

Lestrade, G. P. (1937). 'Domestic and Communal Life', in *The Bantu Speaking Tribes of South Africa*, I. Schapera ed. London: Routledge & Kegan Paul.

Léveillé, L. & Fortin, R. (1971). 'Pour une conquête du Nouveau Quèbec', *La Revue de géographie de Montreal* 25, pp. 59–66.

Levi, Arrigo (1974). *Journey among the Economists*. London: Alcove Press.

Lewis, D. (1972). *Louder Voices: The Corporate Welfare Bums*. Toronto: James Lewis & Samuel.

Lewis, Oscar (1967). *La Vida*. London: Secker & Warburg.

Lewis, W. Arthur (1966). *Development Planning: the essentials of Economic Policy*. New York: Harper & Row.

Leyton, E. (1970). 'Spheres of Inheritance in Aughnaboy', *American Anthropologist* 72, pp. 1378–88.

Little, K. (1965). *West African Urbanization: A Study of Voluntary Associations in Social Change*. Cambridge: Cambridge University Press.

Lloyd, P. C. (1954). 'The Traditional Political System of the Yoruba', *Southwestern Journal of Anthropology* 10, pp. 366–84.

(1960). 'Sacred Kingship and Government among the Yoruba', *Africa* 30, pp. 221–37.

Lusaka, Government Printer (1944). *Report of the Commission appointed to Inquire into the Administration and Finances of Native Locations in Urban Areas*. (The Eccles Report.)

(1957). *Report of the Committee appointed to Examine ways and means by which African residents in Municipal and Township areas should be enabled to take an appropriate part in the administration of those areas*. (Brown Committee Report.)

(1966). *Report of the Commission of Inquiry into the Mining Industry* (Brown Report.)

McLoughlin, P. F. M. (1970). *African Food Production Systems: Cases and Theory*. Baltimore, Md.: Johns Hopkins Press.

Mair, L. P. (1961). 'Applied Anthropology and Development Policies', in *Studies in Applied Anthropology*. L.S.E. Monographs on Social Anthropology. London: Athlone Press.

Malinowski, Bronislaw (1922). *Argonauts of the Western Pacific*. London: Routledge & Kegan Paul.

Malta, Govt of (1970) (1974). *Development Plans*, Valletta: Office of the Prime Minister.

Marris, Peter (1974). *Loss and Change*. London: Routledge & Kegan Paul.

Martindale, D. (1962). *Social Life and Cultural Change*. Princeton N.J.: Van Nostrand.

(1963). 'The Formation and Destruction of Communities', in *Explorations in Social Change*. G. K. Zollschan & W. Hirsch eds. Boston: Houghton Mifflin.

(1966). *Institutions, Organizations and Mass Society*. Boston: Houghton Mifflin.

Mason, P. (1959). *Prospero's Magic*. London: Oxford University Press.

Matthews, R. (1970). *Communities in transition: An Examination of Government Initiated Community Resettlement in Rural Newfoundland*. Ph.D. Thesis, University of Minnesota, Minneapolis.

(1975a). 'Ethical Issues in Policy Research', *Canadian Public Policy – Analyse de Politiques* I, no. II, pp. 204–16.

(1975b). *Paths of Change: Newfoundland Social and Economic Development 1949–957*. Unpublished Manuscript: McMaster University, Hamilton, Ontario.

(1976). '*There's no better place than here*': *Social Change in three Newfoundland communities*. Toronto: Peter Martin Associates.

Meadows, D. H., Meadows, D., Randers, J. & Behrens, W. W. (1972). *The Limits to Growth: a Report for the Club of Rome on the Predicament of Mankind*. New York: Universe Books.

Mesarovic, M. & Pestil, E. (1974). *Mankind at the Turning Point: the second Report for the Club of Rome*. London: Hutchinson.

Mishan, E. S. (1967). *The Costs of Economic Growth*. London: Staples Press.

Morse, C., Hadow, G., Hawes, C. G., Jenkins, O. T. & Phillips, J. F. V. (1960). *Basutoland, Bechuanaland and Swaziland: Report of an Economic Survey Mission*. London: H.M.S.O.

Mortimore, G. E. (1975). *The Road to Eagle Bay: Structure, Process and Power in a Highly Acculturated Ojibwa Band*. Ph.D. Dissertation, University of Toronto.

Municipality of Luanshya (1963–75). Municipal Council Minutes.

Munoz, H. (1960). *Nutritional Survey of Basutoland*. Unpublished Report for W.H.O.

Myrdal, G. (1957). *Economic Theory and Under-developed Regions*. London: Duckworth.

(1968). *Asian Drama: an enquiry into the poverty of nations*. London: Allen Lane.

Nadel, S. F. (1957). *The Theory of Social Structure*. New York: the Free Press.

Nordhoff, C. (1971). *The Communistic Societies of the United States*. New York: Schocken Books.

Nurkse, R. (1953). *Problems of Capital Formation in Under-developed Countries*. Oxford: Basil Blackwell.

O.E.C.D. (1967). *Multidisciplinery Aspects of Regional Development*. Paris: Development Centre of the Organization for Economic Cooperation and Development.

Ogbu, J. (1973). *The Next Generation: an ethnography of education in an urban neighbourhood*. Stanford, Calif.: Academic Press.

Oliver, D. L. (1961). *The Pacific Islands* (Revised Edition). New York: Doubleday Anchor.

Olson, M. & Landsberg, H. (1973). *The No Growth Society*. London: Woburn Press.

Ontario, Public Archives (various dates). *Hudson's Bay Company fur trade records*.

Paul, Ben, (ed.) (1955). *Health, Culture and Community*. New York: Russell Sage Foundation.

Peel, J. D. Y. (1968). *Aladura: a Religion Movement among the Yoruba*. London: Oxford University Press.

Perroux, F. (1955). 'Notes sur la notion de "pole de croissance"', in *Economie appliquée*, janvier–juin 1955, pp. 307–20 translated into English as 'Notes on the Concept of "Growth Poles"', in *Regional Economics*, David McKee *et al.*, eds. pp. 93–103. New York: Free Press 1970.

Peterson, J. (1974). *Status and Conflict: An Ethnographic Study of an Independent Hawaiian Church*. Ph.D., Dissertation: University of Hawaii, Honolulu.

Phidd, R. W. (1974). 'Regional Development Policy', in *Issues in Canadian Public Policy*, eds. G. B. Doern & S. Wilson, pp. 166–202. Toronto: Macmillan of Canada.

Philpott, S. B. (1968). 'Remittance obligations, social networks and choice among Monserratian migrants in Britain', *Man 3*, pp. 465–76.

Pim, Sir A. (1935). *Financial and Economic Position of Basutoland*. London: H.M.S.O.

Poetschke, L. E. (1971). 'Region Planning for Depressed Rural Areas: The Canadian Experience', in *Poverty in Canada* J. Harp & J. Hofley, eds. pp. 270–81. Scarborough, Ontario: Prentice Hall of Canada.

Popper, Sir Karl (1957). *The Poverty of Historicism*. London: Routledge & Kegan Paul.

(1968). *The Logic of Scientific Discovery*. London: Hutchinson.

(1972). *Objective Knowledge: an evolutionary approach*. Oxford: Clarendon Press.

Prince, R. (1966). *An Ecological Study of Social Pathology in Montreal*. Montreal: Urban Social Redevelopment Project.

Radcliffe-Brown, A. R. (1952). *Structure and Function in Primitive Society*. London: Cohen and West.

Redfield, R. (1970). *A Village that chose Progress: Chan Kom revisited*. Chicago: University Press.

Richardson, B. (1972). *James Bay: The Plot to Drown the North Woods*. San Francisco: The Sierra Club, and Toronto: Clarke Irwin.

Robertson, H. (1973). *Grass Roots*. Toronto: James, Lewis & Samuel.

Rostow, W. W. (1956). 'The Take-Off into Self-sustained Growth', *The Economic Journal* II, pp. 25–48.

(1964). *The Stages of Economic Growth; a non-Communist Manifesto*. Cambridge: Cambridge University Press.

Rubin, N. (1971). *Cameroun: an African Federation*. London: Pall Mall Press.

Rudin, H. (1938). *Germans in the Cameroons, 1884–914: a case study in modern imperialism*. London: Jonathan Cape.

Salisbury, R. F., Filion, F. G., Rawji, F. & Stewart, D. (1972). *Development and James Bay*. Montreal: McGill University, Programme in Anthropology and Development.

Sanders, Peter (1975). *Moshoeshoe, Chief of the Sotho*. London: Heinemann.

Schapera, I. (1956). *Migrant Labour and Tribal Life*. London: Oxford University Press.

Schapera, I. & Goodwin, A. J. H. (1937). 'Work and Wealth', in *The Bantu speaking Tribes of South Africa*, I. Schapera, ed. London: Routledge & Kegan Paul.

Schneider, P., Schneider, J. & Hansen, E. (1972). 'Modernization and development: the role of regional elites and non corporate groups in the European Mediterranean, *Comparative Studies in Society and History* 14 (3), pp. 328–50.

Schumacher, E. F. (1973). *Small is Beautiful*. London: Abacus.

Schwab, W. (1955). 'Kinship and Lineage among the Yoruba', *Africa 25*.

Service d'urbanisme, Ville de Montreal (Août 1968). *Critères d'Amenagement: Quartier Ste Famille*. Montreal: Plan-Amur.

Service, E. R. (1971). *Primitive Social Organisation*. New York: Random House.

Sindell, P. S. (1968). 'Some Discontinuities in the Enculturation of Mistassini Cree Children', in *Conflict in Culture*, N. A. Chance, ed. Ottawa: St Paul University.

Sklair, L. (1970). *The Sociology of Progress*. London: Routledge & Kegan Paul.

Southall, A. (ed.) (1961). *Social Change in Modern Africa*. London: Oxford University Press.

Spicer, E. H. (ed.) (1967). *Human Problems in Technological Change*. New York: Wiley.

Spindler, G. D. (ed.) (1963). *Education and Culture*. New York: Holt Reinhart & Winston.

Statistics Canada (1971) *Census*. Ottawa: Queens Printer.

Stavenhagen, R. (1971). 'Decolonialising the Applied Social Sciences', *Human Organisation* 30: pp. 333–44.

Sternlieb, G. (1966). *The Tenement Landlord*. New Brunswick, New Jersey: Urban Studies Center, Rutgers University.

Stoevesendt, G. (1934). 'The Sect of the Second Adam', *Africa* 7, pp. 479–82.

Sykes, P. (1973). *Sellout: The Giveaway of Canada's Energy Resources*. Edmonton, Alberta: Hurting.

Tawney, R. H. (1948). *Religion and the Rise of Capitalism*. Harmondsworth: Penguin.

Teilhard de Chardin, Pierre (1955). *The Phenomenon of Man*. London: Collins.

Thomas, M. D. (1972). 'Growth Pole Theory: An Examination of some of its Basic concepts', in N. M. Hansen, ed. *Growth Centre in Regional Economic Development*. New York: Free Press.

Thompson, Leonard (1975). *Survival in Two Worlds: Moshesh of Lesotho*. London: Oxford University Press.

Turner, B. (1971). 'A Fresh Start for the Southern African Customs' Union', *African Affairs* 70, no. 280.

Valentine, C. (1968). *The Culture of Poverty critique and counter-proposals*. Chicago: University Press.

Vaux, H. (1932). *Intelligence report on the Bakossi Clan, Kumba Division*. Yaounde: Government of Cameroun.

Verdon, M. (1974). *Anthropologie de la Colonisation au Quèbec*. Montreal: Presses de L'Université de Montreal.

Vickers, G. (1972). *Freedom in a Rocking Boat*. Harmondsworth: Pelican.

Vonnegut, Kurt, Jnr. (1969). *Slaughterhouse Five* or *the Children's Crusade*. New York: Dell.

Wallace, A. F. C. (1970). *Culture and Personality*. New York: Random House.

Wallerstein, I. (1961). *Africa: The Politics of Independence*. New York: Vintage Books.

Wallman, S. (1965). 'The Communication of Measurement in Basutoland', *Human Organisation* 24, pp. 236–43.

(1966). Review of Aron & Hoselitz (1965). *Man* (N.S.) I: 117–18.

(1968). 'Lesotho's *pitso*: Traditional meetings in a modern setting', *Canadian Journal of African Studies* 2, 167–73.

(1969). *Take out Hunger: two case studies of rural development in Basutoland*. L.S.E. Monographs on Social Anthropology. London: Athlone Press.

(1970). 'Notes on three innovators' *Journal of Modern African Studies* 8, 3.

(1972). 'Conditions of non-Development: the case of Lesotho', *Journal of Development Studies* 8, 251–61.

(1973). 'Preliminary notes on *Soprannomi* in a part of Piedmont', *Studi Piemontesi* (Turin) vol. II, fasc. I.

(1974). 'Status and the Innovator', in *Choice and Change*, J. Davis, ed. L.S.E. Monographs on Social Anthropology. London: Athlone Press.

(1975). 'Kinship, a-kinship, anti-kinship: variation in the logic of kinship situations', *Journal of Human Evolution* 4, 331–41.

(1976). 'Commentary: New Dilemmas of Application?' *Urban Anthropology* 5, 4.

Ward, Barbara (1965). 'Varieties of the Conscious Model: the fishermen of South China', in *The Relevance of Models for Social Anthropology*, M. Gluckman & F. Eggan, eds. Association of Social Anthropologists Monograph No. 1. London: Tavistock.

Wertheim, W. F. (1973). *Evolution and Revolution: the rising waves of emancipation.* Harmondsworth: Penguin.

Wilkinson, R. G. (1973). *Poverty and Progress.* London: Methuen.

Wilson, Francis (1971). 'Farming 1866–1966', in *Oxford History of South Africa*, vol. 2 *1870–966*, M. Wilson & L. M. Thompson, eds. Oxford: Clarendon Press.

Index